PACIFIC

OCEAN

Equator

INDIAN

OCEAN

CABERNET SAUVIGNON

Harry Eyres

Series editor: Harry Eyres

VIKING

VIKING

Published by the Penguin Group
Penguin Books Ltd, 27 Wrights Lane, London W8 5TZ, England
Penguin Books USA Inc., 375 Hudson Street, New York, New York 10014, USA
Penguin Books Australia Ltd, Ringwood, Victoria, Australia
Penguin Books Canada Ltd, 10 Alcorn Avenue, Toronto, Ontario, Canada MV4 3B2
Penguin Books (NZ) Ltd, 182–190 Wairau Road, Auckland 10, New Zealand

Penguin Books Ltd, Registered Offices: Harmondsworth, Middlesex, England

First published 1991
1 3 5 7 9 10 8 6 4 2

Set in 9/12 point Linotron Janson Text 55 by Wyvern Typesetting Ltd, Bristol
Printed in Great Britain by Butler & Tanner Ltd, Frome and London

A CIP catalogue record for this book is available from the British Library

ISBN 0-670-82481-X

To my father,
who introduced me to the
taste of Cabernet Sauvignon
at a suitably tender age

CONTENTS

MAPS

ACKNOWLEDGEMENTS

I could not have written this book without the generous assistance of Food and Wine from France (special thanks to Catherine Manac'h), the Wine Institute of California and Wine of Australia (special thanks to Hazel Murphy). In Bordeaux Bruno Prats, Roger Zuger, Jean Depiot and Christian Laberrère kindly provided château-bottled accommodation. The regional committees of the Médoc and Graves performed the Herculean task of arranging over 100 appointments. Too many producers to mention were generous with their time and hospitality.

In the UK thanks to the following individuals and firms: David Balls, Fiona Campbell, David Gleave, John Hawes, Andy Henderson, Pam Holt, Donald Mason (Wines from Spain), Manuel Moreno, Jancis Robinson, David Russell, Catherine Scott, Margarit Todorov (Bulgarian Vintners); Avery's, Michael Druitt, Ehrmanns, Hedley Wright, Majestic, Oddbins, Sainsbury's, H. Sichel, Waitrose.

INTRODUCTION

Cabernet Sauvignon is the world's most successful wine grape. It is not the most widely planted – that dubious honour goes to the insipid Spanish Airén. It may not be, at the moment, quite the most fashionable – in a world which craves white wine, that honour is Chardonnay's. But not even Chardonnay has been transplanted with such notable success to quite so many corners of the earth.

Cabernet Sauvignon's homeland is Bordeaux, and especially the Médoc and Graves areas which surround the city and extend sixty miles north on the left bank of the Gironde. It is there, still, that the world's most satisfyingly complex, elegant and long-lived red wines are made. This guide reflects the continuing primacy of Bordeaux, which accounts for nearly half the producer entries. You will never see, however, a 100 per cent varietal Cabernet Sauvignon in Bordeaux. Following the traditional practice of the region, Cabernet Sauvignon is blended with Merlot, Cabernet Franc and Petit Verdot in ever-changing proportions. 'We do not make Cabernet Sauvignon wines,' I was told repeatedly while visiting Bordeaux châteaux.

The Napa Valley in California, as different a landscape as could be imagined, with its conifers, crags and intense light, from the flat and Dutch-looking Médoc, is the place to find 100 per cent Cabernet Sauvignons bursting with ripe fruit. California Cabernet Sauvignons, like other American products, can be larger than life and excessively glossy; wines to admire but lacking the quirks which compel love. The best, though, produced by the world's most articulate and technically advanced wine-makers, are magnificent by any standard.

Australian Cabernet Sauvignon can be as vividly, vibrantly fruity as any in the world. There is, naturally, a great range of styles in the span of an entire continent, but the refined yet intense Cabernets of Margaret River in Western Australia, the startlingly vivid mint-and-berry-flavoured wines of central Victoria and the complex, sharply etched flavours of Coonawarra all deserve mention. There is also a tradition of blending wines from different regions to produce some of the most seductively drinkable Cabernet Sauvignon wines you will find anywhere.

Spain and Italy both feature some highly distinguished Cabernet Sauvignons amid a good deal that is ordinary. Italy has both a longer tradition of planting the grape and a greater number of important producers, with Sassicaia still supreme, but Spain's short list of Torres, Jean León and Marqués de Griñón is impressive as far as it goes.

The Central Valley area of Chile may well offer the most perfect conditions for the cultivation of Cabernet Sauvignon anywhere in the world. Unfortunately, wine-making skills continue to lag behind natural endowment, though great progress has been made in the last decade. The ripe fruit and easy-going complexity of the best wines are immensely appealing; it is a shame that certain producers found it necessary to enhance these natural qualities with an illegal though harmless additive, Sorbitol.

Eastern Europe has emerged as the leading supplier of bargain-priced Cabernet Sauvignon. Bulgaria has led the way, with other countries such as Romania, Yugoslavia and Hungary some way behind, and now has ambitions to compete in the higher reaches of the market.

Of all the wine regions in which Cabernet Sauvignon is a relative newcomer, Washington State in the north-western USA seems to me to have the most exciting potential. The best wines from here have a firmness of structure that brings them closer to Bordeaux than any other New World wines I have tasted.

The wine world, like the world in general, is nothing if not dynamic. A £100-a-bottle Bulgarian Cabernet Sauvignon has been promised in the next decade. Perhaps the vast Russian plantings will yield something exciting too. That leaves China . . .

The Character of Cabernet Sauvignon

Cabernet Sauvignon for red wine is like Mozart for music or Sophocles for drama: universally recognized as classic. If you think in terms of the classic–romantic opposition, Cabernet Sauvignon stands for balance and appeals to the intellect while Pinot Noir produces wine of sensual excess. Such a generalization is dangerous, however, in the case of a grape variety that has travelled so successfully to all parts of the wine world: Cabernet produced in Lebanon or Chile tastes markedly different from Cabernet grown in its homeland of Bordeaux. Yet Cabernet Sauvignon is the most recognizable of the red wine grapes. Where others seem to change their character, schizophrenically, as they travel (how much does Hunter Valley Shiraz have in common with Hermitage?), Cabernet Sauvignon, despite a fascinating range of styles, remains identifiably itself. Having a strong identity is clearly an advantage, but it must also be the right sort of identity. Cabernet's combination of sharply defined blackcurrant fruit with overtones of tobacco, dust and cedarwood, held together in a tight-knit structure, has established a classic quality. Other vines may sometimes be more exciting, sexier even (Pinot Noir in Burgundy, Syrah in the Rhône), but nothing else matches the completeness, the combination of solidity and elegance, of power and subtlety, of complexity and balance, which is Cabernet Sauvignon's hallmark.

Being a classic can have its drawbacks. As with Mozart and Sophocles, it can be difficult to know what to say about Cabernet Sauvignon: for many wine-makers it is simply the best, and that is all there is to it. Even those wine-makers who agree that it is the best can show more affection for other, more difficult, more temperamental vines. The quixotic pursuit of Pinot Noir, whose success rate is so much lower than Cabernet Sauvignon, in all parts of the globe, is the most obvious case in point. It is like parents who with apparent perversity prefer their problem kids to their paragons. One does not always want to listen to Mozart: there are times when only Puccini or Gershwin will do.

Of course, as with Mozart and Sophocles, there is a good deal to say, and to work on in performance, and fortunately there are wine-makers who find the challenge of Cabernet Sauvignon endlessly fascinating. The result is that more great red wines are made from Cabernet Sauvignon than from any other grape variety in the world today.

Cabernet Sauvignon is not the easiest of grapes to appreciate. Cabernet wines are not for beginners. Cabernet Sauvignon has fruit, generally the deep and rather tight fruit of blackcurrant, rather than the sweeter strawberry or more charming raspberry, but except in the case of certain wines from Chile and Australia it is not the soft, juicy fruit that makes instant friends. Most Cabernet Sauvignons have a certain austerity and indeed astringency. They can be dustily dry. One American wine guide goes even further: 'Cabernet Sauvignon is a wine for people who like to sleep on the ground, play rugby, climb mountains, eat Brussels sprouts, anything in which some punishment is part of the pleasure.' This is a rather shrewd summing-up of the masochism of the English ruling class – the class that established the pre-eminence of Cabernet Sauvignon, or claret, long ago. It is also something of an exaggeration: the positively unpleasant side of Cabernet Sauvignon, the mouth-puckering astringency of traditional club claret, is largely a thing of the past. Better wine-making techniques and the salutary example of New World Cabernet Sauvignon, with its unmistakable ripe fruit, are putting paid to that sort of wine even in its traditional stronghold, the Médoc.

The complexity of Cabernet Sauvignon is something intrinsic to the grape, though it can be enhanced by skilful wine-making. In this sense the closest white equivalent to Cabernet Sauvignon is Riesling, not Chardonnay. Cabernet Sauvignon's complexity and structure depend on tannin. To describe this complexity, this dense concentration, the image of a very tightly furled bud comes to mind. Cabernet as a flower would have many, closely packed petals, like a peony. It would take a

long time to open out. Other flowers/grapes would bloom
earlier and create great splashes of colour while Cabernet
Sauvignon was still closed and unyielding. In the end, if you had
the patience to wait, the Cabernet-flower would make the most
majestic, many-layered bloom. Others might prefer the vivid
transience of a poppy. Another image is of a face with beautiful
bone structure. Such a face may never be exactly pretty, but its
virtues are more than skin-deep, and they are made to last. So it
is with Cabernet Sauvignon, which gives the most firmly structured and long-lasting of red wines.

Blending

Probably the most difficult and controversial aspect of
Cabernet Sauvignon is the question of blending. Of the world's
top four grape varieties (the others being Chardonnay, Pinot
Noir and Riesling), it is the only one which is regularly 'cut'
with other varieties (making an exception of the blending of
Chardonnay and Pinot Noir in champagne). This cutting
could, if you were a purist, make you question the *raison d'être*
of this guide. But blending of grape varieties is a characteristic
procedure of the Bordeaux area, where Cabernet Sauvignon
originated. Not only the reds but the whites also are almost
always made from a mixture of usually three varieties. In the
case of the whites, the predominant Sémillon is traditionally
mixed with Sauvignon Blanc and Muscadelle (the new wave of
100 per cent Sauvignon Blanc is a very recent phenomenon).
With reds, the blend is made up of Cabernet Sauvignon,
Merlot and Cabernet Franc, with smaller quantities of Petit
Verdot and Malbec.

Now there are several reasons for regarding the best wines of
the Médoc and Graves (though not of course the St Emilion
and Pomerol, where Merlot reigns supreme) as predominantly Cabernet Sauvignon wines. For a start, practically no one

disputes that the best grape of those regions is Cabernet Sauvignon. The main reason for the planting of the other varieties is that the late-ripening Cabernet Sauvignon cannot be relied upon to ripen fully every year. The mixture of grape varieties provides a built-in insurance policy against the failure of any one grape. Merlot, for instance, is particularly prone to *coulure*. It must be said that, whatever the reasons, the effect of blending in Bordeaux is highly beneficial. Even the best 100 per cent Cabernet Sauvignons in good vintages in Bordeaux, as I was able to verify at a monumental vertical tasting by variety at Léoville-Las Cases, have a bony austerity.

The vogue for blending other varieties with Cabernet Sauvignon in the New World is more recent – so recent, in fact, as to be difficult to assess – and based on other premises. Cabernet never has difficulty ripening fully in the Napa Valley, though it may occasionally in Coonawarra. The reason for blending in Cabernet Franc and Merlot in California (where these grapes produce very different results from the Cabernet Franc of Touraine or the Merlot of St Emilion) is to produce subtler and earlier-maturing styles than the big, tannic, block-buster Cabernet Sauvignons of yesteryear. Some of these wines are certainly very successful, but it is still the case that many of the top California Cabernets (all those of Joe Heitz, for instance) are 100 per cent Cabernet Sauvignon.

Cabernet Sauvignon is by no means always the dominant variety in a blend, and its function varies from place to place. In the Midi, for instance, it is increasingly used as a *cépage amélio-rateur*, in small quantities, to give colour and depth to a blend, while in Tuscany, Cabernet is considered to round out the harsh flavours of Sangiovese. In Australia, the Cabernet–Shiraz blend has acquired an identity of its own: the sharply defined fruit of the Cabernet Sauvignon complements the power and chocolatey richness of the Shiraz, and poses us a philosophical problem. Neither variety dominates the other.

THE MAIN VARIETIES BLENDED WITH CABERNET SAUVIGNON

Merlot

Merlot may be a less ancient and less noble variety than Cabernet Sauvignon, only cultivated on a large scale in Bordeaux since the late nineteenth century, but it covers nearly twice as much of the Bordeaux *vignoble*: 32 per cent as opposed to 18 per cent. In terms of Bordeaux viticulture, Merlot's two great advantages are first that it ripens roughly two weeks ahead of Cabernet Sauvignon, and thus can be counted on to give reasonable degrees of sugar, and secondly that it is more resistant than Cabernet Sauvignon to the disease oïdium (powdery mildew). As for its contribution to the blend, Merlot gives deep-coloured wine which is softer and rounder than Cabernet Sauvignon, generally lower in tannin and acidity. It tends to have a jammier character, suggesting at times strawberries rather than Cabernet's blackcurrants. Merlot can lack structure and tends to develop more quickly than Cabernet Sauvignon, though at its best, in Pomerol, it can produce wine of the highest class.

Merlot is on the increase in the New World, as it is seen to be a more sophisticated blending partner for Cabernet Sauvignon than Shiraz or Malbec. Californian Merlot, however, can be big, beefy and just as tannic as Cabernet Sauvignon. There is not very much Merlot in Australia at present, but plantings are increasing rapidly. Merlot is extensively cultivated in northern Italy and in eastern Europe, where it is more often seen as a single varietal.

Cabernet Franc

Cabernet Franc is so prone to mutation that Jean-Bernard Delmas of Château Haut-Brion feels the variety should be referred to in the plural. Variable as it may be, it produces a lighter wine in the Médoc than either Cabernet Sauvignon or

Merlot. Cabernet Franc, an ancient Bordeaux variety which used to be known as Gros Cabernet because of its larger berries, ripens between Merlot and Cabernet Sauvignon. It is highly susceptible to grey rot, and for that reason is often harvested before it is fully ripe. Its contribution to the blend, usually in the region of 5 per cent in the Médoc, can be underrated. Cabernet Franc is notably aromatic and possesses a lightness and freshness which can be lacking in Cabernet Sauvignon and Merlot. Michel Delon of Château Léoville-Las Cases feels that the effect of Cabernet Franc in lifting the nose and adding elegance on the palate is important. At a tasting of separate varieties made at Las Cases, the Cabernet Franc of 1986 was exceptional. In lesser years it can be grassy and excessively light; the finish is generally short.

Cabernet Franc is grown extensively in northern Italy, and makes up 20 per cent of the blend of the great Sassicaia, but has not travelled as successfully as Cabernet Sauvignon. New World wine-makers do not favour this variety.

Petit Verdot

This is a much misunderstood variety. The myth is that Petit Verdot (an ancient Bordeaux grape whose name suggests unripeness) ripens only one year in five, and produces astringent, tannic wines. In reality, at least during Bordeaux's recent sequence of balmy vintages, Petit Verdot ripens two years out of three, and produces the most full-bodied, rich wine of any of the Bordeaux varieties; indeed, it was always known as the grape variety that could produce a complete wine on its own. It is a late ripener, usually being picked a little later than Cabernet Sauvignon. However, in years like 1983 and 1986, Petit Verdot produced wine of great power and almost fat body, whose only defect was a lack of elegance.

There are signs of a minor Petit Verdot revival, not just in Bordeaux, where properties such as Léoville-Las Cases and Léoville-Poyferré are increasing their plantings, but also in California, where one or two wineries including Newton have planted Petit Verdot with notable success.

Malbec, or Côt

This variety, very widely planted all over France in the eighteenth century, is now very much on the decrease in Bordeaux, though it continues to hold its own in Cahors. Malbec is an earlier-ripening variety even than Merlot, which probably accounted for much of its popularity. It produces wine of good colour and adequate sugar, but with a tendency to excessive softness and lack of acidity and tannin. Authorities such as M. Delmas do not consider it suitable for the Médoc, and very few properties claim to have more than the odd 1 per cent.

Outside France, Malbec is quite common in Australia, where it is used as a blending partner for Cabernet Sauvignon, though it is giving way to Merlot. The country to which Malbec seems most suited is Argentina, where it produces rich wines of great colour and fruit intensity.

Syrah, or Shiraz

In 1865 Dr Guyot recommended a blend of Cabernet Sauvignon and Syrah for the rocky hillsides of Provence, and earlier in the nineteenth century it was common practice to cut claret, even the lofty Lafite, with a percentage of Hermitage to add body and richness. With Syrah, Cabernet Sauvignon, usually the dominant partner in blends, meets its match: Syrah's character – pungent, deep and full-bodied – is even stronger than that of Cabernet Sauvignon. All the same, Georges Brunet, in his time at Château Vignelaure, and Eloi Durrbach, at Domaine de Trévallon, have been extremely successful with their sophisticated blends of Cabernet Sauvignon and Syrah, where neither variety seems to dominate the other.

It is in Australia that the blend of Cabernet Sauvignon and Shiraz has become most popular and widespread. The sometimes caramelly warmth and richness of Shiraz is thought to fill out the 'hollow middle palate' of Cabernet Sauvignon. A wine like Brian Croser's 1979 Petaluma Coonawarra (60 per cent Shiraz, 40 per cent Cabernet Sauvignon) shows the virtues of this arrangement, with a wonderful array of tarry, minty, chocolatey Shiraz flavours held together in a tight Cabernet Sauvignon structure. Croser, like other advanced Australian wine-makers, has subsequently abandoned Shiraz as a blending partner for Cabernet Sauvignon in favour of Merlot – though whether he has yet made a better wine than the 1979 is a moot point.

Sangiovese

Cabernet Sauvignon's success in Tuscany has been achieved mainly in partnership with Sangiovese, the leading local grape variety. According to Marchese Piero Antinori, one of the pioneers of Cabernet Sauvignon in Tuscany, the Bordeaux grape softens the sometimes unpleasantly harsh flavours of Sangiovese. It will be noticed that this is the role Merlot is thought to play in the Médoc with the excessively tough and tannic Cabernet Sauvignon! It is also said that Cabernet Sauvignon rounds out the hollow middle flavour of Sangiovese – the role played by Shiraz, again with Cabernet Sauvignon, in Australia. All the same, the Sangiovese–Cabernet blend (first used at Carmignano and brilliantly exemplified by Contini Bonacossi's Tenuta di Capezzana) is an extremely satisfying addition to the world's store of red wine styles.

The Making of Cabernet Sauvignon

Wine-making consists of a string of decisions, each taken with a view to the kind of wine sought as an end-product. The first and most important is the timing of the harvest. In Bordeaux, the harvesting of Cabernet Sauvignon is poised between underripeness and the threat of heavy rain: Cabernet Sauvignon is almost always picked well into October, when the chances of bad weather are increasing daily. Even so, the grape will struggle, in moderate vintages, to reach 10° potential alcohol. In California and some parts of Australia, the main concern is the opposite one, that the grapes will become too rich in sugar and low in acidity – though Joe Heitz can still be picking in November.

After harvest, the wine-making process has become fairly standardized. Cabernet Sauvignon grapes are almost always de-stemmed (by being passed through a crusher–de-stemmer) and pumped into fermenting tanks. The question here is whether the wine is intended for long cellaring or early consumption. If the latter, the fermentation will be short and there will be no strenuous attempt to extract more colour. Indeed Mitchelton in Victoria use the Beaujolais method of whole-berry fermen-tation, or *macération carbonique*, to produce the wine they call, with true Antipodean charm, Cab Mac. I do not find Cabernet Sauvignon made by *macération carbonique* convincing. The innate complexity of the grape remains, albeit in diluted form, and fights with the easy-drinking style imposed by the wine-making method.

Fine Cabernet Sauvignon wines, though, are intended to age a minimum of five years and sometimes much longer. Its great ageing capacity is, after all, one of Cabernet Sauvignon's trump cards. In the case of these wines, there will be vigorous attempts during fermentation to extract maximum colour and a good dose of tannin from the skins by keeping the 'cap' of skins and pips in contact with the juice. This is generally done either by pumping-over (the commonest method) or by the older method of punching down the cap. The fermentation itself generally lasts a week; in Bordeaux, the traditional practice is to keep the wine macerating with the skins and pips for anything up to three weeks thereafter. The origin of this practice was simply that after fermentation was complete the cellar-workers shut up the vats and went off hunting for three weeks. The Californians have recently discovered it by a very different route, and extended maceration is a buzz idea in the Napa Valley. The theory is that longer chains of tannin are formed, which leads to a more harmonious, velvety wine. Others dispute this theory. Extended maceration is very much less prevalent in Australia. Penfolds, for example, do not use it for their top wines, Grange Hermitage and Bin 707 Cabernet Sauvignon.

When the results are so rich, powerful and long-lasting, I can imagine a laid-back, hard-hatted figure like David Slingsby-Smith remarking, why bother? The technique which Penfolds do use, and which I have not come across elsewhere, is the finishing of fermentation in new oak barrels.

Temperature of fermentation is another important variable. More matter can be extracted at higher temperatures, though to the possible detriment of aromatic freshness. Traditionally in Bordeaux, without sophisticated control of temperature, fermentations were conducted fairly hot, up to 35 °C and beyond. Now, every leading property is equipped with some form of temperature control and most aim for around 30 °C as a maximum.

MALOLACTIC FERMENTATION

Malolactic fermentation is the process whereby sharp malic acid is converted into smoother lactic acid. It occurs naturally with most wines at warmish temperatures; the problems come when the malolactic process stops before the conversion is complete because of cold weather, then restarts in the spring. The malolactic fermentation, which was only identified as a chemical process in the 1960s, is an essential part of the making of Cabernet Sauvignon wines. It can take place at the same time as the alcoholic fermentation (convenient for the wine-maker) or immediately afterwards, either in tank or cask. Sometimes it has to be induced by the injection of special bacteria.

PRESS WINE

After the *cuvaison* (the process of fermentation and maceration), the mass of skins and pips left in the bottom of the tanks or vats is removed and pressed. The resulting 'press wine' is generally deep-coloured and tannic; it is regarded by many wine-makers as an essential ingredient of the blend, adding substance and structure in lesser years. The proportion of press wine in the final blend can be as high as 15 per cent; in some years, at leading properties, no press wine is added (less grand ones cannot afford to waste it).

THE OAK FACTOR

With the *cuvaison* completed, classic Bordeaux practice is to pass the newly made wine into the 225-litre oak barrels called *barriques*. Cabernet Sauvignon's relationship with oak is as crucial as Chardonnay's. Well, almost. It is true that every top Cabernet Sauvignon in the world is aged in small oak barrels, whereas there do exist top Chardonnays which never see oak (the Chablis of Louis Michel comes to mind), but very good Cabernet Sauvignon can be made without oak, as I discovered one day in the Southern Graves with M. Jean Sévenet of Château Toumilon. Oak with Cabernet should never be a dominant influence. If you can taste or smell the new oak on a first-growth claret, as I do on Château Margaux 1978, the wine is either too young or has been over-oaked. It is probably for this reason that so many Cabernet-makers in the New World prefer the subtler flavours of French oak, generally from the forests of Nevers and Allier, and from Limousin (which has a coarser grain), despite the fact that it costs four times as much as American oak. Yet several of the greatest New World Cabernets (BV Georges de Latour, Ridge Monte Bello) are matured in American oak; they have so much power and concentration of fruit that the pronounced spicy, vanilla taste of new American oak does not stand out. Oak adds a subtle spiciness to Cabernet Sauvignon, but, more importantly, maturation in small barrels helps to round out the rough edges and soften the toughness. In this case oxygen is as much a factor as oak. New oak barrels have the further effect of contributing extra tannin, which is why new oak should be used only for wines with the inherent structure to take it.

RACKING AND FINING

In their first year, Cabernet Sauvignon wines made by the classic Bordeaux method are racked (transferred from one barrel into another, clean one, leaving the lees behind) every three months. The barrels are kept with the bungs at the top, and loose. The ultra-traditional way of seeing when the wine ceases to be clear is to hold a candle behind it. I have seen this being performed at Château de Pez in St Estèphe. At the end of the first year, the wine will be fined using beaten whites of egg, which fall through the barrel taking with them any loose particles. After fining and subsequent racking, the barrels are turned over with the bungs to the side, or *bondes de côté* (and, of course, firmly closed). They will spend a further six months to one year in this position.

This is the textbook method. A number of shortcuts are used these days. In most Californian wineries, there is no barrel-to-barrel racking, and the wine spends all its time in barrels on their side. In many classed-growth Bordeaux châteaux, the wine will spend only one year or even less in *barriques*. It will be transferred from tank to barrel and back to tank, to give an oak-aged flavour at lower cost.

AGEING

Exactly how long a wine will last is difficult to predict, and is in any case partly a matter of taste. The French drink their clarets at an age (three to five years on average) which has traditional English claret buffs, who regard ten years as a minimum maturing period for *cru classé* claret, crying 'Infanticide!' It is very difficult to find older vintages of California Cabernet Sauvignons, so one assumes that they too are drunk fairly young – probably before their fifth birthday. The Georges de Latour Private Reserve, from Beaulieu, can age well for at least twenty years, but on the whole, California Cabernet Sauvignons do not improve much beyond their tenth birthday. Australian Cabernet Sauvignons age rather more quickly;

certainly, they are easier to drink young. A few firms, notably Lindemans, have made a point of holding back reserves of special vintages for up to ten years. These certainly prove that the best Antipodean Cabernet Sauvignons can age remarkably well. The fact remains, however, that the great majority of Cabernet Sauvignons, including *cru classé* claret, are drunk too young.

The Cabernet Vine

Cabernet Sauvignon is a member of a family of vines that also includes Merlot, Cabernet Franc, Petit Verdot and Carmenère. All have in common certain characteristics of taste and appearance, but it is Cabernet Sauvignon, both for reasons of adaptability as well as quality, that has achieved pre-eminence among red wine grapes. As on the British Empire in the time of Victoria, the sun never sets on the empire of Cabernet Sauvignon. Voices have been raised in concern that Cabernet Sauvignon's grip on the wine world is becoming too strong. Native varieties are being uprooted; the rich diversity of indigenous styles is threatened. These are valid concerns, but I see evidence from Tuscany, where after the Cabernet rage of the late 1970s the tide has turned and the native Sangiovese is back in fashion, that fears of a world-wide Cabernet invasion are exaggerated.

CULTIVATION

The Cabernet is a vigorous vine with hard wood. Its leaves are quite small and dark green and can be distinguished by the peculiarity of having four or five 'holes' around the stem. The bunches of grapes are smallish, cylindrical and tailing to a point; they sometimes have distinct wings. The stems from which these bunches hang are long but ripen hard and are thus tough to cut. Harvesters in the Médoc need strong scissors. The berries are small and quite closely packed. What gives the Cabernet its notable resistance to rot is the thickness of these berries' skins, which are also rich in colouring compounds. Cabernet berries often have two pips – the proportion of pulp to pip is exceptionally low (12:1, according to the oenologist Professor Peynaud, as opposed to 25:1 for Sémillon), and the amount of tannin correspondingly high.

Cabernet is a relatively late-ripening variety. This gives it an advantage when it comes to spring frosts (its hard wood also protects it against severe winters), but a disadvantage in inclement autumns. The Cabernet Sauvignon harvest in Bordeaux begins, usually, around the end of September and continues into mid-October. In some parts of California, the harvest can continue into November, and in Coonawarra, South Australia, into May. The ripening process with Cabernet is delicately poised. The variety needs to ripen fully, or else the results will taste aggressively herbaceous, with strong notes of green pepper and even asparagus (a speciality of Cabernet from Monterey County, California). On the other hand, excessive ripeness leads to wines which lack length and vitality. The yield can vary enormously. The average in good conditions in Bordeaux is about 50 hectolitres per hectare, while in parts of Chile, the yield can be as high as 200 hectolitres per hectare. Over-production is certainly a problem in parts of northern Italy.

Although Cabernet Sauvignon is reasonably resistant to grey rot, it is prone to certain other diseases, notably oïdium. The outbreak of oïdium in France in 1852 reversed the trend of planting Cabernet Sauvignon in favour of Merlot so decisively that to this day there is twice as much Merlot as Cabernet in France. A new threat to Cabernet has emerged recently: the fungus disease Eutypiose, which enters the vine at the point of pruning and is invariably fatal, is now reckoned to affect 3–4 per cent of the vines in Bordeaux.

Preferred soil

Bordeaux claims, not surprisingly, that the poor, well-drained, deep gravelly soil of the Médoc and Graves is the best of all terrains for Cabernet Sauvignon. The wonderful results achieved from the deposits left by the Garonne and the Dordogne cannot be denied, but a quick glance around the rest of the world will show that Cabernet Sauvignon can thrive in markedly different conditions. The famous Rutherford Bench at the heart of the Napa Valley does have a component of gravel, and the ground is quick to drain. The main component, however, is loam and the soil is considerably richer than that of, say, Margaux. Some fine Cabernet Sauvignons are made from the heavy clay soil of the valley floor, but the new wave of hillside growers claim that the volcanic soils of the hills surrounding the Napa Valley make the best wine; Mayacamas, Dunn and Newton, among others, put up a strong case.

Australia's most famous Cabernet Sauvignon region, Coonawarra, consists of a narrow strip of *terra rossa* soil covering porous limestone, with ample water underground for irrigation. The problem facing Coonawarra's wine-growers is excessive vine growth.

The soils in the Central Valley of Chile are light but fertile – and irrigated by the melted glaciers from the Andes. The problem here is excessive yields, which dilute flavour and character.

Rootstock

Most Cabernet Sauvignon vines are grafted on to American rootstock, which is resistant to the deadly vine aphid, *Phylloxera vastatrix*. Exceptions are the vineyards of Chile, where phylloxera has never penetrated, and Australia, where it has yet to pose a major problem. The matching of rootstock to vine in a particular locality is a sensitive business to which increasing attention is being paid. Among the most common types of rootstock used in Europe are SO4 and 3309. Two common Californian rootstocks are Rupestris St George and Aramon Rupestris Ganzin 1. Fears of a second phylloxera invasion have recently surfaced; infestations have been reported in California and New Zealand. In general, Cabernet Sauvignon needs weak rootstock.

Clonal selection

Clonal selection has not been as important an issue with Cabernet Sauvignon as with certain other varieties such as Pinot Noir and Riesling, where different clones can give markedly different flavours. All the same, considerable attention is being paid to clonal selection of Cabernet Sauvignon in both Bordeaux and California. M. Aimé Guibert of Mas de Daumas Gassac is a passionate believer in the use of non-selected vines. He feels that clonal selection leads to a disastrous standardization. Twenty-four clones have been officially approved; two much used in Bordeaux are 337 and 341.

Density of planting

The classic Bordeaux vineyards are planted in 1 × 1m rows, giving a density of 4,000 vines per acre. Considerably less dense planting, but still high, of around 2,500 vines per acre, is employed at a number of leading châteaux. At the other extreme are some of the Californian vineyards, planted in rows three or four metres apart to allow the big American tractors to pass through. In the Penedès area of north-eastern Spain, Miguel A. Torres is a passionate proponent of high-density planting, around 2,000 vines per acre, as opposed to the 800–1,200 per acre planted by most Penedès farmers. He feels that if the vines are planted too far apart, the ground in between loses its moisture.

Training and pruning

Cabernet Sauvignon vines are generally trained on wires and pruned by the Guyot method, leaving either a single or double cane. The bilateral Cordon Royat system is used also, notably by Torres in Penedès. The canes need to be relatively long to ensure a decent yield, because the buds near the junction with the trunk give little fruit. Mechanical pruning is now widely in use in Australia and, though it leaves the vines looking as if they have been struck by a whirlwind, seems to give good results.

Harvesting

Mechanical harvesting is very widely employed in America and Australia, and in Spain, where Miguel Torres professes himself very satisfied with the results. Such wine-makers as David Hohnen in Western Australia and Janet Trefethen in the Napa Valley say they prefer mechanical to manual harvesting because of the greater flexibility of timing it offers – also because mechanical harvesters do not strike. The thick-skinned berries of Cabernet Sauvignon are especially well suited to mechanical harvesting because they do not break easily. All the same, most of the leading Bordeaux châteaux continue to pick by hand.

HISTORY

Like those of most grape varieties, the origins of Cabernet Sauvignon are lost in prehistory. Professor Olmo of Davis University told me that he found a trailing vine by the side of a road in Afghanistan. It caught his attention because its leaves had the characteristic Cabernet holes. When he tasted its fruit and found the herbaceous and blackcurranty flavours of the Cabernet family, the Professor thought he might be on to something. He brought the plant back to California and has propagated some crossings which continue to give Cabernet-like fruit. This wild Afghan vine may or may not be the father of Cabernet. Certainly Professor Olmo believes that the name Cabernet Sauvignon implies a wild vine (Sauvignon = *sauvage*).

Wherever Cabernet Sauvignon originated (Edward Hyams conjectures Lydia), its adolescence and development are firmly situated in Bordeaux. There is a frail etymological link between the name of the tribe who founded Bordeaux, the Bituriges, and the old name of Cabernet – Vidure, or Petit Vidure. De Secondat, son of Montesquieu (a native of the Graves region), produced another, more likely, etymology: *vidure = vigne dure*.

The pre-eminence of Cabernet Sauvignon is actually quite a recent phenomenon. It only became very widely planted in its home area, Bordeaux, in the late eighteenth century. It had been planted in Bordeaux long before that, of course, but had disputed its position with other grape varieties of the same family, some still widely planted, like Cabernet Franc, others more or less forgotten, like Carmenère. It is quite possible that the great wines of Bordeaux would be greater still if the main variety was Carmenère, whose decline is due to its low yield and poor resistance to disease, nothing at all to do with quality. J.-B. Delmas, the talented *régisseur* of Château Haut-Brion, who keeps some Carmenère in his vine nursery, believes that it could give better-quality wine than Cabernet Sauvignon.

From Bordeaux, as will be detailed in the country-by-country sections, Cabernet Sauvignon was exported to all parts of the wine world where there was a will to produce excellent red wine. According to Count Ugo Contini Bonacossi, it reached Tuscany in the early eighteenth century, Piedmont in the early nineteenth century, Australia in the early-to-mid nineteenth century, California and Chile around 1850. The eastern European countries, especially Bulgaria, jumped on the Cabernet Sauvignon bandwagon after the Second World War and, with their centralized, state-controlled systems, soon had massive acreages. More recent converts to the Cabernet Sauvignon cause include Washington State in the north-west of the USA and Penedès in north-eastern Spain.

CROSSINGS

Ruby Cabernet. Professor Harold Olmo created this cross between Carignan and Cabernet Sauvignon at Davis University, California, in 1946. The aim was to combine the high yield of Carignan with the high quality of Cabernet Sauvignon. According to Jancis Robinson, the result is 'more ruby than Cabernet', but growers in California's Central Valley obviously have some faith in the crossing since there were more than 12,000 acres planted there in 1983.

Magaratch Ruby. The Institute Magaratch in the Crimea produced its version of Ruby Cabernet with this crossing of Cabernet Sauvignon with the indigenous grape, Saperavi. The

Russians appear to have been more successful than the Americans in this instance, for the crossing, according to Jancis Robinson, gives good levels of sugar and acidity, deep colour and an authentic Cabernet character.

Carnelian. Another Olmo crossing, this time between the 1936 Carignan–Cabernet Sauvignon crossing, called F 2–7, and Grenache. In California, 1,600 acres have been planted, but the vine has much more of the Grenache than the Cabernet Sauvignon character.

Centurion. This crossing has the same parents as Carnelian, but is easier to harvest.

Carmine. A Californian crossing between Cabernet Sauvignon and Merlot.

In the Glass, on the Table, in the Cellar

THE TASTE SPECTRUM

Unripe	Green/ Herbaceous/Spicy	Fruity	Mature
Asparagus	Green pepper	Blackcurrant	Cedar
	Tobacco	Blackberry	Cigar-box
	Mint	Plum	Incense
	Eucalyptus		
	Clove		
	Vanilla		

Such a spectrum as this only begins to describe the range of scents and flavours offered by the best Cabernet Sauvignon wines. One of the distinguishing marks of fine Cabernet Sauvignon is the co-existence of different kinds and orders of taste: there is a fruit component, but also a herbaceous one (tobacco, mint, green pepper), together with various kinds of spice (vanilla, clove) and an overall impression which is different from any of these individually. Age tends to reduce the primary fruit impact, but to add endless nuances of graceful decay.

Cabernet Sauvignons from different parts of the world do tend to have different profiles. Wine from the Médoc tends towards leanness and austerity, with primary fruit flavours (except in certain Pauillacs) less marked than a subtle interplay of flavours. A Frenchman would say they expressed the *terroir* rather than the *cépage*: the wines of St Estèphe certainly often possess an earthy taste. A number of Californian and Australian Cabernet Sauvignons are marked by strong aromas of mint and eucalyptus (two different aromas which are often confused). Californian and Australian, especially Australian, Cabernet Sauvignons are also notable for vivid, immediate, fruit character, seldom found in the Médoc. The best Chilean Cabernet Sauvignons combine luxuriant fruit with layers of tobacco and cedarwood. A not altogether flattering descriptor for the taste of Bulgarian Cabernet Sauvignon is boiled blackcurrant. One could say in general that the less obvious and more complex the aroma and flavour, the greater the wine, but one might be left with an awkward question regarding the piercingly clear, not especially complex, blackcurrant nose found on some vintages of Mouton-Rothschild, clearly one of the great Cabernet Sauvignon wines.

Herbaceousness, obviously an intrinsic part of the flavour of Cabernet Sauvignon, must not dominate the wine. The Cabernet Sauvignons of northern Italy and New Zealand can be unpleasantly weedy, while those of Monterey County, California, can be marked by a strong and undesirable note of asparagus. However, subtle additions of tobacco, mint and green pepper (though the latter must not be too assertive) are desirable in adding complexity.

At the other end of the ripeness scale, the taste of ripe blackberry or plum shades into cooked fruit. Cabernet Sauvignon should not taste too jammy.

With great, fully mature wines, aromas and tastes have become both so developed and so integrated as to be virtually indescribable. Indeed, to pick out individual elements of taste seems impertinent, since the whole point is that a wonderful harmony has been created in which the parts merge with the whole.

IDENTIFYING THE TASTE OF CABERNET SAUVIGNON

Château Palmer 1979 (Margaux, troisième cru classé)

Appearance. Fairly deep, bright blood-red colour, with purplish rim indicating youth. A typical youngish Cabernet Sauvignon colour (in fact remarkably youthful for an eleven-year-old wine), lacking the really dense concentration of a great vintage.

Bouquet/nose. The first impression is of ripe berry-fruit (possibly blackcurrant), strongly indicative of Cabernet Sauvignon (though this château has a quite high proportion of Merlot!). New oak is present but very well assimilated; it does not stand out as a separate element. Overall there is a chocolatey richness characteristic of this château.

Palate. Once again, ripe berry-fruit predominates. The flavour is quite rich, not at all thin, but the structure is too firm for it to be anything but Bordeaux. This is a medium-weight, not a big heavyweight wine: though high-class, it could not be a massive château like Latour or Mouton-Rothschild. There is some tannin at the finish, but the wine could be considered ready to drink. A very attractive claret from Margaux, of a good if not great vintage.

Storing and serving. This is wine just reaching maturity, which will hold its quality for another three to five years. As a medium-weight claret it would make a perfect lunch wine. It has a powerful enough flavour to go with beef or lamb, but would perhaps show to best advantage with duck or chicken.

Heitz Martha's Vineyard Cabernet Sauvignon 1982 (Napa Valley, California)

Appearance. Deep, dense colour (what port-shippers call 'solid'), but beginning to turn from deep blood-red at core to a browner, bricky tone at the very rim. Strangely, contrary to the view that California Cabernet Sauvignons keep their dense colour longer than clarets, this is turning much more quickly than the Palmer. This may reflect the fact that 1982 in the Napa Valley was a somewhat variable vintage.

Bouquet/nose. An extraordinary, intense burst of mint and eucalyptus, with blackcurrant, cedar and tobacco in the background. No other wine in the world smells quite like this one (though several Australian Cabernet Sauvignons have a more obvious, chewing-gum mintiness). A bouquet of great power and dramatic intensity, rather than the civilized, subtle balance of the Bordeaux.

Palate. The mint-and-eucalyptus character comes through again on the palate. This is a big, powerful, ripe wine, less elegant than the Palmer and, as wine writers used to say, masculine rather than feminine. There is tough tannin at the finish. Clearly a serious wine intended for long keeping, this is a stern, almost forbidding wine, but it has immense character.

Storing and serving. This is just beginning to be ready to drink, but will benefit from further cellaring, for anything from two to ten years. Whether it will ever mellow completely remains to be seen. Such a massive, uncompromising wine demands similar food – good roast beef or Châteaubriand. The minty nose would also lead to an interesting combination with lamb. Strictly red meat here.

Orlando St Hugo Coonawarra Cabernet Sauvignon 1986 (South Australia)

Appearance. Good, deep, almost thick colour, still with a youthful purple hue, though it does not have the blue of extreme youth. The concentration of colour is promising and suggests a good vintage (as 1986 was in Coonawarra).

Bouquet/nose. There is an arresting intensity of aroma, partly fruity (blackcurrant), partly herbaceous (mint, just a touch of green pepper). This is still a young wine, with vivid fruit character.

Palate. The initial impression is sweet ripe fruit. The middle flavour is impressively concentrated and tight-knit, with some astringency. At the finish, however, tannin is overwhelmed by the sheer ripeness of the fruit and attendant glycerol (natural, of course). A young wine made in a coolish region from ripe grapes, showing excellent intensity of varietal character with the promise of greater complexity to come.

Storing and serving. The wine is still young, but is already drinking beautifully because of the ripeness of the fruit. It will develop over the next five years, but will lose some of its fruit intensity. This is a wine whose sharply defined flavours seem to demand savouring on their own, or with mild, hard cheese (Cheddar or Manchego – a ewes'-milk cheese from central Spain).

CABERNET SAUVIGNON WINES AND FOOD

Anyone expecting to find the answer to the matching of Cabernet Sauvignon wines with appropriate food in the grape variety's homeland, the Bordeaux region of south-western France, is likely to be disappointed. For a start, the cuisine of Bordeaux is not particularly varied or exciting. Specialities include *entrecôte* steak (which should be grilled over vine prunings) and the pale, milk-fed lamb of Pauillac. The fish speciality is lamprey cooked in red wine, with which the best wine is probably a simple claret from Bourg or Blaye rather than a *grand cru classé*.

In some ways, the cuisine of Bordeaux resembles that of Britain, the country where the great clarets found their earliest market. It is difficult to beat roast beef as a background to an array of top-class clarets or California Cabernet Sauvignons. For the more delicate clarets, certain Margaux and St Juliens for instance, the more delicate flavour of young lamb is better suited. White meats such as chicken and, more especially, guinea-fowl allow the full range of flavours of the less powerful Cabernet Sauvignon wines to express themselves.

Not recommended with Cabernet Sauvignon wines are hot or spicy dishes, where Riesling, with a touch of residual sweetness, is often the best solution.

The suitability of cheese as an accompaniment to red wine of all kinds is often taken for granted. In fact, being extremely highly flavoured and having undergone several fermentations, cheese is extremely difficult to match with red wine. In particular, the soft, white-rinded cheeses such as Brie and Camembert completely alter the taste of red wine, making it sweet and soapy. The best cheeses to eat with Cabernet Sauvignon wines are hard and relatively mild: apart from the semi-mature Cheddar and semi-dry Manchego already mentioned, hard Italian cheeses such as Pecorino and Parmigiano are quite suitable.

SERVING

Temperature

Cabernet Sauvignon wines should be served, in general, at room temperature (18–20 °C) or, as the French say, *chambré*. It is always better to err on the cool rather than the warm side: wine can be warmed up by the heat of the hand on the glass but not nearly so easily cooled. To achieve room temperature in cold weather, the wine should be warmed as gently as possible, either by being kept in a warm room for several hours or (an expedient common in my family) in the airing cupboard. Wines should never be warmed by baking or by being placed next to very hot fires.

Certain youthful, unoaked Cabernet Sauvignon wines are best drunk cool, though never cold. Mitchelton's Cab Mac is an obvious example; others are the lighter Cabernet Sauvignon wines of northern Italy.

Decanting

Decanting is a necessity for fine older clarets and other unfiltered Cabernet Sauvignon wines that have thrown a substantial deposit. However, the purpose of decanting is not just to separate the wine from the deposit; it is also to give it some aeration, which has a softening effect on young, tannic wine. This is a tricky area, for excessive aeration can destroy a wine, particularly an older wine. Previous experience is the only safe guide. My advice is to decant younger Cabernet Sauvignon wines of high quality about an hour to an hour and a half before drinking, older ones (pre-1970 in the case of clarets) at most half an hour before drinking.

Glasses

The Austrian glass-making firm Riedel has shown in comparative, blind glass tastings that the choice of glass can substantially affect the taste of the wine. Experienced tasters, asked to rate the same wine from four different glasses (not knowing that it is the same wine) have consistently given 15 per cent higher marks to the wine in the 'best' glass. Glasses with reasonably sized bowls (though not necessarily the vast, 37 fl. oz capacity of Riedel's Sommelier Grand Cru range), tulip-shaped to keep aroma in and designed to be easily twirled, are the most satisfactory. Cut crystal glasses are not recommended: they obscure the wine's appearance. It is essential not to fill glasses too full – between a third and a quarter is ideal.

STORING

Cabernet Sauvignon wines which require long ageing, such as *cru classé* Bordeaux (at least ten years to reach maturity) and top California Cabernet Sauvignons (five to seven years), are best kept in a cool, humid, underground cellar. Absence of temperature variation and freedom from vibration are two important requirements. The importance of humidity is in preventing the corks from drying out; the disadvantage is that it destroys cartons (wine must be binned, racked or kept in wooden cases) and labels.

Few people in the late twentieth century possess underground cellars. Dark, relatively cool places such as cupboards under the stairs are a reasonable short-term solution, but it is not advisable to keep valuable wine in such places for more than a few weeks. In the UK, specialist wine merchants such as Lay & Wheeler, Berry Bros & Rudd, Justerini & Brooks, the Wine Society and many others can arrange storage of customers' wine, at around £3.50 per case per annum. Alternatively, it is possible to arrange private storage with firms such as Smith & Taylor or Trapps Cellars.

GAZETTEER

KEY TO RATING SYSTEM

Quality

🍇 indifferent

🍇🍇 average

🍇🍇🍇 good

🍇🍇🍇🍇 very good

🍇🍇🍇🍇🍇 outstanding

Price

★ cheap

★★ average

★★★ expensive

★★★★ very expensive

★★★★★ luxury

AUSTRALIA AND NEW ZEALAND

Australia

Total vineyard area: 170,000 acres
Area planted to Cabernet Sauvignon: 11,406 acres

The streamlined, high-tech Australian wine industry has a longer history than many realize. Vines were brought out by Captain Phillip on the first expedition in 1788. Though these did not flourish, those planted a few years later by John Macarthur, paymaster of the Rum Corps, on his estate south of Sydney, were more fortunate. Macarthur went to France in 1815 to collect cuttings, which included Cabernet Sauvignon, and so in 1830 did the remarkable man known as the father of Australian viticulture, James Busby. Despite these promising early beginnings, the development of quality table wine production in this country which has so many suitable sites for viticulture was slow to materialize. It was only in 1971 that the production of table wine overtook that of fortified wine.

Cabernet Sauvignon, with over 11,000 acres, is now the second most widely planted of red wine grapes in Australia after Shiraz. South Australia is by far the most important state with 65 per cent. Next come New South Wales and Victoria with 15 per cent each. In terms of quality Cabernet Sauvignon is considered by Australians to be their premium red wine grape (though foreigners are often equally impressed by the undervalued Shiraz). This rise to prominence is a recent phenomenon. Even in Coonawarra, the Australian Cabernet Sauvignon vineyard *par excellence*, Cabernet has only recently

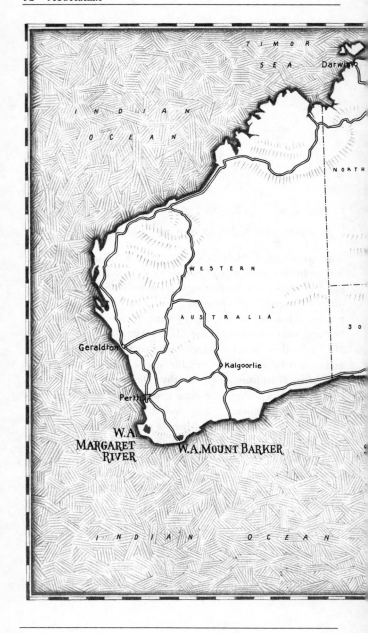

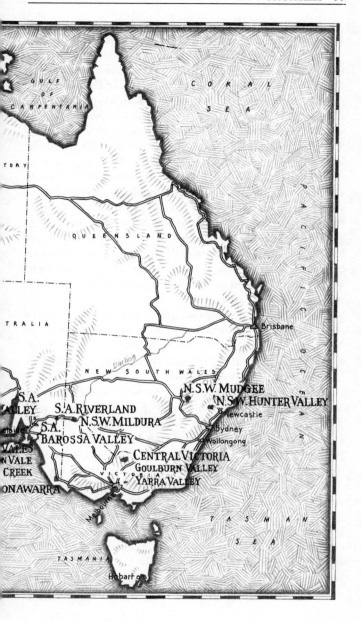

GULF OF CARPENTARIA

CORAL SEA

TORY

QUEENSLAND

TRALIA

PACIFIC OCEAN

Darling

NEW SOUTH WALES

Brisbane

S.A. VALLEY

S.A. RIVERLAND

N.S.W. MILDURA

S.A. BAROSSA VALLEY

N.S.W. MUDGEE

N.S.W. HUNTER VALLEY

Newcastle

Sydney

Wollongong

ALES

N VALE

CREEK

ONAWARRA

CENTRAL VICTORIA

GOULBURN VALLEY

YARRA VALLEY

VICTORIA

Melbourne

TASMAN SEA

TASMANIA

Hobart

outstripped Shiraz. For a long time, of course, Australian wines were sold under misleading labels such as Burgundy, Claret and Chablis. Clarets often contained a percentage of Cabernet, but usually a majority of Shiraz, hardly a Bordelais variety.

When table wine production expanded in the 1960s, the emphasis was on quantity. Most of the wine was everyday stuff destined to be sold in 'casks', the Australian term for bags-in-boxes. Choice of vineyard location was somewhat haphazard. The story of the last fifteen years has been increasingly careful matching of grape variety to vineyard site, combined with remarkable technological advance in the winery. On the whole this has meant a search for cooler locations in a country whose southernmost (therefore most temperate) parts lie on the corresponding latitude to that of southern Spain. Many of the early Australian vineyards were planted close to the major cities, yet areas like the Swan Valley near Perth, parts of the Barossa an hour from Adelaide and, arguably, the Hunter two hours from Sydney are too hot to produce subtle, complex wines, at least from certain grape varieties.

There are now three regions recognized as being in a class of their own for the production of Cabernet Sauvignon: the Margaret River in Western Australia, Coonawarra in South Australia and the Yarra Valley near Melbourne, Victoria. This is not to say that very fine Cabernets are not made elsewhere, in the Clare Valley in South Australia, for instance, the Goulburn Valley in central Victoria and other spots in this most variegated of Australian wine states and, somehow, against the odds, in the Hunter Valley in New South Wales. Showing great promise also are the Mount Barker and Frankland River areas of Western Australia and, coolest of all Australian regions, Tasmania. Good Cabernets are also made in the McLaren Vale and Langhorne Creek areas of South Australia, Mudgee in New South Wales and, for good-value, simple, varietal fruit, the irrigated areas of the Murray and Murrumbidgee Rivers.

This move to cooler regions implies a change towards lighter styles. There has been a concerted effort from the new generation of Australian wine-makers to get away from the big, bold, heavy (and indeed sweaty) stereotype of Australian red wine, based on the produce of famous, hot areas like the Barossa and the Hunter. In the winery, stress has been laid on cooler fermentation temperatures, the avoidance of excessive tannin extraction, and the subtler flavours of French as opposed to American oak. The pursuit of elegance and refinement is both commendable and understandable – big, heavy red wines may be well suited to Australia's export markets but are hardly ideal for the baking heat of the Australian summer. However, the lightening has in some cases gone too far; early-picked grapes have been simply unripe, the results unpleasantly green and thin. The best of the modern wine-makers, such as Brian Croser of Petaluma, have sought refinement with ripeness.

There is an intriguing debate in Australia, not often publicly aired, between those who favour what are in effect single-appellation wines and the advocates of inter-regional blending. The former, backed by the example of France, seem to be winning the day: certainly a Coonawarra Cabernet Sauvignon label is a *sine qua non* for practically every major producer. However, there are some very powerful voices ranged on the other side. The most voluble is Wolf Blass, sometimes derided as a self-publicist but, with his string of award-winning red wines, not a man to be lightly dismissed. Blass is strongly convinced that, with Cabernet Sauvignon, a blend of, say, Langhorne Creek and McLaren Vale with Coonawarra makes a more balanced wine than straight Coonawarra. His beautifully mellow Black Label Cabernet Sauvignons provide cogent support for his argument. My feeling is that 100 per cent Coonawarra Cabernets are often too sharp and angular for comfort.

The main variety traditionally blended with Cabernet Sauvignon in Australia has for many years been Shiraz. Shiraz is thought to fill out the 'hollow middle palate' of Cabernet Sauvignon. Certainly the result can be very satisfying, combining the chocolatey richness of Shiraz with the firm bone structure of Cabernet. The Shiraz tends to dominate the flavour, if not the structure – but with a wine as delicious as Petaluma's 1979 Coonawarra (60 per cent Shiraz, 40 per cent Cabernet), one may not complain. All the same, the tendency, at Petaluma and other premium wineries, has been to abandon blending with Shiraz and to follow the French path with Merlot and (to a lesser extent) Cabernet Franc. Merlot does seem to provide forward, sappy fruit to round out Cabernet's bony contours. Peter Douglas, manager of Wynns, Coonawarra, which produce some of Australia's finest Cabernets, is flatly against blending, however. He considers that Merlot and Cabernet Franc simply dilute great Cabernet. Malbec is still quite widely planted in Australia and blended in small quantities with Cabernet; it seems to contribute the same kind of upfront fruit as Merlot, possibly with a slightly coarser accent, though Stanley Leasingham in the Clare produce an excellent example.

It is difficult to generalize about the flavour characteristics of Australian Cabernets – wines grown all the way across a continent from Margaret River in the far south-west to the Hunter in the east. If Australian Cabernets have anything in common, it is a direct vividness of blackcurrant fruit which this grape nowhere else produces quite so uncompromisingly. Sophisticated producers try to tone down this effect. The Margaret River, in some ways Australia's answer to Monterey County, California, seems naturally to produce Cabernets with a strong herbaceous tone, as well as lifted fruit and a stylish, cedary elegance. Mount Barker's Cabernets are less immediately appealing, and sternly tannic, but have an impressive purity of fruit.

Coonawarra, the isolated strip of *terra rossa* on limestone in the flat lands of south-eastern South Australia, has the largest plantings of top-quality Cabernet in Australia. Wines from this region tend to express themselves intensely on the nose, with a combination of blackcurrant fruit and leafy herbaceousness – sometimes recognizable as green pepper or even asparagus. They are relatively light in alcohol and sometimes uncomfortably high in acidity. It seems to me a mistake to pick Coonawarra Cabernet slightly unripe, as firms such as Mildara have done in the past and Hardy's (or their suppliers, the Coonawarra Machine Company) continue to do with Reynella. Cabernets from other South Australian regions such as McLaren Vale, Langhorne Creek and the Barossa tend to be in complete contrast – rich, plummy, sometimes soft-centred.

Clare, although a warmish region, is capable of producing finely structured Cabernets.

A strongly minty nose is a feature of several Victorian Cabernets, particularly that of Brown Brothers. Coming from a warmer region, the Cabernet of Château Tahbilk is richer and earthier, with massive tannic structure. The cool Yarra Valley, a fine wine region with a long history, is becoming increasingly well known as the source of some of the finest, most subtle and refined red wines in Australia.

Hunter Valley Cabernets tend to show hot-climate characteristics – an almost toffee-like nose, softness and lack of structure. In general, the higher, cooler vineyards of Mudgee show greater promise, producing rich, intense and tannic Cabernets such as those of Montrose.

The best Australian Cabernets come closer to the French ideal of elegance, refinement and length in the mouth than any others made outside Bordeaux. Not many may achieve the complexity of a top *cru classé* , but the progress made in the last decade suggests that the full potential of Australian Cabernet has not yet been realized.

Vintage Guide

1990. I was present in several Australian regions during the 1990 harvest, which had South Australian wine-makers exclaiming over what was possibly the most promising vintage they had ever seen. The picture in the Hunter Valley could hardly have been more different: torrential summer and autumn rain led to severe problems of rot.

1989. Bizarre weather conditions, including a cool rainy summer, in many regions led to variable quality. Some excellent wines were made, but care is needed in selection.

1988. Frost affected quantity in some regions, but the growing season was warm, the harvest early and the quality of Cabernet Sauvignon very good.

1987. A much cooler growing season produced some fine, elegant wines. Coonawarra Cabernet Sauvignons can taste green and astringent. The best are subtle and long.

1986. A superb vintage for Cabernet Sauvignon in most regions.

1985. A cool year; particularly good quality in New South Wales. A good but not great vintage for Cabernet Sauvignon.

1984. A very large crop led to lack of concentration. Some Cabernet Sauvignons drinking very well, however.

1983. A vintage marked by torrid heat, leading to a baked and sometimes dried-out character in many wines. Skilful wine-makers were able to make some intense, full-flavoured wines.

1982. A warm year which gave some exceptionally soft, rich wines.

ANDREW GARRETT. See Garrett, Andrew

BALGOWNIE

Victoria

> Hermitage Road, Maiden Gully, VIC 3551
>
> Vineyard: *c.* 15 acres
>
> Production: 24,000 bottles
>
> Quality: 🍇🍇🍇   Price: ★★★
>
> Best vintages: 1984, 1985, 1986, 1987

The Balgownie style, established by Stuart Anderson, founder of the winery, is big, concentrated, extracted and full of charac-ter. Whether this will change now that Balgownie belongs to the Mildara group remains to be seen: I have heard murmur-ings among senior Mildara personnel that a somewhat lighter, less extracted style might be desirable. A slightly lighter hand with tannin might not be a bad thing, but I feel it would be a shame to change the essence of the Balgownie style. Wines like the 1985 and 1987 Estate Cabernets are impenetrably deep in colour, with mint on the nose and a peppery texture on the palate, long and concentrated.

BERRI-RENMANO

South Australia

> Berri, SA 5343
>
> Production: not released
>
> Labels: Berri Estates, Barossa Valley Estates, Renmano Chairman's Selection
>
> Quality: 🍇 Price: ★★
>
> Best vintages: 1983

The best wines from this gigantic co-operative in the Riverland are sold under the Renmano Chairman's Selection label. The Cabernets are light and cedary (surprising from one of Australia's hottest wine regions), with some elegance but no great depth. The problem, I suspect, is high yields from the Riverland's irrigated vineyards. Production is on a factory scale and not pretty to look at, though the wines are cleanly made.

BLASS, WOLF

South Australia

> Bilyara Vineyards, 97 Sturt Highway, Nuriootpa, SA 5355
>
> Production: 1.4 million bottles
>
> Labels: Yellow Label, Grey Label, Black Label President's Selection
>
> Quality: 🍇 Price: ★★ – ★★★
>
> Best vintages: 1984, 1986

Wolf Blass is undoubtedly a marketing genius. You may find everything about him – the bow-tie, the kitschy labels, even the obviously oaky wines – in poor taste, but you cannot deny that he has discovered a style which a great many people like. The secret – and it is no great secret, for Blass owned practically no vineyards until he acquired Quelltaler in 1987 – lies in blending and the use of oak, both barrels and chips. Even the basic Yellow Label Cabernet Sauvignon–Shiraz spends up to eighteen months in barrels, mainly American oak. It has an attractive, easy-going mixture of toffee and blackcurrant on the nose; on the palate it is oaky, loose-knit and drinkable. The 1986 Grey Label Cabernet Sauvignon–Shiraz (blended 80/20 per cent from 100 per cent Langhorne Creek fruit) is much livelier and fresher, with a minty nose, good fruit on the palate, soft tannin and a good deal of oak coming through on the finish. The 1984 Black Label President's Selection Cabernet Sauvignon–Merlot–Shiraz (75/15/10 per cent) has quite a developed colour, a nose dominated by sweet vanilla oakiness, with just a touch of Cabernet blackcurrant fruit underneath, and a sweet, mellow, attractive flavour. It may not be the most complex or demanding of wines, but it is wine that one wants to go on drinking, and who can blame Blass for providing that?

BROWN BROTHERS

Victoria

Glenrowan-Myrtleford Road, Milawa, VIC 3678
Production: not released
Quality: 🍇🍇🍇   Price: ★★★
Best vintages: 1984, 1985, 1986, 1987, 1988

Brown Brothers, established in 1889, is probably Australia's best-known family winery. The Browns regard themselves as 'varietal wine specialists', making 'deeply flavoured varietal wines rather than generic styles or copies'. Certainly their wines always seem to have vividly defined varietal character-istics, and their Cabernet Sauvignons, almost a parody of the grape variety with their mint-and-blackcurrant character, are no exception. The single-vineyard Koombahla Cabernet, from the relatively cool King Valley, is minty on the nose, medium-weight on the palate, with intense fruit and moderate tannin.

BOWEN ESTATE

South Australia

> Naracoorte Road, Penola, SA 5277
> Vineyard: 15 acres
> Production: not released
> Quality: 🍇🍇🍇🍇🍇   Price: ★★★
> Best vintages: 1987

Doug Bowen is currently producing some of the best Cabernets in Coonawarra – which is to say in Australia – with a combination of ripeness and refinement that eludes many better-known names. His Cabernet is blended with 10 per cent Merlot – both varieties grown on the Bowens' own vineyards at the southern end of Coonawarra – and there is definitely a Bordelais touch to its subtlety and refinement.

CAPE MENTELLE

Western Australia

> Wallcliffe Road, Margaret River, WA 6285
> Vineyard: 32 acres
> Production: 30,000 bottles
> Quality: 🍇🍇🍇🍇🍇   Price: ★★★★
> Best vintages: 1984, 1986, 1987, 1988

The laconic David Hohnen, founder of Cape Mentelle, and of Cloudy Bay in New Zealand, is one of Australia's most impressive wine-makers. Among Margaret River's colourful collection of doctors, millionaires and eccentrics, Hohnen stands out for his sheer professionalism. He believes strongly in the particular virtue of the Margaret River's combination of ocean-influenced climate and ancient soil, especially for the Cabernet Sauvignon grape – in his view the Margaret River speciality. Hohnen's Cabernet is, like the man himself, impressive but reserved. It can show the herbaceous, green-pepper character which is obtrusive in some Margaret River Cabernets, but there is berry-fruit ripeness also, creamy texture and considerable tannin. The 1983 has a rich, minty nose and is big and powerful, and still tannic on the finish. The 1986 is beginning to show some cedary character, and is lean and well structured. Hohnen looks for 'fine-grained tannin which supports the wine like a coat-hanger'. Both the 1987 and 1988 seem to have a degree of extra fruit ripeness and intensity. Cape Mentelle Cabernet has about 5 per cent Merlot added in for complexity, and spends fourteen months in French oak *barriques*, renewed in thirds.

CHÂTEAU TAHBILK

Victoria

Tabilk, VIC 3607

Production: not released

Quality: 🍇🍇🍇   Price: ★★

Best vintages: 1976, 1984, 1985

This is not only the oldest family-owned winery in Victoria, dating back to 1860, but also the most obstinately old-fashioned. The Cabernets are made by traditional Bordeaux methods – that is to say, fermentation in wooden vats without much recourse to cooling. The result is some of the most long-lasting Cabernets in Australia, making up for any lack of refinement with character and guts. To give an idea of how long they can last, the 1968 Cabernet Sauvignon, tasted in 1989, had a lovely soft, sweet, cedary character on the nose and gentle, ripe fruit on the palate. In some years, like 1979, roasted, gamy aromas and flavours predominate. Among more recent vintages, the 1984 has a minty nose and is a big, solid, tannic wine which obviously needs more time. The 1985 is much lighter, surprisingly delicate, with a floral character on the nose.

CHITTERING ESTATE

Western Australia

Chittering Valley Road, Lower Chittering, WA 6084
Vineyard: 6 acres
Production: 24,000 bottles
Quality: 🍇🍇🍇   Price: ★★★
Best vintages: 1987, 1988

Chittering Estate has one of the most beautiful settings of any Australian wine estate, in a green, parrot-filled valley of the Darling range north of Perth on which man has scarcely impinged. Money was obviously no object when Stephen Schapera, a young South African engineer, and George Kailis, one of the biggest names in the Western Australian fish industry, set up this operation in 1981. Schapera, who has attended Davis University in California but is in some respects an autodidact, runs the winery more or less single-handed. As a wine-maker he favours soft, rich styles, which this fairly warm region naturally produces. His 1987 Cabernet–Merlot (80/20 per cent) is minty on the nose, rich and not hard on the palate, but with sufficient tannin. The 1988 is even richer, almost sweet, with luscious fruit. These are unusual wines; it will be interesting to see if they have the structure for extended life.

COLDSTREAM HILLS

Victoria

> Lot 6, Maddens Lane, Coldstream, VIC 3770
>
> Production: not released
>
> Quality: 🍇🍇🍇   Price: ★★★★
>
> Best vintage: 1988

The combination of lawyer and writer on wine is not uncommon, but the additional move from writing about wine to making it is much rarer. It has been accomplished with some brilliance by Australia's leading wine writer, James Halliday (can Château Parker be far away?). Halliday's first efforts were a beautifully structured Chardonnay and an even better Pinot Noir. He has now begun producing a Cabernet Sauvignon, with a little Cabernet Franc and Merlot in the blend, from three vineyards in the Yarra Valley. Initial impressions of the 1988 are very deep colour and a rich, toasty nose (the wine is matured for one year in new Nevers *barriques*). On the palate this is a Cabernet for Pinot Noir-lovers – aromatic and elegant with raspberry fruit.

CULLEN

Western Australia

> Caves Road, Cowaramup, WA 6284
>
> Vineyard: 8 acres
>
> Production: 24,000 bottles
>
> Quality: 🍇🍇🍇   Price: ★★★
>
> Best vintages: 1986, 1987, 1988

Di Cullen is one of the great individuals in the Australian wine scene, a courageous and talented woman who has taught herself to be a very good wine-maker. The first vines she and her doctor husband Kevin planted in 1971 were Cabernet Sauvignon and Riesling. The Cullen portfolio is now much wider, but Cabernet, blended with Merlot and Cabernet Franc to achieve greater finesse, is still an important part of the range. The Cullen Cabernets can be very good – ripe, creamy, long and complex, with moderate tannins – without ever reaching the heights of the best from Moss Wood, Cape Mentelle or Vasse Felix, or, for that matter, of the excellent Cullen Chardonnays and Sauvignons.

DROMANA ESTATE

Victoria

Harrison's Road, Dromana, VIC 3936

Vineyard: 4 acres

Production: 14,000 bottles

Labels: Dromana Estate, Schinus Molle

Quality: 🍇🍇🍇   Price: ★★★

Best vintages: 1987, 1988, 1989

Garry Crittenden is a horticulturalist turned wine-grower and wine-maker in the Mornington Peninsula south of Melbourne, one of the coolest viticultural regions in Australia. The 1988 Dromana Estate Cabernet–Merlot (the proportion of Merlot stands at 8 per cent but is expected to rise) has a green aspara-gusy character on the nose and notes of tobacco on the palate. I prefer the riper 1989, still closed on the nose but showing promising, juicy fruit and medium-weight elegance. Crittenden also produces wine from bought-in fruit under the Schinus Molle (Peppercorn tree) label. The 1988 Schinus Molle, made from 55 per cent Mornington Peninsula and 45 per cent Coonawarra fruit, has a tremendous burst of blackcurrant on the nose, with some tobacco and a firm but not hard structure. This is Crittenden's best Cabernet.

GARRETT, ANDREW

South Australia

> Kangarilla Road, McLaren Vale, SA 5171
>
> Production: 72,000 bottles
>
> Quality: 🍇🍇🍇   Price: ★★★
>
> Best vintages: 1985, 1986

This fast-growing enterprise, based at a country club in McLaren Vale just south of Adelaide, is the brainchild of two men in their early thirties – Andrew Garrett himself and wine-maker Warren Randall, perhaps Australia's leading expert in *méthode champenoise*. The sparkler is by far Garrett's most important line, but his Cabernet–Merlot (75/25 per cent), blended from fruit from Currency Creek, McLaren Vale, Coonawarra and Clare (most parts of South Australia, in fact), is a reliable, easy-drinking, relatively soft commercial wine, well made to show attractive berry-fruit flavours and a long finish.

GOUNDREY WINES

Western Australia

> Langton, Muir Highway, Mount Barker, WA 6324
>
> Production: 30,000 bottles (rising fast)
>
> Labels: Windy Hill, Chapel View, William's Rest
>
> Quality: 🍇🍇🍇   Price: ★★★
>
> Best vintages: Windy Hill, 1985, 1986, 1987, 1988

Mike and Alison Goundrey have come into wine-growing from sheep-farming – the activity for which the rolling hillsides of Mount Barker look more obviously suited – but they have ambitious plans for expanding their crush from 400 to 2,000 tonnes by 1998. Cabernet Sauvignon is their most important single varietal and shows the firm, tight character which seems typical of Mount Barker. French oak is used for the top-of-the-range Windy Hill label and, in wines like the austere but complex 1987 Cabernet Sauvignon, is well integrated with the fruit. The 1986 Cabernet is riper wine with an intense black-plum character. Best so far may turn out to be the 1988 Cabernet, with its combination of vivid, upfront fruit and tannic structure. The cheaper Chapel View Cabernet is softer and more approachable, with a certain sweetness from American oak.

HARDY (THOMAS) & SONS

South Australia

Reynell Road, Reynella, SA 5161

Production: not released

Labels: Nottage Hill, Moondah Brook, Château Reynella, Hardy Collection

Quality: 🍇🍇–🍇🍇🍇   Price: ★–★★★

Best vintages: 1987, 1988

Now the third-largest Australian wine conglomerate (having purchased Reynella in 1982 and Houghton and Stanley Leasingham in 1988), the family-owned Hardy group has a fine reputation for clean, reliable and sometimes exciting wine-making across its range. I must say I find the Cabernets generally disappointing: the style aimed for is light and 'elegant', but the result seems to be blandness and lack of character. The Nottage Hill Claret has vivid fruit on the nose but lacks flesh and substance on the palate. The 1986 Château Reynella Cabernet Sauvignon has a Bordeaux-like lead-pencil nose but is too thin on the palate, fading away and drying out. The 1988 Château Reynella Coonawarra has an attractive 'Murraymint' nose with vivid fruit intensity, but greenness on the palate betrays lack of real ripeness in the fruit. The 1988 Hardy Collection Cabernet Sauvignon is a little richer, with a fair amount of oak, but once again lacks character.

HOLLICK

South Australia

> Racecourse Road, Coonawarra, SA 5263
>
> Vineyard: 28 acres
>
> Production: 75,000 bottles
>
> Quality: 🍇   Price: ★★★
>
> Best vintage: 1988

Ian Hollick, formerly national vineyard manager with Mildara, has enjoyed considerable success with his winery, founded in 1982, especially in the award of the prestigious Jimmy Watson Trophy for the 1984 Cabernet. Current releases seem less impressive: the 1987 Cabernet–Merlot is surprisingly forward and developed, medium-bodied and quite elegant, but not distinguished. The 1988 Cabernet (blended with 5 per cent Merlot and 5 per cent Cabernet Franc) has greater fruit intensity and complexity, with a fair amount of oak and highish acidity.

HOUGHTON

Western Australia

> Dale Road, Middle Swan, WA 6056
>
> Production: c. 300,000 bottles
>
> Labels: Moondah Brook, Margaret River, Frankland River, Gold Reserve
>
> Quality: 🍇 – 🍇   Price: ★★ – ★★★
>
> Best vintages: 1987, 1988

Western Australia's largest winery, owned since 1976 by Hardy's and beautifully situated on the Swan River, is noted more for its whites, in particular the admirable Houghton

Supreme (White Burgundy in Australia), than its reds. The Moondah Brook Cabernet, made from 80 per cent Frankland River fruit, I find cheesy and unconvincing. The Frankland River Cabernet Sauvignon, which spends a year in French oak, has more fruit intensity, in a lightish style. The top-of-the-range Gold Reserve Cabernet 1986 is disappointingly vegetal and thin. The best Houghton Cabernet I have tasted is the 1986 Margaret River – a pronounced minty nose and medium-weight on the palate with relatively soft tannin.

KNAPPSTEIN, TIM

South Australia

2 Pioneer Avenue, Clare, SA 5453

Vineyard: *c.* 50 acres in Clare

Production: 180,000 bottles

Labels: Cabernet Sauvignon–Merlot, Cabernet Sauvignon

Quality: 🍇🍇🍇🍇   Price: ★★★

Best vintages: 1986, 1987, 1988

Tim Knappstein, whose family owned the Stanley Wine Company until 1971, began producing his own wines in the old Enterprise brewery building in Clare in 1976. Although Wolf Blass bought 51 per cent of the winery (but not the vineyards) in 1986, Knappstein, one of Australia's most perspicacious wine men, remains conspicuously at the helm. The Cabernet–Merlot and the Cabernet are important lines, accounting for nearly half the winery's production. Knappstein is a particular admirer of 1978 Bordeaux, and with his best wines achieves the same combination of fruit intensity, elegance and balance, with moderate tannin.

The 1987 Cabernet–Merlot (85/15 per cent) has a soft, subtle nose with a hint of oak, and is an elegant wine with good natural balance. Ten per cent of the Cabernet is fermented by *macération carbonique*. The 1987 Cabernet Sauvignon (which in fact contains 10 per cent Cabernet Franc and 8 per cent Merlot) has a cedary character typical of this producer and a velvety mouth-feel. Three-quarters of the fruit for these reds comes from Knappstein's own holdings in Clare, with the remaining quarter being bought in from local growers.

KRONDORF

South Australia

Krondorf Road, Tanunda, SA 5352
Production: 150,000 bottles
Labels: Limited Release, Show Reserve
Quality: 🍇🍇🍇   Price: ★★ – ★★★
Best vintages: 1985, 1986, 1987, 1988

The high quality of the Krondorf range, now part of the Mildara group and unflatteringly presented behind ugly Germanic labels, is not sufficiently well known. The star attraction may be the rich, unctuous Chardonnays, but the Cabernets are not far behind. The secret of both the Limited Release and Show Reserve labels is a judicious mixture of Coonawarra and McLaren Vale fruit – the former giving intensity and backbone, the latter filling this out with richness and softness. The 1986 Limited Release is quite rich, but still reserved on the nose, and soft-textured with smooth tannin. The 1985 Show Reserve has a toast-and-tobacco character on the nose and combines power and smoothness on the palate. The ageing potential of these wines is shown by the 1980 Show Reserve, with its minty nose, still possessing good structured fruit.

LEEUWIN ESTATE

Western Australia

Gnarawary Road, Margaret River, WA 6285

Vineyard: 70 acres

Production: 100,000 bottles

Quality: 🍇🍇🍇   Price: ★★★★

Best vintages: 1982, 1983, 1987

The best wine made at Leeuwin Estate, showpiece of Margaret River, is undoubtedly the brilliantly structured, long-lasting Chardonnay. The Cabernet can be excellent too, but is not consistently in the top league. Green, herbaceous tones can be obtrusive, though wines like the 1982 Cabernet Sauvignon, with its very deep colour, fascinating lifted tarry nose and great intensity and depth on the palate disarm criticism. A testament to this wine's quality is the fact that the oak flavours from two years in new French *barriques* have been completely digested. The 1983 Cabernet Sauvignon is much lighter, with toasty-oak and red-berry characters on the nose, elegant and nicely developed on the palate. The light-coloured, slightly fizzy 1984 is not recommended.

LEHMANN, PETER

South Australia

Para Road, Tanunda, SA 5352

Production: 65,000 bottles

Quality: 🍇🍇   Price: ★★

Best vintages: 1987, 1988

Peter Lehmann promotes himself as 'the character of the Barossa', and anyone who has seen him in his vine-covered weighbridge, receiving the grapes and the grape-growers of the area, can vouch for his stature, both physical and metaphorical. Whether the character of the Barossa Valley fruit he buys from over 200 growers is suitable for top-quality red wine production is more questionable. I find that his 1987 Cabernet Sauvignon, though quite complex and deep-flavoured, lacks fruit and freshness on the palate.

LINDEMANS–ROUGE HOMME

South Australia

Naracoorte Road, Coonawarra, SA 5263

Vineyard: 150 acres

Production: not released

Labels: St George, Pyrus, Rouge Homme

Quality: ♟♟♟♟♟ Price: ★★★★

Best vintages: 1980, 1982, 1984, 1985, 1986, 1987

It makes sense to deal jointly with all the wines made under the highly skilled direction of Greg Clayfield at the Rouge Homme winery in Coonawarra. Lindemans bought Rouge Homme in 1965 and since 1990 the whole concern has been part of the Penfolds group. Rouge Homme, founded by Bill Redman (a witty man, obviously) in 1908, was one of the first commercial wine companies in Coonawarra. The Rouge Homme Estate Cabernets are complex, cedary wines, with a classic balance of ripeness and austerity and long ageing potential. The 1986 Rouge Homme has a rich, ripe-berry nose, cedary complexity on the palate and particularly good texture. To show how well these wines age, the 1978 Rouge Homme, one of the Classic Releases of which Lindemans admirably hold back small quantities until they are considered mature, is drinking superbly – a warm, gamy, cedary wine which caresses the mouth.

At the very top of the Lindemans range are the single-vineyard wines from Coonawarra. The thirty-acre St George vineyard produces wines of great refinement, subtlety and power, expertly vinified by Greg Clayfield and matured, since 1984, in 100 per cent French oak. The style is pure and intense, and the wines tend to be very closed and tight when young. The

1980 St George (winner of the Jimmy Watson Trophy in 1981) exhibits an extraordinary asparagus tone on the nose, but has memorably intense redcurrant fruit on the palate. Both the 1985 and 1986 are firm, powerful wines, the latter especially perfumed. From the Pyrus vineyard comes a Bordeaux blend, roughly three-quarters Cabernet Sauvignon with the remaining quarter split between Merlot and Cabernet Franc: the 1985 vintage is deep-coloured, with a remarkably concentrated nose and a surprising hint of anchovies – a very impressive wine.

McWILLIAM

New South Wales

Mount Pleasant, Marrowbone Road, Pokolbin, NSW 2321

Production: 400,000 bottles

Labels: Hanwood, Coonawarra, Mount Pleasant Limited Release

Quality: 🍇   Price: ★★

McWilliam is one of the biggest and most ramified Australian wine companies, with wineries in the Riverina area and in the Hunter Valley, where most of the best wines are made. The Hanwood Cabernet from Riverina has a 'Murraymint' nose and is a soft, approachable, commercial wine – no more. The 1985 Coonawarra Cabernet has a deep colour and decent concentration and fruit intensity – good but not great. The 1986 is more solid and more powerful – quite impressive. The Mount Pleasant Cabernet–Merlot is light and gamy, slightly hollow but attractive in this hotter style.

MILDARA

Victoria/New South Wales

> Wentworth Road, Merbein, VIC 3505
> Production: not released
> Labels: Flower Label, Coonawarra, Alexander's
> Quality: 🍇🍇🍇   Price: ★★
> Best vintages: 1986, 1987, 1988

This large company, based in the Riverland, has extensive vineyard holdings in Coonawarra. The Flower Label Cabernet–Merlot is a pleasant enough, lightish, softish commercial. The Coonawarra Cabernet Sauvignon is generally admired, but I have found it too lean and green in several vintages. Mildara's head wine-maker, Mike Press, comments: 'We used to pick Cabernet too green, at 11° Baumé. Now we are aiming for 12.5°.' This change certainly shows in the 1988, which is the most powerful vintage for some time, combining ripe berry-fruit with leafy tobacco tones. Top of the Mildara range is Alexander's, a Bordeaux blend: the 1986 is very deep-coloured, with a complex, dusty nose, fresh mintiness and smooth texture on the palate, and a pretty tight structure leading to a tannic finish.

MITCHELTON

Victoria

> Mitchellstown, Nagambie, VIC 3608
> Production: 130,000 bottles
> Labels: Mitchelton, Print Label, Classic Release
> Quality: 🍇🍇🍇   Price: ★ – ★★★
> Best vintage: 1986

The best wines from this showpiece winery on the Goulburn River in central Victoria are its Rieslings and Marsannes, but Cabernets can be interesting too. The Print Label Cabernet–Merlot 1985 is in a vivid, lightish style, with a strong minty tone on the nose. Considerably more impressive is the Mitchelton 1986 Cabernet Sauvignon, a blend of 55 per cent Coonawarra and 45 per cent Nagambie (Victoria) fruit, with its minty, dusty nose and excellent fruit definition. The Mitchelton Classic Release Cabernet Sauvignon 1982 has a very mature, minerally nose – on the palate it is quite loose-knit and fully developed, with some complexity and a sweet finish. Worth a brief mention is Mitchelton's most notorious wine, Cab Mac. This is a Beaujolais-style light red, made by *macération carbonique* from Cabernet Sauvignon, Shiraz and Grenache, and showing, despite the wine-making and perhaps the intention, a certain amount of Cabernet structure.

MONTROSE

New South Wales

Henry Lawson Drive, Mudgee, NSW 2850

Production: not released

Labels: Cabernet–Merlot, Special Reserve Cabernet Sauvignon, Craigmoor Cabernet Sauvignon

Quality: 🍷🍷🍷   Price: ★ – ★★★

Best vintages: 1986, 1987, 1988

This winery, founded in 1974, belongs to the Wyndham Estate group, now owned by Orlando. Most of the fruit for its Cabernets comes from its own vineyards in Mudgee, and the style is unusually rich and powerful in these days of elegance at all costs. The Cabernet–Merlot 1986 gives a burst of jammy fruit on the nose but is quite astringent on the palate, and needs time. The superior 1986 Cabernet Sauvignon is deep-coloured wine of impressive richness. The 1985 Special Reserve

Cabernet Sauvignon is a mighty monster indeed – impenetrable in colour, porty on the nose and massively concentrated on the palate. More elegant is the Craigmoor 1986 Cabernet Sauvignon – creamy on the nose, with satisfying substance and length.

MOSS WOOD

Western Australia

> Metricup Road, Willyabrup, WA 6284
> Vineyard: 8 acres
> Production: 24,000 bottles
> Quality: 🍇🍇🍇🍇🍇   Price: ★★★★
> Best vintages: 1985, 1986, 1987, 1988

This winery, founded by Bill and Sandra Pannell (the first vines were planted in 1969) and now owned by wine-maker Keith Mugford, is one of the least pretentious you could find. It looks like what it is, an old cowshed. From these rustic surroundings, however, come some of the finest Cabernets in Australia. David Hohnen of Cape Mentelle envies Moss Wood its sheltered vineyard, with deep loam soil. What this produces is a softer, suppler style of Cabernet than Cape Mentelle's, with a special texture which reminds me of a great red Bordeaux from the Graves. Keith Mugford ferments at a fairly high temperature with frequent plunging of the cap, in order to 'highlight ripe fruit and go for richness'. Some vintages of Moss Wood Cabernet, like the 1987, have a herbaceous tone, but there is always ripe fruit and silky texture on the palate. The 1988 has a roasted, smoky character, with lovely structure and balance.

MOUNTADAM

South Australia

> High Eden Ridge, Eden Valley, SA 5253

Vineyard: 4 acres
Production: 6,000 bottles
Quality: 🍇🍇🍇　　Price: ★★★
Best vintages: 1986, 1987

The winery, set up high above the Eden Valley by David and Adam Wynn from the proceeds of the sale of their family business, Wynns in Coonawarra, specializes in voluptuously rich Chardonnay and Pinot Noir. The Cabernet Sauvignon, made in small quantities, does not yet reach anything like such heights, but the spicy, cigar-box character of the 1987 is attractive, while the 1986 is richer and sweeter, with blackberry fruit. Adam Wynn is encouraged enough by these essays to wish to double production to 1,000 cases.

ORLANDO

South Australia

Barossa Valley Highway, Rowland Flat, SA 5352
Production: *c.* 1 million bottles
Labels: RF, St Hugo, Jacaranda Ridge
Quality: 🍇🍇🍇　　Price: ★ – ★★★
Best vintages: 1985, 1986, 1987, 1988

Orlando was founded by Johann Gramp, who planted the first commercial vineyard in the Barossa in 1847. Now Australia's second biggest, this vast winery is notable above all for the consistency and good value of its range, the lower-to-mid-price RF series and the upper-to-mid-range Saints series in particular. RF Cabernet Sauvignon is made from fruit from a wide range of South Australian vineyards – Padthaway and Coonawarra in the south-east and Langhorne Creek and Southern Vales closer to Adelaide. It is aged for a year in French and American oak, mainly new.

The 1986 RF has a minty nose with excellent varietal definition; on the palate it is loose-knit and ready to drink. The 1987
is in a lighter, greener style, which reflects the cooler vintage.
The 1988 RF is a much bigger, richer wine, still quite tannic. St
Hugo Cabernet Sauvignon is 100 per cent Coonawarra, aged in
new oak, mainly American. The 1986 St Hugo has splendid
depth of colour, a complex nose with herbaceous tones and a
hint of tar. On the palate it is a big wine, packed with fruit, still
tannic. The 1987 is leaner, balanced by the sweetness of the
American oak. I have not been able to taste Orlando's top-of-
the-range Jacaranda Ridge Coonawarra Cabernet Sauvignon,
which has won many plaudits.

PENFOLDS

South Australia

> Penfold Road, Magill, SA 5072
>
> Production: not released
>
> Labels: Killawarra, Eden Valley, Seaview, Bin 389, Bin 707
>
> Quality: 🍇🍇🍇 – 🍇🍇🍇🍇🍇   Price: ★ – ★★★★★
>
> Best vintages: 1982, 1986, 1988

Penfolds is a remarkable and uniquely Australian phenomenon
– the country's largest wine company, making an unimaginable
150 million bottles of wine a year, which also produces arguably
the greatest Australian red wines. The enormous complex at
Nuriootpa in the Barossa is hardly a prepossessing sight –
something between a biscuit factory and a petrol refinery. The
Grange room, the inner sanctum where Grange Hermitage,
Australia's most celebrated wine, is matured, is a corrugated-
iron shack. All this shows is that Penfolds is a no-nonsense, no-
frills operation, which does not waste money on making things
look pretty. If Penfolds is most famous for its Shiraz, the company is no slouch at Cabernets, which, like all Penfolds red
wines, have a distinctive, rich fullness.

The basic Killawarra Cabernet, made from Southern Vales and Barossa fruit, has good fruit intensity and much more richness and substance than many wines in its class. The Eden Valley Cabernet has ripe berry-fruit on the nose and a rich, soft, velvety texture with no hard edges. Seaview Cabernet is made in a lighter, more elegant (though not weedy) style from McLaren Vale fruit, aged in second-hand American oak. The 1987 Seaview is a pleasant, soft, balanced wine with a touch of oak vanilla, rounded at the finish. Bin 389, known as the poor man's Grange, is a Cabernet–Shiraz blend, a winning mixture of toasty oak and full, soft, plummy fruit, with a quite powerful tannic finish.

Penfolds' top Cabernet is called Bin 707 (apparently an ex-director of Qantas joined Penfolds as marketing manager). It is based on fruit from the Kalimna vineyard in the Barossa (which also provides the backbone of Grange), and is topped up with other fruit from the Barossa and an increasing amount from Coonawarra, made at Wynns. Bin 707 also shares with Grange a wine-making technique apparently pioneered by Grange's inventor, Max Schubert – the finishing of fermentation in new American oak barrels. The 1986 Bin 707 is very deep in colour, and has a nose dominated by toasty, smoky American oak. However, deep blackberry fruit comes through too and, on the palate, this is a very rich, concentrated, cedary, long wine – most impressive. Among other recent vintages the 1987 is more closed and less oaky on the nose, with a minty character; it is less rich and more tannic on the palate than the 1986. The 1982 Bin 707 has a rich, ripe nose and is plush and velvety on the palate, with no hardness – not unlike a 1982 Bordeaux. Normally, Bin 707 has an ageing potential of at least ten years. Penfolds Clare Estate is mainly Merlot and Cabernet Franc, with just 15 per cent Cabernet Sauvignon. Aged in French oak, the 1986 is medium-bodied, soft, complex and elegant.

PETALUMA

South Australia

> Lot 6, Spring Gully Road, Piccadilly, S A 5151
>
> Vineyard: 100 acres in Coonawarra
>
> Production: 120,000 bottles
>
> Labels: Petaluma, Bridgewater Mill
>
> Quality: 🍇🍇🍇🍇   Price: ★★★
>
> Best vintages: 1986, 1987

Brian Croser is one of the most dynamic figures the Australian wine industry has produced, and also one of the most controversial. No one doubts his technical expertise – and few in their right mind would dispute the fact that he has raised the whole standard of Australian wine-making – but some accuse him of a soulless, sterile approach. I have even heard him likened to a phobic hand-washer. Outside the bitchy world of Australian wine-making, Croser's achievement can perhaps be appreciated more clearly. His relentlessly perfectionist approach, starting in the vineyards, has brought a new level of refinement to the Australian wine scene. All the Petaluma wines are notable for their purity of fruit and clarity of construction – Apollonian rather than Dionysian, without doubt.

Petaluma is better known for its whites than its reds, but my feeling is that the Coonawarra red, generally 70 per cent Cabernet Sauvignon, 30 per cent Merlot (though the first vintage, 1979, contained 60 per cent Shiraz and is still delicious), has been underrated. In most years it achieves both refinement – a combination of mint, tobacco and blackcurrant on the nose – and ripeness, avoiding the hollowness which afflicts many Coonawarra Cabernets. As Croser explains: 'Coonawarra Cabernet needs filling out with richness in the middle. Merlot gets ripe early and is rich and supple.' A fine example is the 1987, deep purple in colour, with a nose combining a herbaceous, leafy element and great fruit intensity, packed with fruit on the palate and very long, with ripe tannin. Croser produces a second label, Bridgewater Mill, named after the converted flour mill not far from the Petaluma winery in the Adelaide Hills, which has a truly splendid mill-wheel and houses an excellent restaurant.

PETER LEHMANN. See Lehmann, Peter

PLANTAGENET

Western Australia

46 Albany Highway, Mount Barker, WA 6234

Vineyard: 16 acres

Production: 22,200 bottles

Labels: Plantagenet, Bouverie

Quality: 🍇 Price: ★★

Best vintages: 1986, 1988

Plantagenet, the pioneering winery of the remote Mount Barker region, is the creation of the Smith and Meredith-Hardy families, descendants through a tortuous line of the Plantagenet kings of England. Mount Barker happens to be the centre of the Western Australian shire of Plantagenet. Tony Smith is the man in charge – a quiet, seemingly shy man who has completely kicked over the traces of his privileged English background (he is a nephew of Lord Radnor and Lord Hambledon) and seems happiest driving a fork-lift truck. The winery, a converted apple-shed with a jerry-built air, is also far from showy. However, the wine-making is by no means amateurish and, under John Wade, formerly head wine-maker for Wynns, looks set to scale new heights. Cabernet Sauvignon is regarded by many as Mount Barker's most successful grape: the style is harder and more austere than that of Margaret River, sometimes uncomfortably so. The 1986 Plantagenet Cabernet Sauvignon has a lovely deep, plummy character on the nose and a big, dusty flavour, with fruit intensity and quite hard tannin at the finish. The 1988 Cabernet, the first made by John Wade, has an extra dimension of ripeness and richness, plus a considerable element of new oak. Wade believes in long maceration after fermentation, which seems to give the wine a more velvety texture. A very small quantity of a special reserve is produced under the Bouverie label, named after the family of Tony Smith's mother. The 1989 Bouverie, tasted from cask, had a lovely combination of toasty oak and ripe berry-fruit, with remarkable length. As part of his contract with Plantagenet, John Wade is given fruit with which to make his own wine, under the Howard Park label. About 3,000 bottles of a dense-textured, complex Cabernet Sauvignon are produced. 'No one in Australia has made complex Cabernet like the French,' claims Wade. His own efforts deserve to be taken very seriously.

ROSEMOUNT

New South Wales

> Rosemount Road, Denman, NSW 2328
>
> Production: not released
>
> Labels: Estate Cabernet Sauvignon, Show Reserve Coonawarra Cabernet Sauvignon, Kirri Billi Coonawarra Cabernet Sauvignon
>
> Quality: 🍇🍇🍇🍇   Price: ★ – ★★★
>
> Best vintages: 1985, 1986

Rosemount may be best known for its Chardonnays – the rich Show Reserve and the powerful, intense Roxburgh – but this successful company's reds are not to be overlooked. The basic Estate Cabernet Sauvignon has a remarkably deep colour and is very well made in a soft, forward style. The Show Reserve Coonawarra Cabernet Sauvignon has a complex nose, with hints of tobacco and blackcurrant, and a touch of typical Coonawarra greenness on the palate. The newly introduced Kirri Billi Cabernet Sauvignon 1986, from a single vineyard in Coonawarra, is opaque in colour and has a medicinal nose. This is a thick, dense-textured wine of considerable complexity, still rather tannic and not yet in balance.

SALTRAM

South Australia

Angaston Road, Angaston, SA 5353

Vineyard: 18 acres

Production: 350,000 bottles

Labels: Cabernet Sauvignon, Reserve, Mamre Brook, Pinnacle Selection

Quality: 🍇🍇🍇🍇   Price: ★★ – ★★★

Best vintages: 1984, 1986

Founded by the resourceful settler William Salter in 1859, after he had tried his hand at arable and livestock farming and mining, Saltram was bought by Seagram in 1978. The reputation of these wines is not as high as it should be. The generic Cabernet Sauvignon is well made, from McLaren Vale and Barossa fruit; a medium-to-light-weight wine for early drinking, with a touch of oak. But the real star is the Mamre Brook Cabernet Sauvignon–Shiraz (80/20 per cent). Named after Salter's solid five-gabled stone house (itself named after the biblical home of Abraham) at Angaston in the Barossa, this is an unashamedly big, rich, toasty, full-bodied wine from vineyards around the house. This may be one of Australian wine's best-kept secrets. The Pinnacle Selection Coonawarra Cabernet Sauvignon is in a firmer, more elegant style than the Mamre Brook, with impressive fruit intensity and tight structure. The 1984 is just beginning to open up.

SANDALFORD

Western Australia

> West Swan Road, Caversham, WA 6055
>
> Vineyard: 62 acres
>
> Production: 120,000 bottles
>
> Labels: Caversham Estate, Margaret River, Reserve
>
> Quality: 🍇   Price: ★★
>
> Best vintage: 1987

This old-established winery, based at the idyllic Caversham winery on the Swan River, does not seem very sure of its identity. Its wine-making has been rather too commercial for my liking, resulting in light, soft, easy-drinking wines of no distinction. The 1987 Caversham Estate Cabernet Sauvignon, made from Swan Valley fruit, is typically soft, medium-bodied, with little tannin. Christian Morlaes, the articulate French wine-maker, says this will be the last vintage for the time being, as he is not happy with the style. The Margaret River Cabernet (Sandalford have considerable holdings in Margaret River) has, on the nose, the combination of lifted fruit and herbaceousness typical of the region. It starts off quite soft on the palate, then develops some fruit intensity and finishes with some tannin: a lively medium-weight wine without any great complexity – I am sure Sandalford could do better.

SEPPELT

South Australia

> Seppeltsfield, SA 5352
>
> Vineyard: very various
>
> Production: *c.* 1 million bottles
>
> Labels: Gold Label, Black Label, Premier Vintage, Dorrien,
>   Padthaway, Drumborg, Great Western

Quality: 🍇🍇🍇 – 🍇🍇🍇🍇   Price: ★ – ★★★
Best vintages: 1984, 1986

Seppelt produce a bewildering variety of wines from their vast spread of vineyards extending from the Barossa, the Adelaide Hills and Padthaway in South Australia, to Drumborg and Great Western in Victoria and Barooga in New South Wales. They are best known for their sparkling wines, and so the reliable and sometimes excellent table wines may be unfairly overlooked. The basic Gold Label Cabernet has a pleasant, bright, berry-fruit character on the nose and is a drinkable, soft wine with fair varietal character. Much better is the Black Label Cabernet (made mainly from Padthaway fruit), which is rich on the nose, with some mint, and substantial and well structured on the palate, with the tannin to age further. In their Premium Range, Seppelt produce (in very small quantities) a Premier Vineyard Selection Cabernet Sauvignon–Malbec–Merlot (proportions roughly 65/20/15 per cent). The 1986, made from a mixture of Coonawarra and Langhorne Creek fruit, has good complexity on the nose and is rich, soft, almost sweet on the palate, with toasty oak and no hard tannin. Finally, in tiny quantities also, there are the single-vineyard selections. From the Dorrien vineyard on the Barossa Valley floor comes a dense, deep-flavoured, oaky but elegant wine, clearly Seppelt's answer to Penfolds' Bin 707. The Drumborg Cabernet from southern Victoria is in complete contrast – lean, intense, high in acidity. The Great Western Cabernet is too astringent and unripe for my taste, but the 1987 Padthaway Cabernet is long, lively and elegant.

STANLEY WINE COMPANY

South Australia

7 Dominic Street, Clare, SA 5453
Vineyard: 79 acres

Production: 84,000 bottles
Label: Domaine
Quality: 🍇🍇🍇   Price: ★★
Best vintage: 1987

This famous old company went through a bad patch in the 1970s under the ownership of Heinz, who concentrated on inexpensive cask wines. Thomas Hardy came to the rescue in 1987 and decided to separate the cask production, under the Leasingham label, from the bottled wines made in the old winery at Clare. The Domaine series is currently one of the jewels in Hardy's crown and, at a big horizontal tasting, the Domaine Cabernet–Malbec (the same wine as the old Leasingham Bin 56) stood out as the best Cabernet-based wine in Hardy's portfolio. It is made entirely from Clare fruit; the 20 per cent of Malbec seems to give it upfront, accessible fruit, while the remaining 80 per cent Cabernet provides firm tannic structure. Anyone who has tasted the magnificent Leasingham Bin 49 Cabernet Sauvignon 1980, with its splendidly vivid blackcurrant-and-mint nose and beautiful freshness and definition on the palate, will join me in hoping that a straight Cabernet will be reintroduced.

THOMAS HARDY & SONS.
See Hardy (Thomas) & Sons

TIM KNAPPSTEIN. See Knappstein, Tim

TISDALL

Victoria

Cornelia Creek Road, Echuca, VIC 3564
Production: 160,000 bottles
Labels: Tisdall, Mount Helen

Quality: 🍇🍇 – 🍇🍇🍇   Price: ★ – ★★★
Best vintage: 1988

The glory of the winery founded by Dr Peter Tisdall in 1979 is its Mount Helen Chardonnay; I find the Cabernet–Merlot from this high, cool vineyard excessively green-peppery and sharp. The lower-priced Tisdall Cabernet Sauvignon, made with fruit coming mainly from Rosbercon in northern Victoria, is somewhat coarse. Greatly preferable is the Tisdall Cabernet–Merlot (blended 60/40 per cent), with its more complex nose and softer and more supple palate.

VASSE FELIX

Western Australia

Harman's South Road, Cowaramup, WA 6284

Vineyard: 15 acres

Production: 84,000 bottles

Quality: 🍇🍇🍇 – 🍇🍇🍇🍇   Price: ★★★
Best vintages: 1977, 1978, 1982, 1988

Named after a French seaman from the *Géographe* who was drowned off Cape Leeuwin in 1801, this was the first winery to set up shop in Margaret River back in 1967. It is now managed by Englishman David Gregg. Gregg can seem like a restless innovator, but the secret of the sometimes baffling changes of style apparent in his Cabernet Sauvignon is the light, sweet, burgundian Cabernet he made in 1977. Gregg has been trying to re-create this style for years, not always with success and I sometimes feel misguidedly; for the best Vasse Felix Cabernets, which stand comparison with any in Australia, are the powerful, complex wines of years like 1978 and 1982. The nose is characteristically minty and dusty, the palate long, minerally, with a fine poise between fruit and tannin. The 1988 looks highly promising, while the 1989 seems on the light side.

WOLF BLASS. *See* Blass, Wolf

WYNDHAM ESTATE

New South Wales

> Government Road, Dalwood, via Branxton, NSW 2321
>
> Production: not released
>
> Labels: Bin 888 Cabernet Sauvignon–Merlot, Bin 444 Cabernet Sauvignon
>
> Quality: ♟♟♟   Price: ★★ – ★★★
>
> Best vintages: 1985, 1986, 1987

The Hunter Valley's largest producer, since 1990 part of Orlando, is hard to beat in the lower-to-middle part of the market: the Wyndham reds are extremely well made and offer excellent value for money. The Bin 888 Cabernet–Merlot has a winning combination of chocolatey richness and freshness. The Bin 444 Cabernet Sauvignon is a more serious wine, with a minty nose, pure vivid fruit and a velvety texture. Though these wines seem soft and approachable early on, they can age grace-fully too, at least on the evidence of a Bin 444 1979 tasted in 1989 – a big, powerful wine with a lovely chewy density.

WYNNS

South Australia

> Memorial Drive, Coonawarra, SA 5263
>
> Vineyard: *c.* 400 acres in Coonawarra
>
> Production: not released
>
> Quality: ♟♟♟♟   Price: ★★ – ★★★
>
> Best vintages: 1982, 1984, 1985, 1986

It was David Wynn who bought a considerable vineyard holding in Coonawarra in 1951 and established the reputation of this largest and most famous of Coonawarra producers. The firm was sold, first to Tuohys and finally to Penfolds, but still operates from the gabled stone cellar built in the 1890s by John Riddoch, founding father of Coonawarra viticulture. Wynns may be part of the vast Penfolds group, but in remote Coonawarra, under the sturdy direction of Peter Douglas, the firm maintains its own identity. Wynns Cabernets which are not blended with Merlot are in a full-bodied, ripe style (for Coonawarra) which goes against the trend towards etiolated elegance. He favours picking when the grapes are fully ripe.

The 1986 Wynns Coonawarra Estate Cabernet has a really intense blackcurranty, dusty nose, considerable depth and complexity on the palate and a firm tannic finish. Top of Wynns' range is the John Riddoch Limited Release Cabernet Sauvignon: the 1986 is impenetrably deep in colour and has a lovely cedary, blackcurranty nose. On the palate this is a long, velvety, dense-textured wine which needs at least five, possibly ten years in bottle.

YALUMBA (S. Smith & Sons)

South Australia

Eden Valley Road, Angaston, SA 5263

Production: not released

Labels: Hill-Smith Estate, Yalumba Coonawarra Reserve, Heggies Vineyard, Pewsey Vale, Yalumba Signature Reserve

Quality: 🍇🍇🍇 – 🍇🍇🍇🍇   Price: ★ – ★★★★

Best vintages: 1986, 1987

Founded by the English brewer Samuel Smith in 1849, Yalumba (which means 'all the land around' in aboriginal) is now one of the largest Australian wine companies remaining under family control. Production is quite diverse, with two-litre varietal casks, or wine-boxes, playing an important role, and sparkling wines (in particular the highly successful Angas Brut) accounting for nearly 40 per cent of bottled wines. Under the managing directorship of Robert Hill-Smith and with the wine-making expertise of Brian Walsh, renewed attention has been paid to premium table wine: exciting single-vineyard ranges from the Heggies and Pewsey Vale vineyards in the Adelaide Hills have been introduced, and the top-of-the-range Signature Reserve series has been revamped.

The basic Hill-Smith Estate Cabernet Sauvignon has a mint-and-berry nose and is quite attractive in a lightish, lively style. More interesting is the Yalumba Coonawarra Reserve, which is something of a compromise between the very green style favoured recently by, for instance, Château Reynella and the bigger, richer style of Wynns. The 1988 works well, with intense berry-fruit on the nose and medium-weight with soft tannin on the palate. More distinctive still are the single-vineyard wines: Heggies (the blend is normally 75 per cent Cabernet Sauvignon, 15 per cent Cabernet Franc and 10 per cent Merlot) is the most elegant and 'French' of all Yalumba's Cabernets. The 1987 is very herbaceous and green, but elegant with soft tannin. The 1986 has a minty nose with lovely berry-fruit intensity and is very attractive to drink already. Pewsey Vale seems to give a somewhat lusher, richer wine; both the 1986 and 1988 have impressively concentrated fruit. The Yalumba Signature Reserve is deliberately made in a quite different, bigger, more old-fashioned style. The 1986, 1987 and 1988 are massive, chunky, dense-textured wines, blended with 15 per cent Shiraz, aged in new American oak barrels and designed to benefit from ten years' cellaring.

YARRA YERING

Victoria

| Briarty Road, Gruyere, VIC 3770

Vineyard: 30 acres total (varieties not released)

Production: not released

Quality: 🍇🍇🍇🍇🍇   Price: ★★★

Best vintages: 1982, 1984, 1986, 1987

The retired research viticulturalist Dr Bailey Carrodus, with his reserved manner in the image of an English country gentleman, is one of the more unusual Australian *vignerons*. His powerful, complex, Yarra Yering Dry Red No. 1 (80 per cent or more Cabernet Sauvignon, with the remainder split between Merlot and Malbec) is perhaps the closest Australian approximation to the great growths of the Médoc. The 1986, with its very deep colour and terrifically dense, opulent, concentrated lead-pencil aroma, is the Yarra Valley's answer to Mouton-Rothschild.

Carrodus's wines are notable for their ageing potential: the magnificent 1982, with its perfumed nose, lively balance and velvety texture, will last many years yet. The somewhat lighter 1981 is, perhaps, in French terms, still more classic. Vintages from the 1970s can show high levels of volatile acidity and occasionally an old, musty wood tone. If you comment on this to Dr Carrodus, he is likely to reply: 'Squeaky clean wines are a bit of a bore.'

New Zealand

Total vineyard area: 13,585 acres

Area planted to Cabernet Sauvignon: 978 acres

The youthful and pioneering New Zealand wine industry, which has enjoyed such success with white varieties, especially Sauvignon Blanc and Chardonnay, has been markedly slower to come to grips with red wine-making. The cool climate which has been advertised as a great advantage for the whites has not been such a boon for makers of properly constituted red wines. Cabernet Sauvignons from New Zealand have been, with very few exceptions, light and herbaceous, lacking the concentration which wines from this variety, and indeed any serious red wines, need.

However, there are signs of improvement, most importantly a recognition that the best areas for growing Cabernet Sauvignon are Hawke's Bay and Waimaku in the North Island. There seems little future for Cabernet Sauvignon in the cooler conditions of Marlborough in the South Island.

CLOUDY BAY

Cape Mentelle New Zealand, PO Box 376, Blenheim

Production: not released

Quality: 🍇🍇🍇   Price: ★★★

Best vintage: 1988

The astute David Hohnen of Cape Mentelle has added a Bordeaux blend to the world-beating Sauvignon Blanc and excellent Chardonnay which have made Cloudy Bay famous. The 1988 Cabernet Sauvignon–Merlot–Cabernet Franc is deep-coloured and combines herbaceous and red-berry notes on the nose. On the palate it is elegant rather than powerful – not yet a match for the whites but, as you would expect, stylish and well made.

MATUA VALLEY

Waikoukou Road, Waimaku, Auckland

Vineyard: 50 acres

Production: 60,000 bottles

Quality: 🍇🍇🍇   Price: ★★

Best vintages: 1985, 1986, 1987

Wine-maker Ross Spence produces one of New Zealand's few worthwhile Cabernet Sauvignons, with fruit from Hawke's Bay (90 per cent) and Matua Valley's estate in Waimaku (10 per cent). It has decent colour, a pleasant tobaccoey nose and attractive ripe berry-fruit on the palate. Fourteen months in Nevers oak does not give excessively oaky flavours.

TE MATA

PO Box 335, Havelock North (Hawke's Bay)

Vineyard: 25 acres

Production: 120,000 bottles

Quality: 🍇🍇🍇🍇   Price: ★★★

Best vintage: 1985

New Zealand's oldest winery, established in 1896, was bought by the English wine merchant John Buck in 1978. It is now run by John and his wife Wendy, together with Michael and June Morris. The Coleraine Cabernet–Merlot, from Te Mata's own vineyards in Hawke's Bay, has consistently been New Zealand's finest red wine. Deep in colour, it combines new oak with subtle, refined fruit on the nose; on the palate it comes closer to the firm structure of classic Bordeaux than any Cabernet Sauvignon from the New World I know, with the possible exception of a top Coonawarra wine such as Bowen Estate.

AUSTRIA

| Total vineyard area: 145,000 acres

I have come across one interesting producer of Cabernet Sauvignon in a country much better known for white wine than red, and where Cabernet Sauvignon only exists in tiny quantities.

SCHLOSSWEINGUT MALTESER RITTERORDEN-MAILBERG

A-3495 Rohrendorfer-bei-Krems, Lenz-Moser-Strasse 4–6

Vineyard: 11 acres

Quality: 🍇 Price: ★★★

Best vintages: 1986, 1988

Cabernet Sauvignon has been cultivated at the wine estate of the Knights of Malta at Mailberg, north-east of Vienna, since 1981. Since 1969 the Lenz Moser family have been in charge of vineyards and wine-making; Lenz Moser IV has conducted research into the use of oak from different French forests and with different degrees of toast. The Kommende Mailberg Cabernet Sauvignon–Merlot shows the influence of Limousin oak in its sweet, vanilla nose, but there is also, in good years, an attractive combination of tobacco and cherry. My only misgiving concerns a highish level of acidity, but this is a worthwhile and unusual addition to the world's store of Cabernets.

EASTERN EUROPE

Bulgaria

Total vineyard area: 200,000 acres

Area planted to Cabernet Sauvignon: 45,000 acres

The remarkable success story of Bulgarian wine, and Bulgarian Cabernet Sauvignon in particular, is a post-war phenomenon. Wine was undoubtedly made in Bulgaria from early times, but Turkish domination between 1396 and 1878 put an end to wine production (except, one may assume, for unofficial home brews). In 1944, wine became a state-controlled industry. Vineyards were planted on a large scale, with rows two metres apart to allow tractors to pass between them. Efficient mechanization is one key to the success of the Bulgarian vineyards. More important still was the choice of grape varieties. With great foresight, Cabernet Sauvignon was chosen as the main red variety, and it still holds the position of number one grape variety in Bulgaria.

Initially, most of this very large quantity of wine was exported to other Eastern-bloc countries. In the 1970s, exports to the West started and, during the 1980s, increased at a dramatic rate. Even so, with the UK now consuming nearly 2 million cases of Bulgarian wine a year, exports to the West still account for only 10 per cent of the total. Bulgaria, exporting 85 per cent of her production, is the fourth-largest wine exporter in the world.

Bulgarian Cabernet Sauvignon has been successful because it has offered excellent value for money: ripe, rather plummy but well-balanced wine, with typical Cabernet flavours and a touch of oak (almost all Bulgarian Cabernet Sauvignon is aged for a

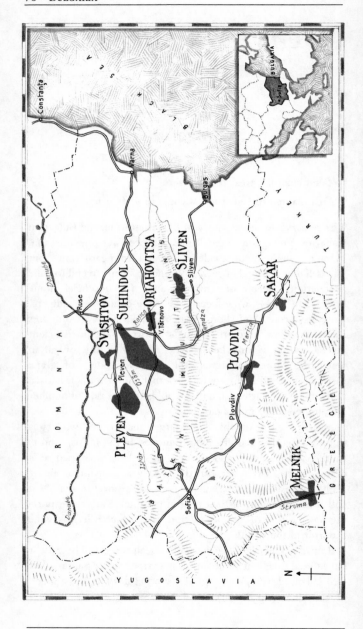

while in oak, usually in large 3,000–7,000 litre vessels), at a price comparable with cheap French *vin de table*. Until recently, almost all the Bulgarian Cabernet Sauvignon on the market was priced at the bottom end. More recently, however, a wider range of wines, both in terms of geographical area and quality, has been offered. Under the charismatic (and highly entrepreneurial) direction of Mr Margarit Todorov, a move towards higher quality has been initiated. Mr Todorov said to me, with a touch of Balkan exaggeration perhaps, that 'there will be Bulgarian wines selling at £100 a bottle before long – and they will be good value'. Under the new non-Communist order, it is expected that moves towards higher quality and greater differentiation will gather pace.

Given their highly centralized system of production and the concentration on value for money rather than top quality, Bulgarian wines have not merited the detailed descriptions of, say, the *crus* of Bordeaux. In 1991, this system was privatized with as yet unforeseeable effects. However, brief comments on the different areas of production and quality levels are in order. It is worth noting that in order to be labelled as varietal wines, Bulgarian wines need to consist 100 per cent of the named variety. Pure varietals are considered to be of higher quality than blends.

Areas of production

Melnik in the south-west of the country produces big, power-ful, plummy, full-bodied Cabernet Sauvignon, close to the character of Plovdiv.

Oriahovitza is situated in central Bulgaria. The Cabernet Sauvignon, usually seen as an oak-aged Reserve, is an elegant, medium-weight, cedary wine of some class. The Controliran Cabernet–Merlot is highly reputed.

Plovdiv, in the south of the country, produces an entirely dif-ferent, hotter style of Cabernet Sauvignon, deep in colour, with flavours of stewed plums. The hotter wines from the south are more highly prized in Bulgaria but were initially not thought suitable for export.

Sakar is situated in mountainous country in the south. The high altitude tempers the heat of the climate, and Sakar Mountain Cabernet has very well-defined blackcurrant fruit flavours.

Sliven is close to Oriahovitza and produces a similar style of Cabernet Sauvignon.

Suhindol, in north central Bulgaria, was the original source of relatively light, cedary Cabernet Sauvignon, high in acidity. These can still be some of the best balanced and best defined of Bulgarian Cabernets, though some recent examples have lacked concentration.

Svishtov, even further north, produces richer and more powerful Cabernet Sauvignon, especially in its Controliran form.

Quality levels

Country Wines carry a district appellation or DGO (Declared Geographical Origin). Wines in this category, such as the Pavilenki Cabernet–Merlot and the Petrich Cabernet–Melnik, can offer good, uncomplicated quaffing.

Varietal Wines are of better quality and have usually been aged for longer.

Reserve Wines must (in the case of the reds) spend at least three years in oak. The usual practice is to blend together wines which have spent varying lengths of time in different sizes of American and Bulgarian oak.

Controliran Wines, the highest level of quality, must be made from specified grape varieties grown in certain DGOs. The nearest equivalent in the rest of Europe is Italy's DOCG. Wineries must apply for Controliran status, which is only granted when three vintages have been assessed. It must be said that both Reserves and certain Controliran wines are often over-oaked, to modern Western taste.

Hungary

Total vineyard area: 345,800 acres

Area planted to Cabernet Sauvignon: 440 acres

Production of Cabernet Sauvignon: 1,200,000 bottles

Only a small proportion of Hungary's considerable acreage of vineyards is planted to Cabernet Sauvignon. This is not a traditional variety in Hungary, and the examples I have tasted have not been impressive. A Cabernet Sauvignon from Villány in the south was light and cedary; one from Kiskörös, also in the south, had lively fruit and acidity. Hajós region in the south-west seems to produce a richer, jammier style, while the Cabernets I have tried from the big state farm at Eger in the north have been big, coarse and obvious. Perhaps Hungary's espousal of the free market will lead to greater things.

Romania

Total vineyard area: 743,470 acres

Area planted to Cabernet Sauvignon: 24,700 acres

Romania not only has the sixth-largest vineyard area in the world and the joint fourth-largest area planted to Cabernet Sauvignon; it can also produce wine of excellent quality. The Cabernet Sauvignon wines I have sampled, one from the Dealul Mare district north of Bucharest, the other from Murfatlar on the Black Sea near Constanta, were both well made and enjoyable to drink, on a par with the better quality Bulgarian Cabernets. The Dealul Mare had a distinctively Balkan resiny character, but also the more classic Cabernet cedar; on the palate it had good plummy fruit. The Murfatlar was somewhat richer and more sophisticated, and well preserved at seven years of age. It is a shame these wines are not better marketed, but the travails which have afflicted this unfortunate country have undoubtedly hampered efforts to export wine.

USSR

Total vineyard area: 3,458,000 acres
Area planted to Cabernet Sauvignon: 112,355 acres

The Soviet Union has one of the largest areas planted to Cabernet Sauvignon in the world. The grape was introduced into Russia at the beginning of the nineteenth century and is cultivated in Moldavia, the Ukraine, Georgia, Kazakhstan, Kirghizia, Azerbaijan and part of the Russian Republic around Krasnodar. The only examples to have come my way are from Moldavia: a straight Cabernet Sauvignon from Tchouma Taraklia in the district of Suvorovo in southern Moldavia had good colour but was light in bouquet and flavour and seemed to have spent too long in oak. The Kodru Cabernet Sauvignon–Merlot blend had more attractive, plummy, soft fruit but was hardly distinguished.

Yugoslavia

Total vineyard area: 600,000 acres
Area planted to Cabernet Sauvignon: 24,700 acres

Yugoslavia is another country with a vast vineyard area and considerable plantings of Cabernet Sauvignon. The examples that have come my way have been distinctly thin and inferior to those from Bulgaria and Romania, though Jancis Robinson speaks of 'light, toothsome' Cabernets from Serbia.

FRANCE

| Total vineyard area: 2,264,990 acres
| Area planted to Cabernet Sauvignon: 88,920 acres

Discussion of Cabernet Sauvignon in France concentrates on Bordeaux, the area where the variety is most widely planted (60,947 of the 88,920 planted acres are in the Département du Gironde) and where it achieves, indisputably, its greatest heights. However, there are a number of other regions where Cabernet Sauvignon is planted in significant quantities. Plantations are on the increase especially in the southern areas of Languedoc-Roussillon and Provence, where the grape is used primarily as a *cépage améliorateur* to improve blends, though notable examples of straight varietals or Cabernet-based blends have begun to appear, especially in Provence. The grape itself goes by a variety of names in different parts of France. In central France it is variously called Petit Cabernet, Petite Vidure, Vidure and Sauvignon Rouge. In the Gironde it is known as Bouché, and in St Emilion and Pomerol as Bouchet or, sometimes, Petit Bouchet.

Cabernet Sauvignon is definitely a variety in vogue. Plantings have increased by over 50 per cent in the last decade, a percentage surpassed only by Syrah among classic red grapes. It is now the eighth most planted variety in France.

Bordeaux

Bordeaux, homeland of Cabernet Sauvignon and the other grape varieties of the Cabernet family, is the fine-wine capital

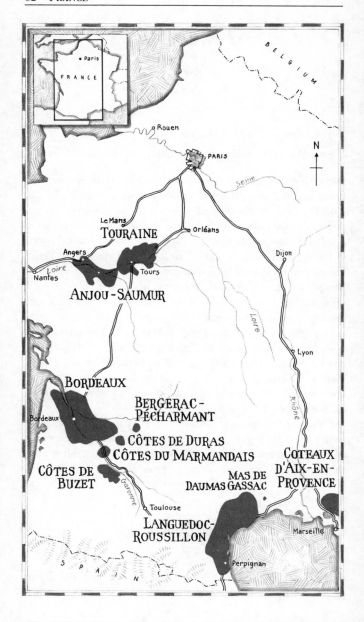

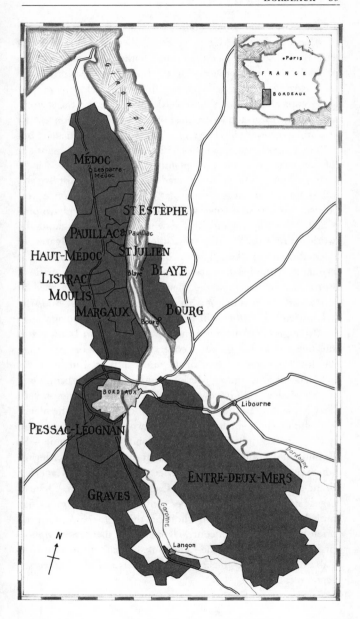

of the world. The Bordeaux region, which stretches from the northern tip of the Médoc, seventy miles north of Bordeaux city, to well south of Langon in the Southern Graves, and from the Atlantic coast in the west to the borders of Périgord in the east, is the largest great-wine region in the world (the greater geographical extent of Vinho Verde country in northern Portugal can be forgotten – like most of the wines). It produces vast quantities of everyday red and white wine, much smaller, but still very significant, quantities of fine red wine, small quantities of fine sweet wine and tiny quantities of fine dry white wine.

It is with the fine red wines, made for keeping at least five and often fifteen or more years, that we are mainly concerned. These châteaux (the concept will be explained later) have provided the model for quality red wine-making throughout the world. From California to Chile, and from Bulgaria to Australia, wine-makers have set out to emulate the aristocratic refinement, the balance and longevity of the great growths of Bordeaux. Rather than the blend of grape varieties used in Bordeaux, these imitators have generally used just one, the acknowledged aristocrat of the region, Cabernet Sauvignon.

Although Cabernet Sauvignon is recognized in Bordeaux as the finest red wine grape, it covers many fewer hectares than Merlot. Eighteen per cent of the vines cultivated in Bordeaux are Cabernet Sauvignon; Merlot accounts for 32 per cent. Only in the Médoc and Graves regions is Cabernet Sauvignon very heavily planted. In the other regions it forms part of the blend, but often only a small part. In the two regions of very high quality on the right bank of the Gironde and Dordogne – St Emilion and Pomerol – the dominant grape variety is Merlot, which performs better in the heavier, clayey soil, with Cabernet Franc usually being preferred to Cabernet Sauvignon. Château Figeac in St Emilion, with 35 per cent Cabernet Sauvignon, has probably the highest proportion on the right bank. Its proprietor, Thierry Manoncourt, claims that Cabernet Sauvignon ripens perfectly well on the right bank, but rather too long after Cabernet Franc to make retaining a team of *vendangeurs* economical.

Fair amounts of Cabernet Sauvignon are grown in those two

neglected regions opposite the Médoc – Bourg and Blaye. There must be potential there for producing something more exciting than the very agreeable easy-drinking red for which they are known these days. In the Entre-deux-Mers region, Cabernet Sauvignon often forms up to 60 per cent of the blend of the reds, which, however, can only carry the appellations Bordeaux or Bordeaux Supérieur.

The château

What is a château? It certainly is not always a castle; it may not even be a house. Cos d'Estournel, one of the Médoc's grandest wines, has an admittedly very splendid set of warehouses and outbuildings, but no dwelling. In fact, the château on the label of a Bordeaux wine may have no relation to any construction except a mental one – try finding Château Clairefont (second wine of Château Prieuré-Lichine), for example, on a map.

Even more strangely, 'château' does not necessarily mean a particular piece of land. It means, as Hugh Johnson has put it, 'the property on the land' – in other words, the estate. Now estates can grow and diminish, and a brief comparison of the production figures given in an early edition of *Cocks et Féret* with present ones will show that almost all the Bordeaux châteaux have changed considerably in size over the last hundred-odd years. Most of them have grown, by the expedient of the owner buying land from a neighbour and including it in his château. What was Château X has become Château Y. Henri Martin created Château Gloria very largely out of fragments of *crus classés*; several *crus classés* have more than doubled in size, swollen with the land of non-classified châteaux. In terms of the 1855 classification this raises all sorts of questions.

The 1855 classification and the crus classés

The classification of all the main Médoc châteaux, with the solitary Graves Château Haut-Brion, into five classes, undertaken by the Bordeaux Chamber of Commerce for the Paris Universal Exhibition of 1855, was by no means the first attempt to put the Médoc châteaux in order of merit. Previous classifications had been made by Jullien (1816), Franck (1824) and Paguierre (1827). However, the 1855 list has acquired a quality of immutability which it does not deserve – not because it is a bad list but because human things change. There have been attempts to revise it. In 1960 the INAO established guidelines for a new ranking, but the very thought of changing the 1855 list caused a political storm, and the matter was dropped. More recently, Alexis Lichine drew up his own personal classification, divided up into Outstanding, Great, Superior and Good Growths, but this has not been widely followed. It seems that the prestige of Bordeaux itself has become bound up with the immutability of the 1855 list (which, of course, given the promotion of Mouton-Rothschild from a second to a first growth in 1973, is not immutable anyway). This is regrettable, but the same thing probably occurred with the Ten Commandments.

Second wines

The idea of the *grand vin*, or principal wine, of a château goes back two hundred years or more. It seems to imply the existence of a second, or not-so-*grand*, *vin*. However, the widespread marketing of second wines – the contents of the vats rejected from the assemblage of the *grand vin* – is a very recent phenomenon. The pioneer was Les Forts de Latour, the second wine of Château Latour, introduced (with the 1966 and 1967 vintages) in 1972. Now almost all the *crus classés* and not a few *crus bourgeois* have their second label. A château like Giscours, which believes that only wine of *grand vin* standard should be associated with the château, is now the exception. Most, following the lead of Margaux with Pavillon Rouge, Pichon-Lalande with Réserve de la Comtesse and Léoville-Las Cases with Clos du Marquis, lean heavily on the association with the château for the marketing of the second wine. The idea is that you are getting a lighter version of the *grand vin* for about half the price (or less). Very often this is indeed the case, and the wine is good value. It depends a good deal on the vintage, however. In a year like 1985, some second wines, like Les Fiefs de Lagrange, were outstanding. But you need to be very careful with second wines in lighter years like 1987, when the difference between good and less good vats was very considerable.

The crus bourgeois

It is curious that a country whose motto includes the word *égalité* should maintain a rigid distinction between aristocracy and bourgeoisie in the world of wine. It is unfortunate that the word 'bourgeois', with its connotations of cosy philistinism, should be attached to what are often very high-class wines. All this has led to an inferiority complex manifested by some proprietors of *crus bourgeois*, including their president, Jean Miailhe. M. Miailhe feels that the *crus bourgeois* are not well enough known, and that they somehow fall between two stools, being neither extremely expensive and prestigious nor cheap and cheerful. All the better for them, is my immediate response; the very best value wines to be found in Bordeaux today belong to this category. A further manifestation of this inferiority complex is the refusal on the part of some former *crus bourgeois* such as Gloria, Lanessan and de Pez to be considered as such.

Crus bourgeois are exactly like *crus classés*, except that they were not classified in 1855. The first list of *crus bourgeois* was drawn up in 1932 by the Chamber of Commerce and the Chamber of Agriculture of the Gironde, and divided into Crus Bourgeois Supérieurs Exceptionnels, Crus Bourgeois Supérieurs and Crus Bourgeois. It was revised in 1966 and again in 1978, with the categories being renamed Crus Grands Bourgeois Exceptionnels, Crus Grands Bourgeois and Crus Bourgeois. EEC regulations, however, (with some sense) only allow the use of the single category Cru Bourgeois on the label, and this is the style I have followed.

There are a number of *crus bourgeois*, around fifteen, which are quite as good as decent, lower-ranking *crus classés* – and considerably better than a number (around a dozen) of under-performing *crus classés*.

En primeur and investment

The selling of the great growths of Bordeaux is a complicated business which involves two tiers of middlemen. The château proprietors sell the wine to the *négoce* – the merchant houses – of Bordeaux, with *courtiers*, or brokers, acting as intermediaries. The *négoce* then sells on to merchants and retailers throughout the world. For a long time it has been customary for the château proprietors to begin offering the wine to the *négoce* in the spring or early summer following the vintage – though in the 1950s and 1960s it was common for the wine to be sold *sur souche*, before the harvest, obviously for a low price to compensate for the risk.

A more recent phenomenon is the invitation to the consumer to purchase the wine (from merchants, of course; there is very little direct selling of the better wines) as soon as it goes on the market – what is known as *en primeur* purchasing. This system has proved surprisingly popular – I say surprisingly because it benefits the château proprietors more obviously than the consumer. Certainly the price is lower than it will be when the wine is mature, but when the cost of money and storage is taken into consideration, *en primeur* prices are not necessarily a bargain. The 1983 vintage is a case where the punter would have been better advised to wait five years and buy from a merchant or at auction. *En primeur* seems to create a cult of the new vintage, and a relative undervaluation of older vintages, with the exception of highly touted 'vintages of the century' like 1982.

This raises the question of wine as an investment. Certain past vintages such as 1961, 1966 and 1970, originally offered at very low prices by today's standards, even in real terms, have appreciated quite spectacularly in value. The picture today is very different: the opening prices are already so high that it is difficult to imagine anyone paying five times as much in five years' time. I believe that buying wine purely for investment is essentially immoral, being a misuse of something designed to be drunk and appreciated, not locked in a bank vault. Even if you are not convinced by the moral argument, the economic arguments suggest a need for caution. Buying twice as much of a wine as you want *en primeur* with the intention of selling half later (and, if you are lucky, covering your initial purchase) seems to me as far as anyone should go.

Short vintage guide

1990. Another early and exceptionally ripe vintage. So far greeted with refreshingly cautious optimism. Cabernets ripened later than in 1989 and late-picked châteaux did best.

1989. The earliest vintage since 1893, with some of the highest sugar levels seen in the lifetime of many vinifiers, 1989 will certainly have produced some splendidly ripe, complex wines. The obvious comparison is with 1982. One caveat: low levels of acidity have caused doubts to be raised over the long-term ageing potential.

1988. The enthusiastic reports that the 1988s combined the charm and richness of the 1985s with the structure of the 1986s need to be taken with a small pinch of salt. 1988 is, in fact, a very good and in some cases outstanding vintage, but one with its own distinctive character. The wines are notable for very deep colour and exceptional, violety aroma. Some are too hard and tannic, while others are on the light side. But the best, including a number from the Graves region, which was particularly successful in 1988, will be superb. Drink: 1997–2030.

1987. Washed out by torrential October rain, this was certainly not the vintage of the century or the decade. However, 1987 was not a complete disaster: a very warm September had given the grapes some ripeness, and in fact the Merlots, picked before the rain, achieved decent sugar levels. There is a strongly herbaceous tone on many 1987s; others have charming, supple fruit, while lacking something in concentration. A very useful early-drinking vintage, if carefully selected. Drink: 1991–7.

1986. If pushed to name a vintage of the century in the 1980s, I would choose this rather than 1982. The wines may not have the lush ripeness of 1982, but they have concentration, power and depth. They are more reserved, tannic wines than 1982s or 1985s, but promise, in time, even greater complexity. The Cabernet Sauvignon ripened extremely well, and there is a lovely black-plum and blackberry ripeness (as opposed to the red-fruit character of 1985). Drink: 1996–2040.

1985. Another year of exceptional success for the Merlot grape in the Médoc and Graves. These are some of the most immediately seductive and appealing clarets in living memory. The best of them have a vivid red-fruit character on the nose, ripeness, charm and balance. Some, however, lack concentration. Drink: 1992–2020.

1984. The ominous year of Orwell saw severe *coulure* affecting the Merlot grape, whose production was down 40 per cent in the Médoc and 80 per cent in Pomerol. The main problem with the wines when they came on the market, however, was their excessive price. At six years old, a number of these Cabernet-dominated wines were showing well; these are well-structured wines with decent fruit, even if a little angular. Drink: 1991–5.

1983. Another huge vintage in quantity, and, thanks to hot dry weather in September and October, fine in quality. Although the best 1983s are undoubtedly superb, I must admit to some reservations about this vintage. Some wines seem to have developed extremely fast – a number are already *tuilé* in colour – and contradict the widespread view that this is a classic, tannic vintage. There is often a hot, roasted quality on the nose. Still, in the best estates the Cabernet Sauvignon was notably successful and some great classics were made. Margaux is the star commune of the vintage; in St Estèphe, where yields were dangerously high, the wines tend to lack concentration. Drink: 1992–2030.

1982. The first of several 'vintages of the century' in the 1980s produced a very large quantity of wines of exceptional richness and ripeness. Some have an almost Californian character. The Merlot grape in the Médoc was particularly successful, and this means·that the wines do not always have the classic, Cabernet Sauvignon-dominated style. Some châteaux undoubtedly produced great classics, with the tannic structure to last decades, but others are dangerously low in acidity, and may start falling apart in a few years. Drink: 1991–2020.

1981. Somewhat diluted by rain during the harvest, this is nevertheless a good, underrated vintage. The wines are leaner than 1982s or 1983s, but, in general, fuller-bodied and deeper than 1979s. The best of them are extremely stylish and have classic balance – a number are better-balanced than the highly touted 1982s. Drink: 1991–2000.

APPELLATIONS

GRAVES & PESSAC-LÉOGNAN

| AOC under vine (reds): 4,700 acres

The Graves region, which extends from the immediate outskirts of Bordeaux forty kilometres down the left bank of the Garonne, is the oldest-established part of Bordeaux's Cabernet stronghold, which also includes the Médoc. It is also the least known and reputed. This paradox can be simply explained by the Graves' proximity to the city of Bordeaux. It was natural that the first vineyards should be planted close to the city; natural also that the city should expand and swallow many of them up. Châteaux Haut-Brion and La Mission Haut-Brion now sit incongruously amidst urban sprawl, with the jets serving nearby Mérignac airport an added inconvenience. Further south the vineyards take on the aspect of clearings in the endless pine forest which stretches most of the way to Spain.

For some time there was a feeling among the leading red châteaux of the Graves, below the level of the top two, that they were not getting their due. The appellation was tainted by its association with sweet white Graves served in London clubs and restaurants. It took the Napoleonic drive of M. André Lurton to achieve a separation of the northern part of the Graves, where all the growths classified in 1855 and 1953 are situated, and the more straggly southern part. The new Pessac-Léognan appellation for the northern part was officially created on 9 September 1987. It is too early to say whether this communal appellation on the Médocain model will prove beneficial.

Currently the Graves and Pessac-Léognan appellations have 4,700 acres planted with black grapevines – less than half the acreage of a century ago. Of these, a rather lower proportion are planted to Cabernet Sauvignon than in the Médoc. The soil, as the name Graves so unequivocally suggests, is predominantly deep gravel over a subsoil of clay – and not just in the north. Gravel pits at least twenty feet deep were pointed out to me near St Pierre de Mons in the Southern Graves. Most Graves vineyards also contain a good deal of sand.

The character of Graves red wines is often alluded to in a vague sort of way, but is rather hard to pin down. On the whole I find red Graves slightly softer and riper in feel than Médoc, though wines like La Mission Haut-Brion are as tannic as any in Bordeaux. Perhaps Maurice Healy's definition remains the best: 'The Médoc and Graves are like glossy and matt prints of the same negative.' A certain graininess of texture is to be found in some Graves. The region is currently undergoing a renaissance, with the leading properties producing excellent wine on a par with good Médoc *crus classés*. There are still some bargains in the southern part.

Best of the Southern Graves

Château Cabannieux, 33640 Portets. The enthusiastic Dudignacs make a solid, reliable red Graves, whose *encépagement* of 55 per cent Merlot, 45 per cent Cabernet Sauvignon may make it unsuitable for inclusion in this guide, but which deserves mention on account of its considerable complexity and ability to age fifteen years.

Château Magneau, 33650 Labrède. M. Ardilats makes a good, deep-coloured red from roughly equal proportions of Cabernet Sauvignon and Merlot grown on 62 acres.

Château Roquetaillade-La-Grange, Mazères, 33210 Langon. M. Pierre Guignard, leading spokesman of the Southern Graves, makes one of its best wines here in the shadow of the vast medieval castle of Roquetaillade. The grape varieties are Cabernet Sauvignon, Merlot and Cabernet Franc, with slightly more Merlot than the other two, but the wine, with good fruit and the typical Graves minerally tone, has considerable tannic structure.

Château Toumilon, St-Pierre-de-Mons, 33210 Langon. This is the better of the two red labels sold by M. Jean Sévenet (the other is Château Cabanes). Though the wine, made from just over 50 per cent Cabernet Sauvignon, spends no time in *barriques*, it has an attractive warm ripeness and enough structure to last twelve years.

HAUT-MÉDOC

AOC under vine: 8,620 acres

Average annual production: 20.5 million bottles

The appellation Haut-Médoc runs around the fringes of the communal appellations from the north of St Estèphe to the south of Margaux. It is difficult therefore to generalize about the wines produced from varying soils and microclimates in a district 45 km long by 10 km wide. There are two pockets within the appellation where *crus classés* are to be found: in the extreme south, in the communes of Ludon and Macau, which could really be considered as extensions of Margaux; and in the commune of St Laurent, inland from St Julien. Apart from the *crus classés*, there are a number of *crus bourgeois* which approach classified quality. Particularly recommended are **Châteaux d'Agassac, Beaumont, Caronne-Ste-Gemme, Cissac, Citran, Lamarque, Liversan, Ramage-La-Batisse, Sénéjac, La Tour du Haut-Moulin**.

LISTRAC

AOC under vine: 1,530 acres

Average annual production: 3.3 million bottles

The name Listrac conveys to me the hard stringy quality I have often found in the wines. This small inland appellation prides itself on having the Médoc's highest gravel banks, at a vertiginous 43 metres above sea-level. There are no *crus classés* but some excellent *crus bourgeois* (**Château Lestage** is one) – if you can come to terms with the uncompromising, firm, old-fashioned style which the *terroir* seems to impose.

MARGAUX

AOC under vine: 3,110 acres
Average annual production: 7.1 million bottles
Crus classés as proportion of AOC vineyards: 73 per cent

The name Margaux conveys a gracious allure – the scent of violets, the rustle of silk. This is the only Médoc appellation named after a top château; it is also the only one which is not confined to a single commune, but spreads over five: Margaux itself, Cantenac, Labarde, Soussans and Arsac. The first two are the most important in terms of area and quality of vineyards.

The typical Margaux style is considered to be scented and elegant, not as full-bodied as Pauillac. This is an over-generalization. Margaux wines have a wide range of styles, from the big and full-bodied to the ethereally delicate. One more-or-less common factor is an especially fragrant bouquet, which often reminds me of fresh blackcurrants and, more strangely, Murraymints.

Margaux has some clear advantages over other parts of the Médoc. The climate is milder, so that the harvest takes place at least a week earlier, and the soil is particularly poor and well drained – bad news for quantity but good news, you would have thought, for quality. Unfortunately, Margaux does not always make the best use of its natural advantages. It probably contains as many underperforming *crus classés* as the other four classic appellations combined. The biggest technical problem is excessive parcelling of vineyards: the average Margaux *cru* consists of thirty or forty parcels scattered all over the five communes. There is surely a case for a German-style *Flurbeeinigung*, or vineyard rationalization, though that is probably wishful thinking. The good news for Margaux is the excellent performance, since 1978, of the flagship château, now restored to its historic position as leader of the whole region. Less spectacular, but encouraging improvements are going on at various properties (Marquis de Terme, d'Issan, Cantenac-Brown); others still have work to do. Recommended *crus bourgeois* of the appellation are **Châteaux La Gurgue, Labégorce-Zédé, Monbrison, La Tour de Mons**.

MÉDOC

AOC under vine: 9,300 acres

Average annual production: 23 million bottles

The Médoc appellation covers, in theory, the entire region from Blanquefort in the south to Jau-Dignac-et-Loirac in the north. In practice, however, it is confined to the northernmost part of the region, north of St Seurin de Cadourne. There are no *crus classés*, but some more than respectable *crus bourgeois*, making solid, tannic wines, sometimes hard when young and possessing less finesse than those from further south. Because the appellation is less fashionable, there are some excellent bargains to be picked up among the best *crus bourgeois*. Among these are **Châteaux La Cardonne, Lacombe-Noaillac, Loudenne, Les Ormes Sorbet, Pâtache d'Aux, Potensac**.

MOULIS

AOC under vine: 1,260 acres

Average annual production: 2.8 million bottles

Even smaller than Listrac, but somewhat more distinguished, Moulis has a handful of good *crus bourgeois* grouped around the hamlet of Grand-Poujeaux, among them, **Châteaux Branas-Grand-Poujeaux**, **Dutruch-Grand-Poujeaux** and **Gressier-Grand-Poujeaux**. The best of them approach, or indeed attain, *cru classé* standard. The Moulis style is full-bodied but lacks the stringy toughness of Listrac.

PAUILLAC

AOC under vine: 2,640 acres

Average annual production: 6.9 million bottles

Crus classés as proportion of AOC vineyards: 89 per cent

Pauillac, gathering together eighteen of the sixty-two *crus classés* and three of the five first growths, must be considered the Médoc's premier commune. The best wines of Pauillac can offer a combination of blackcurranty power and cedary finesse which makes them the most majestic of clarets. The Cabernet Sauvignon seems to express itself in certain Pauillac vineyards more forcefully than anywhere else in the Médoc.

All the same, it is not easy to pin down a single Pauillac style. There is a wide difference between, say, Grand-Puy-Lacoste, and Haut-Batailley (both under the same ownership), one tending towards the chunky, earthy richness of St Estèphe, the other towards the elegance of St Julien. The commune is notable for having a high proportion of both first and fifth growths, with little in between. It also sports only a handful of *crus bourgeois*. One of them, **Château Pibran**, bought by Jean-Michel Cazes's Axa-Millésimes in 1987, now produces big, opaque, reserved, classy wines, especially the 1988, from 30 acres around Pontet-Canet and Mouton-Rothschild.

Pauillac may boast some of the world's greatest wines, but it is a rather sad, one-horse sort of town. One feels it has never regained its vitality since the disappearance of river traffic on the Gironde.

ST ESTÈPHE

AOC under vine: 3,110 acres

Average annual production: 8 million bottles

This is the most northerly of the communal appellations of the Médoc, and also one of the largest. The soil, mainly gravel on top, with clay subsoil, is considerably more fertile than that of, say, Margaux, and yields tend to be higher.

St Estèphe's speciality is very good *crus bourgeois*; **Châteaux Beausite**, **Le Boscq**, **Le Crock** and **Houissant** are among the best. It has a smaller proportion of classified growths than the other communal appellations. The style tends to be big, hearty and robust, with an earthier texture and less refinement than other Médocs. A number of wines used to be made in an exaggeratedly hard, tannic style, but the trend now is towards a softer, more immediately appealing character.

ST JULIEN

AOC under vine: 1,850 acres

Average annual production: 5.1 million bottles

Crus classés as proportion of AOC vineyards: 84 per cent

St Julien may be the smallest of the Médoc's major appellations, and may have a slightly lower proportion of *cru classé* vineyards than Pauillac, but all the same there is a strong case for saying that St Julien is the epitome of what claret should be. This is largely a question of the style of the wines, which are more homogeneous than those of Pauillac or Margaux. St Juliens tend to be softer than Pauillacs, with a combination of blackcurrant fruit (Cabernet Sauvignon is almost as prominent here as in Pauillac) and cedary finesse which for many is definitive. As Franck said in his *Traité sur les Vins du Médoc*, St Juliens 'combine all the qualities which constitute the very best wines'.

St Julien is also uniquely lucky in having a consistently high standard of wine-making. Since the spectacular renaissance of Lagrange, and the almost equally impressive improvements at Léoville-Barton, Léoville-Poyferré and Langoa-Barton, one can fairly say that there are no disappointing wines in the appellation. The average size of the estates is quite large (around 125 acres), which, compared to the fragmentation of Margaux, has probably helped St Julien to achieve its current high standard. **Châteaux du Glana**, **Hortevie** and **Terrey-Gros-Caillou** are worthwhile *crus bourgeois*.

CHÂTEAUX

CHÂTEAU D'ANGLUDET

Margaux, *cru bourgeois*

> Vineyard: 86 acres (55 per cent Cabernet Sauvignon, 35 per cent Merlot, 5 per cent Cabernet Franc, 5 per cent Petit Verdot)
>
> Production: 140,000 bottles
>
> Quality: 🍇🍇🍇   Price: ★★
>
> Best vintages: 1983, 1984, 1985, 1986

Peter Sichel of Château Palmer bought this property in 1960. It is his family house and the wine benefits from his close care and attention. This is a very stylish and well-made *cru*, whose quality surpasses that of some *crus classés*. D'Angludet does not have quite the richness of Palmer, and tends to be quite hard when young, but in vintages like 1985 (chocolatey rich nose, very elegant and harmonious) and 1986 (deep in colour, backward but powerful, almost meaty) it comes very close to Palmer in both style and quality.

CHÂTEAU BATAILLEY

Pauillac, *cinquième cru classé*

> Vineyard: 123 acres (73 per cent Cabernet Sauvignon, 20 per cent Merlot, 5 per cent Cabernet Franc, 2 per cent Petit Verdot)
>
> Production: 200,000 bottles
>
> Quality: 🍷🍷🍷   Price: ★★★
>
> Best vintages: 1982, 1985, 1986, 1988

This gracious château, not only elegant on the outside but (more unusually in the Médoc) warm and lived-in inside, is situated in the south of the commune of Pauillac, on the road to St Laurent. The proprietor is M. Emile Castéja, owner also of the shipping firm of Borie-Manoux, and a gentleman of the old school. M. Castéja regrets the price rises of recent years which have pushed the top châteaux beyond the reach of non-plutocrats. 'The basis of our market was always the solid professional middle classes; it is dangerous to lose touch with them.'

Batailley has all the solid virtues of the professional classes: it is well made, well constructed and built to last. This is much more of a typical, plummy, Cabernet-dominated Pauillac than Haut-Batailley, but it can lack a little style and elegance. The 1985 has a lovely chocolatey richness, with some new oak apparent. The 1986 has a smooth, creamy texture at first, then shows very closed, with considerable, but not harsh, tannin.

CHÂTEAU BELGRAVE

Haut-Médoc, *cinquième cru classé*

> Vineyard: 130 acres (40 per cent Cabernet Sauvignon, 35 per cent Merlot, 20 per cent Cabernet Franc, 5 per cent Petit Verdot)

Production: 250,000 bottles

Second wine: Diane de Belgrave

Quality: 🍇   Price: ★★★

Best vintages: 1985, 1986

I would have wagered a small fortune that the *maître de chai* of this backwoods château in St Laurent would be a wizened, be-bereted old Frenchman in blue dungarees. Not a bit of it: Merete Larsen, who runs the property owned by a consortium of shareholders and leased to Dourthe-Kressmann, is young, blonde and Danish. Mlle Larsen has succeeded in pulling up the prime candidate for demotion among the *crus classés* to at least good *cru bourgeois* standard. The Belgrave style will always be tough, sinewy and a shade rustic, but vintages since 1984 show the benefits of new oak (up to 50 per cent), careful vinification and stricter selection. The 1985 is particularly attractive, with red-fruit ripeness and a touch of welcome refinement. The 1986 is more backward, but long and powerful, with a ripe finish.

CHÂTEAU BEYCHEVELLE

St Julien, *quatrième cru classé*

Vineyard: 173 acres (65 per cent Cabernet Sauvignon, 27 per cent Merlot, 5 per cent Cabernet Franc, 3 per cent Petit Verdot)

Production: 200,000 bottles

Second wine: Réserve de l'Amiral

Third wine: Les Brulières de Beychevelle

Quality: 🍇🍇🍇🍇   Price: ★★★★

Best vintages: 1982, 1985, 1986, 1987, 1988

This is one of the grandest, most beautiful properties in the Médoc, and it always comes as a surprise to find that it is a relatively lowly fourth growth. An impressive set of iron grilles protects the entrance to the lovely pale-stone *chartreuse* château, before which a cedar of Lebanon spreads its wide branches. At the back is a formal garden. It is good to report that Beychevelle is now on a par with the second growths not only in airs, but also in the quality of recent vintages.

The nautical connection (the second wine, and the label of the *grand vin* depicts a beautiful galley with an absurdly large prow) comes from the fact that the property belonged in the sixteenth century to the Duc d'Epernon, Admiral of France under Henri III. For nearly a century Beychevelle was owned by the Achille-Fould banking family, who sold it in 1987 to the French Civil Servants' Mutual Society. In these unlikely hands it seems to be thriving.

For me, Beychevelle is one of the most immediately appealing of all Médoc wines; 50 per cent new oak contributes to its soft, rich and chocolatey character. It seems to have no hard tannic edges, but it does not lack the structure to age, as the 1970 vintage is currently showing. The 1985 is deep-coloured, with a hint of tobacco on the nose; it is rich and supple on the palate, almost sweet (the cellar master uses the term *moelleux*), but concentrated – an excellent 1985. The 1986 is equally good, with a raisiny ripeness and powerful Cabernet structure. A more surprising success is the chocolatey, rounded 1987.

CHÂTEAU BOYD-CANTENAC

Margaux, *troisième cru classé*

Vineyard: 47 acres (67 per cent Cabernet Sauvignon, 20 per cent Merlot, 7 per cent Cabernet Franc, 6 per cent Petit Verdot)

Production: 80,000 bottles

Quality: 🍇🍇🍇   Price: ★★★

Best vintages: 1982, 1983, 1985, 1986, 1988

The property is named after Jacques Boyd, one of the most prominent members of Bordeaux's Irish community, who purchased it in 1754. It has belonged since 1934 to the Guillemet family. I came upon M. Pierre Guillemet inscribing entries in a ledger which seemed, like the pretty, modest château, to come out of the eighteenth century. M. Guillemet is a charming, old-fashioned wine-grower, who is proud to proclaim a countryman's attachment to his land.

There is something old-fashioned, though not rustic, about the wine-making at Boyd-Cantenac. The wine tends to be hard and somewhat charmless in its youth, but is well and carefully made and comes into its own after a minimum of ten or twelve years. 'You must never drink Margaux wines young,' asserts M. Guillemet. The 1982 is rather an exception – a rounded, velvety wine, ample in the mouth and finishing long. Better defined is the 1983, with the typical roasted aromas of the vintage and big, velvety and powerful in the mouth. The 1985 is attractively ripe and well balanced, with liveliness and verve. The 1986 is very deep-coloured, with a striking nose of violets, blackcurrant and some new oak – a fine, balanced wine of classic Margaux elegance. The 1988 is surprisingly powerful and backward, almost tough.

CHÂTEAU BRANAIRE-DUCRU

St Julien, *quatrième cru classé*

Vineyard: 126 acres (75 per cent Cabernet Sauvignon, 20 per cent Merlot, 3 per cent Cabernet Franc, 2 per cent Petit Verdot)

Production: 200,000 bottles

Second wine: Château Duluc

Quality: 🍇🍇🍇   Price: ★★★★

Best vintages: 1981, 1982, 1983, 1985, 1986, 1988

The neat, classical château (dating from 1780) stands across the road from Beychevelle, but a considerable proportion of the vineyards is much further inland, towards St Laurent. Perhaps this contributes to the very distinctive style of Branaire, not quite like any other St Julien. From tastings in Britain, I would have characterized this style as rich and chocolatey, with a special bouquet. When I tasted at the château, my impressions were rather different; the wines were certainly highly perfumed, but less full-bodied and more delicate than I expected. One point of interest is that the proportion of Cabernet Sauvignon in the wine is even higher than that in the vineyards – 80–85 per cent in a normal year, one of the highest proportions in the Médoc.

The 1982 Branaire has a very deep colour and a pungent, leathery nose; on the palate it has all the 1982 weight and richness, together with classic structure. Both the 1983, which has a lovely roasted bouquet, and the tobacco-scented 1985 are rather lighter. The 1986 is highly aromatic, complex and tannic, but with good ripeness. The 1988 is most promising – aromatic, long and ripe.

CHÂTEAU BRANE-CANTENAC

Margaux, *deuxième cru classé*

Vineyard: 200 acres (70 per cent Cabernet Sauvignon, 15 per cent Cabernet Franc, 13 per cent Merlot, 2 per cent Petit Verdot)

Production: up to 250,000 bottles

Second wine: Château Notton

Quality: 🍇   Price: ★★★★

Best vintage: 1986

I have never had much luck with this large and important property, flagship of the Lucien Lurton empire. Vintages from the 1970s had a farmyardy, manurey quality which did not seem appropriate for a second growth, and while that is missing from more recent vintages, I still fail to detect the concentration and length of a top-class wine. Certainly the Brane-Cantenac style is of the elegant, feminine Margaux school, but I do not find the requisite definition. The 1986, well coloured, with an attractive hint of new oak on the nose, is the best Brane-Cantenac for some years.

CHÂTEAU CALON-SÉGUR

St Estèphe, *troisième cru classé*

Vineyard: 150 acres (70 per cent Cabernet Sauvignon, 20 per cent Merlot, 10 per cent Cabernet Franc)

Production: 275,000 bottles

Second wine: Marquis de Ségur

Quality: 🍇🍇🍇   Price: ★★★

Best vintages: 1986, 1988

This is the most northerly of all the Médoc *crus classés*. The vineyard, partly surrounded by a wall, is just to the north of the village of St Estèphe, whose only notable feature is a tall church tower which looks rather like a bottle. The château at Calon-Ségur is a fine seventeenth-century building whose low end-towers give it a semi-fortified look. This is certainly the most historic vineyard in the commune: its origins go back to the twelfth century and in the eighteenth century it belonged to the Marquis de Ségur, who also owned Lafite and Latour. For the last century it has belonged to the Gasqueton family.

The wine, generally less refined than Cos and less hard than Montrose, went through a dull patch in the 1970s but recent vintages have been much more encouraging. M. Philippe Gasqueton feels that too many châteaux are pushing for excessive extraction these days. 'We haven't wished to push the colour by heating,' he says. 'Wines made in this traditional way are better balanced and age longer.' I was particularly impressed by the 1986 – meaty, ripe and deep – and the 1988 – very concentrated with excellent depth of fruit. The 1985 and 1983 are lighter vintages.

CHÂTEAU CAMENSAC

Haut-Médoc, *cinquième cru classé*

Vineyard: 185 acres (60 per cent Cabernet Sauvignon, 20 per cent Cabernet Franc, 20 per cent Merlot)

Production: 300,000 bottles

Second wine: La Closerie de Camensac

Quality: 🍇 Price: ★★★

Best vintages: 1984, 1985, 1986

The Forners, the energetic family of Spanish origin who also own the innovative Rioja bodega of Marqués de Cáceres, have been proprietors of this quiet château in the St Laurent hinterland since 1964. As they themselves admit, there was a certain disinvestment in Camensac during the 1960s while they were devoting their efforts and resources to the restitution of the large *cru bourgeois*, Château Larose-Trintaudon. More recently, and especially since Larose-Trintaudon was sold in 1986, the Forners have been able to invest heavily in Camensac.

The style is chunky, rich and fruity, but lacking in finesse and breed. Both the 1982 and 1983 are ripe but lacking in structure. The 1984 is remarkably good and solid for the year. The 1985 is the first really classy Camensac I have encountered – an attractive velvety wine with a subtle touch of new oak. The 1986 is closed but has depth, concentration and ripeness. On present form, Camensac is a worthy if not exceptional fifth growth.

CHÂTEAU CANTEMERLE

Haut-Médoc, *cinquième cru classé*

> Vineyard: 136 acres (45 per cent Cabernet Sauvignon, 40 per cent Merlot, 10 per cent Cabernet Franc, 5 per cent Petit Verdot)
>
> Production: 200,000 bottles
>
> Second wine: Baron Villeneuve de Cantemerle
>
> Quality: ♕♕♕♕   Price: ★★★
>
> Best vintages: 1985, 1986, 1987, 1988

Great improvements have been apparent at this lovely property, set among woods in the far south of the Médoc, since its running was taken over by Domaines Cordier in 1981. Cantemerle, despite the fact that many of its vineyards are planted on sandy soil, has always had the potential to produce fine wine, very much in the elegant Margaux style. It had a particularly good run in the 1950s when 1953, 1955 and 1959 were all superb, but things went gradually downhill during the late 1960s and 1970s, and by 1981 the vineyard had been reduced to 50 acres.

Cantemerle has a high proportion of Merlot, which is apparent both in the 1985, with its ripe, roasted aromas and soft, elegant body, and in the remarkably attractive 1987. The 1986 is much deeper in colour and character, pungent and tarry on the nose, powerful, long and mouth-filling. The 1988 was heavily influenced by sweet new oak when tasted from cask, but showed lovely perfumed fruit underneath. This is clearly a château in the ascendant.

CHÂTEAU CANTENAC-BROWN

Margaux, *troisième cru classé*

> Vineyard: 100 acres (67 per cent Cabernet Sauvignon, 25 per cent Merlot, 8 per cent Cabernet Franc)

Production: 120,000 bottles

Second wine: Château Canuet

Quality: 🍇 Price: ★★★

Best vintages: 1986, 1988

I have never been especially attracted by the rustic, hard style of Cantenac-Brown, any more than I am by the imposing but hideous golf-club Tudor nineteenth-century château. However, one cannot fail to be impressed by the investments made since the property was bought in 1987 by Compagnie du Midi, subsequently merged with Axa-Millésimes. Under the direction of Jean-Michel Cazes and Daniel Llose, and with one of the best-equipped *cuviers* in the Médoc, Cantenac-Brown should certainly be a rising star. I find the 1985 big, rich and chunky, with floral scents on the nose – a powerful wine made in a somewhat over-extractive style. The 1986 is actually more elegant and better-balanced, while the 1988 is very aromatic, with violets and toasty oak on the nose, and at the same time powerful and tannic. It may turn out very well, but I have slight doubts about the balance.

CHÂTEAU CARBONNIEUX

Pessac-Léognan, *cru classé de Graves*

33850 Léognan

Vineyard: 100 acres (55 per cent Cabernet Sauvignon, 30 per cent Merlot, 10 per cent Cabernet Franc, 5 per cent Malbec and Petit Verdot)

Production: 240,000 bottles

Second wine: La Tour-Léognan

Quality: 🍇 Price: ★★★

Best vintages: 1986, 1987, 1988

The largest of the Graves classified estates is administered from a splendid fourteenth-century building with three capped towers and an interior courtyard. The vineyard, one of the oldest in the Graves, was developed by the monks from the Abbaye Ste Croix, which purchased it in 1741. There is a tale, surely apocryphal, that the (white) wine of Carbonnieux found its way to the Topkapi Palace in Istanbul under the label 'eau minérale de Carbonnieux'.

On the whole I have found Carbonnieux a rather ordinary wine, lacking character and distinction. The 1985, highly praised by some writers, seemed to me weedy and vegetal on the nose, and light on the palate. The 1987 is gamy and medicinal on the nose, and has a fair structure for the vintage. The 1988, deep in colour, with a plummy nose, appears much more concentrated and promising at this stage. But I remain to be fully convinced of this château's class.

CHÂTEAU CHAMBERT-MARBUZET

St Estèphe, *cru bourgeois*

Vineyard: 37 acres (70 per cent Cabernet Sauvignon, 30 per cent Merlot)

Production: 100,000 bottles

Second wine: Château MacCarthy

Quality: 🍇🍇🍇　　Price: ★★

Best vintages: 1982, 1985, 1986, 1987

This is not, the proprietor M. Duboscq asserts, the second wine of Haut-Marbuzet, but the product of different parcels of vineyard, nearer Cos d'Estournel, with a slightly different *terroir*. Certainly Chambert is a more classic St Estèphe, but that has also to do with the fact that it is aged not in new oak but in the second-year barrels from Haut-Marbuzet. It has much of the chocolatey richness of its companion château, but in lesser vintages the fruit is not dominated by oak – in my view, an advantage.

CHÂTEAU CHASSE-SPLEEN

Moulis, *cru bourgeois*

> Vineyard: 185 acres (60 per cent Cabernet Sauvignon, 35 per cent Merlot, 3 per cent Cabernet Franc, 2 per cent Petit Verdot)
>
> Production: 280,000 bottles
>
> Second wine: L'Ermitage de Chasse-Spleen
>
> Quality: 🍷🍷🍷🍷   Price: ★★★
>
> Best vintages: 1983, 1984, 1985, 1986, 1988

Under the energetic and perfectionist direction of Mme Bernadette Villars, this imposing property has gone from strength to strength since the 1976 vintage. It is now probably the best of all the non-classified châteaux, and in any modern classification it would undoubtedly find a place well above many *crus* classified in 1855.

The Chasse-Spleen style is deep-coloured, big, robust, chocolatey; more notable for power than finesse, but structured to last. It is particularly good in off-vintages like 1977, 1980 and, more recently, 1984. Mme Villars uses 50 per cent new oak even in lesser years. Among the better recent vintages, the 1983 is magnificent – big, rich, full of fruit, still tannic at the finish. The 1982 is relatively disappointing, somewhat lacking in concentration (apparently Moulis suffered some rain during the vintage). Chasse-Spleen is on form, though, in 1985, with a charming, fruity wine not lacking in strength. The 1986 is dark, closed and powerful, while the 1988 is an inky-black, splendidly concentrated, earthy wine.

There are two explanations of the name, both involving splenetic poets. According to the English one, Byron, visiting the property in 1821, exclaimed, 'Quel remède pour chasser le spleen!' The French version is that the château is named after Baudelaire's poem 'Spleen'.

*

CHÂTEAU CLARKE

Listrac, *cru bourgeois*

Vineyard: 356 acres (46 per cent Cabernet Sauvignon, 40 per cent Merlot, 10 per cent Cabernet Franc, 4 per cent Petit Verdot)

Production: 500,000 bottles

Second wine: Château Malmaison

Quality: 🍇🍇🍇   Price: ★★★

Best vintages: 1981, 1982, 1983, 1985, 1986, 1987

It seemed a maverick, almost mad decision of Baron Edmond de Rothschild to purchase a derelict property in the Médoc's least fashionable appellation in 1970, and then invest huge sums in replanting the vast vineyard and installing the most modern equipment. Twenty years on, Clarke is justifying the Baron's faith; it has become one of the Médoc's best and most reliable *crus bourgeois*. Careful wine-making and liberal doses of new oak have reduced the stringy toughness, but Clarke remains a typical firm Listrac with the characteristic, bitter-cherry twist. The 1981 is perhaps the first vintage to show the Rothschild touch: medium-bodied, with a sweet entry and firm backbone, stylish. I prefer the 1983, with its gamy nose and good balance, to the rather bony 1982. Both the powerful, velvety 1985 and the plummy, deep 1986 are impressive.

CHÂTEAU CLERC-MILON

Pauillac, *cinquième cru classé*

Vineyard: 94 acres (75 per cent Cabernet Sauvignon, 15 per cent Merlot, 8 per cent Cabernet Franc, 2 per cent Petit Verdot)

Production: 100,000 bottles

Quality: 🍇🍇🍇   Price: ★★★★
Best vintages: 1982, 1985, 1986, 1988

Baron Philippe de Rothschild bought this rather obscure growth in 1970. Despite considerable investment, and some excellent vintages in the 1980s, it has not had the attention it deserves. Clerc-Milon is in a completely different style from either Mouton; the vineyard is on the gravel ridge nearest to the Gironde, north of Pauillac, and the wine has more than a little in common with those other great growths near the river, Latour and Léoville-Las Cases. This is a big, powerful, concentrated wine – 'archetypal Pauillac', according to the oenologist Bertrand Bourdil. The 1986 is particularly impressive, both ripe and concentrated, though it obviously needs at least fifteen years. The 1988 is also a success, with the concentration which some wines from the vintage lack. Clerc-Milon, which spends twenty months in oak (35 per cent new), is a wine to watch.

CHÂTEAU COS D'ESTOURNEL

St Estèphe, *deuxième cru classé*

Vineyard: 170 acres (58 per cent Cabernet Sauvignon, 40 per cent Merlot, 2 per cent Cabernet Franc)

Production: 300,000 bottles

Second wine: Château de Marbuzet (q.v.)

Quality: 🍇🍇🍇🍇🍇   Price: ★★★★★
Best vintages: 1979, 1981, 1983, 1985, 1986, 1988

The three pagoda-like towers in pale sandstone make one of the Médoc's most eye-catching sights. They are not part of a château, but glorify the working buildings erected in the 1830s by Louis-Gaspard d'Estournel on the ridge north of Lafite. Cos's sweep of south-facing gravel is one of the Médoc's finest and, under the management of Bruno Prats and his brothers (who inherited the estate from their maternal grandfather

Ferdinand Ginestet), has been producing consistently one of the Médoc's best wines.

Cos (you pronounce the 's') is, as is often said, quite different from any other St Estèphe. It is rounder and more refined, yet even off-vintages age extremely well. Wine-making is traditional with modern refinements: fermentation is at 30 °C in squat stainless steel *cuves*; ageing, for top vintages, is in 100 per cent new oak.

A ten-year vertical tasting was one of the most impressive I have had of any property, showing scarcely any disappointments. The 1979 is a lovely ripe wine, with gamy, leathery scents on the nose. The 1981 is excellent also, surprisingly big and powerful. The 1982 is massive and port-like, not as balanced as the superb 1983, which is well structured but without hard tannins. The 1985 is again superb – toasty, full-bodied and ripe, with a beautiful fresh balance. The 1986 is extremely big, powerful and concentrated, the 1987 impressive for the vintage and the 1988 long, elegant and showing classic potential. Just to show how gracefully the wine can age in an off-vintage, M. Prats showed the 1973, which proved to be ripe, soft, gentle yet complete, by no means over the hill. This château is deservedly regarded as a 'super-second'.

CHÂTEAU COS-LABORY

St Estèphe, *cinquième cru classé*

Vineyard: 44 acres (45 per cent Cabernet Sauvignon, 30 per cent Merlot, 20 per cent Cabernet Franc, 5 per cent Petit Verdot)

Production: 100,000 bottles

Quality: 🍇   Price: ★★★

Best vintages: 1981, 1982, 1986, 1988

This is one of the smallest, least pretentious and homeliest of the *crus classés*. Perhaps for that reason it has tended to get an exaggeratedly bad press from certain wine writers. This may not be one of the great wines of the Médoc, or even of St Estèphe, but recent vintages have produced a reliable, chunky wine. The main part of the vineyard is a long thin strip set like a splinter into Cos d'Estournel, the rest being near Lafon-Rochet, so one would not expect the wine to be entirely bad. The owners are the Audoy family, who are making substantial investments: a new *chai* is under construction and up to 50 per cent new *barriques* are being used for the 1988 vintage.

The 1986 is a powerful, animal wine, with a leathery scent and a good deal of tannin. The 1985 is much lighter, but pleasant. The 1988, tasted from cask, promised as much concentration as the 1986 without the hard tannin. Among earlier vintages I particularly like the well-balanced 1981.

CHÂTEAU CROIZET-BAGES

Pauillac, *cinquième cru classé*

Vineyard: 64 acres (54 per cent Cabernet Sauvignon, 30 per cent Merlot, 15 per cent Cabernet Franc, 1 per cent Malbec and Petit Verdot)

Production: 110,000 bottles

Second wine: Château Richebon

Quality: 🍇   Price: ★★★

Best vintages: 1981, 1982, 1985, 1986

The 'château' consists of a number of buildings in the hamlet of Bages. Owned by the Quié family (proprietors of Rauzan-Gassies) since 1945, Croizet-Bages has never achieved anything like the renown of Lynch-Bages. Recently, however, under the directorship of Jean-Michel Quié, considerable improvements have been made, including the construction of a new stainless steel *cuvier* in 1987. The vineyard was heavily replanted in the 1970s: recent vintages are beginning to show the benefit of the older vines.

Croizet-Bages, despite the relatively low percentage of Cabernet Sauvignon, generally has a plummy, blackcurranty fruit typical of Pauillac, though it lacks the depth and staying power of the top *crus*. The 1981 is surprisingly powerful for the vintage, with an animal, gamy nose; it is still unready on the palate. The 1982 is a big, reserved wine with some cassis character. The 1985 is pleasantly fruity and forward, now ready for drinking. The 1986 is the best wine produced at the property for some time, with a true Cabernet nose and firm and backward on the palate.

CHÂTEAU DAUZAC

Margaux, *cinquième cru classé*

Vineyard: 110 acres (57 per cent Cabernet Sauvignon, 37 per cent Merlot, 4 per cent Cabernet Franc, 2 per cent Petit Verdot)

Production: 240,000 bottles

Second wine: La Bastide-Dauzac

Quality: 🍇　　Price: ★★★

Best vintages: 1985, 1986, 1988

The vineyard of this mediocre fifth growth is situated on the flat land near the village of Labarde. Labarde seems to produce soft wines, and Dauzac is no exception. With a rather high proportion of Merlot, the result is a fairly attractive, fruity wine which lacks class and definition. Changes may be on the way since the château's purchase in 1988 by the insurance group MAIF. The owners certainly seem to be enthusiastic; they have lost no time in renovating the buildings. Whether the wine can be improved as rapidly I am not sure.

Among recent vintages, the 1985 is a full, fat wine with a touch of leather on the nose. The 1986 is a more potent, dark wine, but still on the soft side. The 1988, showing some new oak, seems the most complex of recent vintages, though there is still a certain flatness of character.

CHÂTEAU DESMIRAIL

Margaux, *troisième cru classé*

> Vineyard: 42 acres (80 per cent Cabernet Sauvignon, 10 per cent Merlot, 9 per cent Cabernet Franc, 1 per cent Petit Verdot)
>
> Production: 20,000 bottles
>
> Second wine: Château Baudry
>
> Quality: 🍇🍇🍇 Price: ★★★★
>
> Best vintage: 1981

This is a *cru* resurrected by Lucien Lurton after it was dismembered following the Second World War. For many years Desmirail was the second label of Château Palmer. The first vintage of born-again Desmirail is 1981; the wine has attractive, forward fruit, in a lightish style but with a certain body. I considerably preferred this to the 1981 vintage of Durfort-Vivens. As this is the only vintage I have been able to taste, judgement must be suspended, but I find this 1981 more charming than many other wines from the Lucien Lurton stable.

CHÂTEAU DUCRU-BEAUCAILLOU

St Julien, *deuxième cru classé*

> Vineyard: 121 acres (65 per cent Cabernet Sauvignon, 25 per cent Merlot, 10 per cent Cabernet Franc and Petit Verdot)
>
> Production: 240,000 bottles
>
> Second wine: Château La Croix-Beaucaillou
>
> Quality: 🍇🍇🍇🍇🍇 Price: ★★★★★
>
> Best vintages: 1981, 1982, 1983, 1985, 1986, 1988

The perfectionism of Jean-Eugène Borie, equal to but in a very different style from that of Michel Delon at Léoville-Las Cases, has made Ducru one of the top wines not just of St Julien but of Bordeaux. Some may criticize the price rises which have led to the creation of the group of 'super-seconds', but Ducru often reaches the level of the first growths, at about half the price.

The château, a substantial eighteenth-century *chartreuse* with two Victorian end-towers tacked on, is beautifully situated on a terrace overlooking the Gironde. The vineyards surrounding it have a high proportion of clay – you need gumboots on a wet day.

The Ducru style is elegant and subtle, much softer than Las Cases, say, but not without depth and length and staying power. The wine is often very deep-coloured and closed-up when young, but mellows in time to achieve a near-perfect harmony.

The 1981 is deep-coloured; to taste, it is all cedary elegance – classic St Julien and classic claret. The 1982 has a splendidly inky, concentrated, blackcurrant nose and is very rich, almost fat, on the palate. The 1983 has some of the roasted aromas typical of the vintage; this is a very complex, interesting wine, one of the best of the vintage. The 1985 is relatively open on the nose, with tones of red fruits and tobacco – a ripe wine but with firm tannic structure. The 1986 is very deep-coloured and in 1989 smelt quite strongly of new oak (65 per cent was used), though some floral, violet scents were evident too; this is a tightly furled, tannic wine, of great potential. The 1988, dominated by new oak vanilla in 1989, was not quite as power-ful but very long in the mouth.

CHÂTEAU DUHART-MILON

Pauillac, *quatrième cru classé*

Vineyard: 150 acres (70 per cent Cabernet Sauvignon, 20 per cent Merlot, 5 per cent Cabernet Franc, 5 per cent Petit Verdot)

Production: 300,000 bottles

Second wine: Moulin de Duhart

Quality: 🍇🍇🍇   Price: ★★★★
Best vintages: 1984, 1986, 1987, 1988

This somewhat obscure growth (a château without a château) was bought by the Rothschilds of Lafite in 1962. The vineyards border those of Lafite. It has remained less well known than many other Pauillac *crus*, despite producing some excellent vintages in the 1980s.

Duhart-Milon seems to perform particularly well in lesser vintages: the 1987 has an enticing soft nose and is silky and attractive on the palate with good length for the vintage. It may sound sacrilegious, but I prefer this to the Lafite of the same year. The 1986 Duhart-Milon belies the soft, lightish style with which the château had become associated; this is full, powerful, ample and concentrated wine, and the 1988 looks as if it will be similar. Certainly an underrated property at present.

CHÂTEAU DURFORT-VIVENS

Margaux, *deuxième cru classé*

Vineyard: 62 acres (82 per cent Cabernet Sauvignon, 10 per cent Cabernet Franc, 8 per cent Merlot)

Production: 70,000 bottles

Second wine: Domaine de Cure-Bourse

Quality: 🍇🍇   Price: ★★★★

Best vintage: 1986

Another Lucien Lurton property which has failed to inspire me with great enthusiasm. M. Lurton bought the reduced and dilapidated property in 1961 from Pierre Ginestet, with only 27 acres under vines. The vineyard is now more than twice that size, and is planted with a very high proportion of Cabernet Sauvignon – one of the highest in the Médoc. This leads, as you would expect, to a somewhat severe wine. I find the 1981 lacking in focus, but the 1986, though closed, shows good depth of plummy fruit.

CHÂTEAU FERRIÈRE

Margaux, *troisième cru classé*

> Vineyard: 10 acres (46 per cent Cabernet Sauvignon, 33 per cent Merlot, 12 per cent Petit Verdot, 8 per cent Cabernet Franc, 1 per cent Malbec)
>
> Production: 30,000 bottles

A walled vineyard in the centre of Margaux, owned by Mme Durand-Feuillerat but leased to Château Lascombes, Ferrière must win prizes for both smallest and most obscure *cru classé*. The production is sold almost entirely to the French restaurant trade, and I have never seen a bottle in England. From hearsay, the style is lightish and early-maturing, as one might deduce from the *encépagement* and chosen market.

CHÂTEAU DE FIEUZAL

Pessac-Léognan, *cru classé de Graves*

> 33850 Léognan
>
> Vineyard: 72 acres (60 per cent Cabernet Sauvignon, 30 per cent Merlot, 5 per cent Cabernet Franc, 5 per cent Petit Verdot)
>
> Production: 125,000 bottles
>
> Second wine: L'Abeille de Fieuzal
>
> Quality: 🍇🍇🍇🍇   Price: ★★★★
>
> Best vintages: 1985, 1986, 1988

The vineyard of Fieuzal occupies a fine gravel ridge in the south of the commune of Léognan. After a period of relative obscurity, the dynamic new team of owner/managing-director Gerard Gribelin and *régisseur* Michel Dupuy has pushed Fieuzal into the front rank of Graves châteaux.

Fermentation starts at low temperature, which is raised quite high for extended maceration. This certainly seems to achieve the object sought by M. Dupuy of extracting the maximum in both aromas and complexity. The 1986 has a very deep colour and an excellent, complex nose, with leathery and gamy scents. This is a complex, rich wine, with more charm than most 1986 Graves. The 1988 is still richer and more powerful, with a lovely pure blackcurrant fruit. The 1987 is a success for the year – attractive and toasty.

CHÂTEAU FOURCAS-DUPRÉ

Listrac, *cru bourgeois*

> Vineyard: 100 acres (50 per cent Cabernet Sauvignon, 38 per cent Merlot, 10 per cent Cabernet Franc, 2 per cent Petit Verdot)
>
> Production: 250,000 bottles
>
> Second wine: Château Bellevue-Lafont
>
> Quality: 🍇🍇🍇　　Price: ★★★
>
> Best vintages: 1981, 1982, 1983, 1986, 1988

This attractive and well-maintained property, with its vineyard consisting of a single block of Pyrenean gravel, has been administered by Guy Pagès, and then his son Patrick, since 1970. It is certainly one of the best Listrac wines – typically firm and slightly earthy, but with definite class and long ageing potential.

The 1981 is stylish. The 1982 is ripe but has typical earthiness and grip. The 1983 is fresh and well-balanced, with firm tannic structure and good length. The 1986 shows more fruit than the rather dry 1985 and the 1988, showing a fair amount of sweet vanilla new oak, also has attractive cherry fruit, and should be well-balanced.

*

CHÂTEAU FOURCAS-HOSTEN

Listrac, *cru bourgeois*

> Vineyard: 94 acres (50 per cent Cabernet Sauvignon, 40 per
>   cent Merlot, 10 per cent Cabernet Franc)
>
> Production: 200,000 bottles
>
> Quality: 🍇🍇🍇   Price: ★★★
>
> Best vintages: 1981, 1982, 1983, 1985, 1986, 1988

On current form I would place Fourcas-Hosten, which has
belonged since 1972 to a syndicate of American, French and
Danish *négociants*, slightly ahead of Dupré at the top of the
appellation. The style is very distinctive – tough, slightly earthy,
with a bitter twist, but also possessing great depth and staying
power in good vintages. Sometimes I detect a kinship with good
Riserva Chianti; perhaps this has something to do with the
limestone soil which both have in common.

The 1982 is a big, rounded wine, atypically fat but long in
flavour. The 1983 has tones of both toffee and coffee on the
nose, and lots of tannin and acidity on the palate indicating long
ageing potential. The 1985 has an attractive blackcurrant nose,
and is full, long and earthy on the palate. The 1986 smells more
of black cherries than blackcurrants and is just a little riper and
better than the 1985. The 1988 is somewhat lighter with attractive cherry fruit.

A park of interesting mature trees surrounds the low
chartreuse-style château.

CHÂTEAU GISCOURS

Margaux, *troisième cru classé*

> Vineyard: 200 acres (70 per cent Cabernet Sauvignon, 21 per
>   cent Merlot, 7 per cent Cabernet Franc, 2 per cent Petit
>   Verdot)

Production: 300,000 bottles

Quality: 🍇🍇🍇🍇   Price: ★★★★

Best vintages: 1981, 1982, 1983, 1984, 1985, 1986, 1988

Giscours is by far the most important estate in the commune of Labarde. It is indeed an imposing property, with a large nineteenth-century château (well likened by Edmund Penning-Rowsell to a spa hotel), 250 acres under vines (200 entitled to the Margaux appellation) and a polo park. Apparently it was in a sorry state when Nicholas Tari, a *pied-noir* wine-grower with a degree in oenology, bought it in 1952. It is now run by his son Pierre, a high-profile chatelain who jets around the world publicizing not only his château but Bordeaux in general.

The man who makes most of the wine-making decisions is Lucien Guillemet, son of the owner of Boyd-Cantenac and Pouget, and a character of original, deeply held views. 'I distrust hard wines,' says Guillemet, and recent vintages of Giscours have indeed displayed a rich vinosity. This is one of the fullest-bodied Margaux *crus*. Tannic structure is present, but there are no hard edges. 1980s vintages have been consistently good. The 1981 is well balanced, the 1982 big, rich and complex. The 1983 combines sweetness and power, while the 1984 (100 per cent Cabernet Sauvignon) is remarkably ripe and attractive for the year. Both 1985 and 1986 are excellent, with the former a shade livelier, the latter deep and cedary. The 1988 is lighter. Fifty per cent new oak is used. There is no second wine: Guillemet and Tari believe that only wine good enough for the château label should be sold as Giscours.

CHÂTEAU GLORIA

St Julien, *cru bourgeois*

Vineyard: 125 acres (65 per cent Cabernet Sauvignon, 25 per cent Merlot, 5 per cent Cabernet Franc, 5 per cent Petit Verdot)

Production: 250,000 bottles

Second wine: Château Peymartin

Quality: 🍇🍇🍇   Price: ★★★

Best vintages: 1982, 1983, 1985, 1986, 1988

Created in the mid twentieth century, this is perhaps the Médoc's most interesting example of a new *cru*. The man behind it is Henri Martin, scion of a long line of local *maîtres de chai* and barrel-makers and well-known mayor of St Julien. M. Martin, who is still very active in his late eighties, started in his father's barrel-making business but from 1942 began buying parcels of vines. Over the course of twenty years or so, he built Gloria up to its present respectable size, and as for the quality of the vineyards, 80 per cent came from *crus classés*, including Léoville-Barton, Gruaud-Larose, Talbot, Lagrange and Beychevelle. If Gloria, since 1978, has refused to call itself a *cru bourgeois*, it is not without some justification.

The style of Gloria is seductively soft, supple and filled with fruit. It also gains the characteristic St Julien cedary finesse as it ages – not such a long process as with most other St Julien *crus*. One of the secrets of M. Martin's success is judicious control of oak ageing: the wine spends part of its time in *barriques* (30 per cent new) and part in much larger oak *foudres*. The 1986 Gloria has a rich, ripe blackcurranty nose and is smooth, vinous and delicious, with no hard edges, on the palate. The 1988 is highly promising, with a subtle, soft nose and rich blackberry fruit on the palate.

CHÂTEAU GRAND-PUY-DUCASSE

Pauillac, *cinquième cru classé*

Vineyard: 91 acres (60 per cent Cabernet Sauvignon, 40 per cent Merlot)

Production: 140,000 bottles

Second wine: Château Artigues-Arnaud

Quality: 🍇 Price: ★★★

Best vintages: 1982, 1985, 1986, 1988

The château of this fifth growth is a fine eighteenth-century stone building on the quayside in Pauillac: the vineyards are spread all over the commune. There are three main blocks, one in the north between Mouton-Rothschild and Pontet-Canet, one in the south around St Lambert and one adjacent to Batailley in the west.

Grand-Puy-Ducasse used to be one of the less distinguished *crus* of Pauillac. It was bought in 1971 by the Mestrezat group, and considerable improvements have been made, starting in the vineyards and culminating in the construction of a gleaming new stainless steel *cuvier* in 1986.

Recent vintages show marked signs of improvement. The 1985 is attractive in a softish, loose-knit style, while the 1986 is altogether more concentrated, with fine raspberry fruit. The 1988 seems more concentrated still – perhaps too much so, as I find the tannin somewhat rough. I feel the natural style of the wine is elegant rather than big and powerful.

CHÂTEAU GRAND-PUY-LACOSTE

Pauillac, *cinquième cru classé*

Vineyard: 150 acres (70 per cent Cabernet Sauvignon, 25 per cent Merlot, 5 per cent Cabernet Franc)

Production: 180,000 bottles

Second wine: Lacoste-Borie

Quality: 🍇🍇 Price: ★★★★

Best vintages: 1980, 1981, 1982, 1983, 1985, 1986, 1988

The vineyard, in one block, surrounds the substantial nineteenth-century château situated a kilometre or so west of

Pauillac. Jean-Eugène Borie of Ducru-Beaucaillou took a controlling interest in the property in 1978, and now it is his son François-Xavier who is in charge. Like father, like son: the impeccable standards maintained at Ducru are being reproduced, and a string of fine vintages has resulted. Grand-Puy-Lacoste has been one of Bordeaux's most successful properties in the 1980s.

In style, Grand-Puy-Lacoste leans towards St Estèphe. It is substantial, deep-coloured and robust, and sometimes has the raisiny-ripe nose of good St Estèphe. The 1981 is a success – youthful in colour, with a touch of earthiness and considerable ripe fruit. The 1982 is velvety rich and very long on the palate, still somewhat closed on the nose. The 1983 is big and ripe, but still has a good deal of tannin, as has the still somewhat aggressive 1985. The 1986 is deep and rich, marked by attractive vanilla from the oak (Grand-Puy-Lacoste spends 18–20 months in *barriques*, one-third new), with concentrated fruit lying underneath. The 1988 is also most promising, showing toasty oak on the nose with concentrated fruit behind.

CHÂTEAU GRUAUD-LAROSE

St Julien, *deuxième cru classé*

> Vineyard: 207 acres (65 per cent Cabernet Sauvignon, 23 per cent Merlot, 8 per cent Cabernet Franc, 4 per cent Petit Verdot)
>
> Production: 350,000 bottles
>
> Second wine: Sarget de Gruaud-Larose
>
> Quality: 🍇🍇🍇🍇   Price: ★★★★★
>
> Best vintages: 1981, 1982, 1983, 1984, 1985, 1986, 1988

Some criticize the wines of Domaines Cordier, of which Gruaud-Larose is the flagship, for being marked by a house style (Cordierized is the term used by one eminent claret expert). Personally I admire Cordier's meticulous approach, which results in some of the most consistent and admirable wines in Bordeaux. One hopes there will be no changes following the sale of most of the Domaines Cordier to the insurance group ENA in 1984: the Cordier family have retained a 50 per cent share in Gruaud-Larose and Talbot.

Gruaud-Larose is typically a rich, full-bodied, plummy wine – perhaps the most powerful of all St Juliens, with the possible exception of Las Cases. In top years Gruaud-Larose ideally combines fleshy richness with tannic structure. Both the 1961 and the magnificently opulent, mouth-filling 1982 are on a par with the first growths. The château also performs notably well in off-vintages, the 1980 and the remarkably rich and ripe 1984 being good recent examples. The second wine, which together with those of the other Cordier properties helped to set a trend, is often excellent value, and even the *grand vin* offers 'super-second' quality at rather lower price.

CHÂTEAU HAUT-BAGES-LIBÉRAL

Pauillac, *cinquième cru classé*

Vineyard: 57 acres (80 per cent Cabernet Sauvignon, 17 per cent Merlot, 3 per cent Petit Verdot)

Production: 120,000 bottles

Quality: 🍇🍇🍇   Price: ★★★

Best vintages: 1982, 1983, 1985, 1986, 1987, 1988

Haut-Bages-Libéral was a candidate for the title of most obscure *cru classé* of the Médoc when it was bought in 1983 by the Merlaut family consortium. The energetic and impressively committed Mme Bernadette Villars believes that the property has a greater potential than her immensely successful *cru bourgeois*, Château Chasse-Spleen. Certainly the vineyard is extremely well situated, between Latour and the two Pichons.

While having great confidence in Mme Villars, I must admit to certain reservations about Haut-Bages-Libéral – notes on the same vintage vary from tasting to tasting, and I have not formed a very clear idea of the wine's style. It is certainly more in the powerful, plummy, backward style of Pauillac than the more forward, elegant mode. The 1986 is deep-coloured, concentrated and very closed. The 1985 seems initially more forward, with an attractive tobacco tone on the nose; on the palate, however, it is quite severe and tannic. The 1988 seems to be lighter and more aromatic than the 1986, with a suggestion of violets on the nose. This is certainly a promising château, worth watching; it is also relatively inexpensive.

CHÂTEAU HAUT-BAILLY

Pessac-Léognan, *cru classé de Graves*

> 33850 Léognan
>
> Vineyard: 69 acres (65 per cent Cabernet Sauvignon, 25 per cent Merlot, 10 per cent Cabernet Franc)
>
> Production: 200,000 bottles
>
> Second wine: La Parde de Haut-Bailly
>
> Quality: 🍇🍇🍇🍇 Price: ★★★★
>
> Best vintages: 1979, 1981, 1985, 1986

The late Daniel Sanders bought this property in 1955 in a run-down state. Under his son Jean, Haut-Bailly continues to produce a silky, understated red wine, sometimes seemingly light but often one of the most harmonious and complete in Bordeaux. In top years Haut-Bailly has a voluptuous richness which has led to its acquiring the sobriquet of the Pomerol of Graves.

Some find the key to the wine's style in the charm and courtesy of the Sanders, father and son. Another factor is the soil, more sandy in this part of Léognan than gravelly. Wine-making methods are classic: long *cuvaison* of two to three weeks, eighteen months in *barriques* of which up to half are new each year.

Of recent vintages the 1985 is superb, showing concentration and ripe charm; the 1986 is typically more backward, somewhat medicinal, but with good depth; the 1987 has attractive fruit and spicy oak, and is a good wine for the vintage if hardly a classic Haut-Bailly. Among older vintages the 1981 is drinking superbly – gentle, harmonious and complete.

CHÂTEAU HAUT-BATAILLEY

Pauillac, *cinquième cru classé*

Vineyard: 50 acres (65 per cent Cabernet Sauvignon, 25 per cent Merlot, 10 per cent Cabernet Franc)

Production: 130,000 bottles

Second wine: Château La Tour-l'Aspic

Quality: 🍇🍇🍇   Price: ★★★★

Best vintages: 1981, 1982, 1983, 1985, 1986, 1988

This smaller of the two Pauillac *crus classés* belonging to the Bories (it has been in the family since the 1930s) could hardly be more different in style from Grand-Puy-Lacoste. If the latter resembles a St Estèphe, Haut-Batailley, elegant, well-balanced and quite soft, is a Pauillac in the St Julien mode. Some have accused Haut-Batailley of lacking power, but I find recent vintages to be beautifully balanced with a notable purity of fruit. The 1981 has a lovely freshness and acidity, while the 1982 is unusually powerful, with an animal, leathery nose. The 1983 is long and elegant, a success for the vintage, and the 1985 charming and forward. The 1986 is more closed, but not massive, and the 1988 seems gentle and unassertive, with some toasty oak.

CHÂTEAU HAUT-BRION

Pessac-Léognan, *premier cru classé*

> 33600 Pessac
>
> Vineyard: 104 acres (55 per cent Cabernet Sauvignon, 25 per cent Merlot, 20 per cent Cabernet Franc)
>
> Production: 140,000 bottles
>
> Second wine: Bahans-Haut-Brion (60,000 bottles)
>
> Quality: 🍇🍇🍇🍇🍇   Price: ★★★★★
>
> Best vintages: 1979, 1981, 1985, 1986

Haut-Brion was the first of the first growths to be created, by Arnaud de Pontac in the late seventeenth century; in 1960 it became the first château in Bordeaux to install stainless steel fermentation tanks. Thus it justifies its claim to be always at the cutting edge of progress. In 1935 Haut-Brion also became the first *premier cru* to be bought by an American, the banker Clarence Dillon. The proprietor is now his daughter, the Duchesse de Mouchy. Continuity is assured by the devoted, thoughtful care and questing technical approach of the *régisseur*, Jean-Bernard Delmas.

The vineyard, situated in what are now the outskirts of Bordeaux, consists of two deep gravel ridges but also has a proportion of sand. The wine it produces, made with a higher proportion of Merlot than any of the other first growths, is suave and rich, with a distinctive caramelly tone on the nose. It tends to taste softer than the other first growths, and is surprisingly approachable when young. However, it has no difficulty ageing two decades and more. Haut-Brion spends thirty months in 100 per cent new *barriques*.

The 1985 is beautifully complete, if not over-powerful. The 1986 is full in flavour and quite stern. The 1988 seems on the light side. But older vintages like 1978, 1971 and 1961 continue to impress me.

*

CHÂTEAU HAUT-MARBUZET

St Estèphe, *cru bourgeois*

Vineyard: 110 acres (50 per cent Cabernet Sauvignon, 40 per cent Merlot, 10 per cent Cabernet Franc)

Production: 250,000 bottles

Second wine: Château Tour de Marbuzet

Quality: 🍷🍷🍷🍷   Price: ★★★

Best vintages: 1982, 1983, 1985, 1986

M. Henri Duboscq is one of the most articulate and, as he would say, expressive proprietors in the Médoc. He is able to explain exactly what he is aiming to do with his wine, and while you might be tempted to write off his torrents of words as salesman's patter, the wine largely substantiates his claims. Haut-Marbuzet is certainly one of the great maverick wines, not just of St Estèphe, but of Bordeaux. Instead of the dour, firm, masculine style once thought typical of the commune, M. Duboscq produces a chocolatey-rich, spicy, voluptuous wine. 'I am constantly fighting my *terroir*: it is hard and taciturn, while I am voluble and sensual,' he says. His main weapon is oak: he uses 100 per cent new *barriques*, every year, and selects many different qualities and toasts. He finds Allier oak, heavily toasted, gives exuberance; Nièvre is good in lesser vintages, imparting tones of vanilla, cinnamon and honey; Limousin, which gives a harsh and aggressive taste, is excluded.

I found his 1987 very spicy on the nose, and dominated by oak on the palate – a wine for oak-lovers. The 1986, on the other hand, showed a fine balance between the charming toasty character of skilfully applied oak and the firm sinewy fruit of what is undoubtedly a fine vineyard. The 1970 Haut-Marbuzet (aged, like all vintages since 1952, in 100 per cent new oak), with a wonderful ripe gamy nose and a prune-like richness on the palate, is still lively, and proof of the class and staying power of this remarkable wine.

CHÂTEAU D'ISSAN

Margaux, *troisième cru classé*

Vineyard: 69 acres (75 per cent Cabernet Sauvignon, 25 per cent Merlot)

Production: 150,000 bottles

Quality: 🍇🍇🍇 Price: ★★★★

Best vintages: 1981, 1982, 1983, 1985, 1986, 1988

The wine of d'Issan may not quite match the beauty of the seventeenth-century moated château, perhaps the most romantic in the Médoc, but steady and dedicated work by Emmanuel Cruse, his wife and his son Lionel has brought it up to a worthy standard.

With a high proportion of Cabernet Sauvignon, d'Issan is a typical, fragrant, medium-weight Margaux which tends to be quite hard and tannic when young. The 1983, as often in Margaux, is better than the 1982. It has a very distinctive blackcurrant nose and is long and powerful in the mouth with pure, lean fruit. The 1982 is softer and richer but less focused. In 1989 I was more impressed by the 1985 – silky-textured but firm, with more Cabernet character than usual in this Merlot year – than by the 1986, which seemed lighter. The 1986 could have been going through an awkward stage – it showed very well in June 1987. One-third new oak is used.

CHÂTEAU KIRWAN

Margaux, *troisième cru classé*

Vineyard: 79 acres (40 per cent Cabernet Sauvignon, 30 per cent Merlot, 20 per cent Cabernet Franc, 10 per cent Petit Verdot)

Production: 180,000 bottles

Quality: 🍇🍇🍇   Price: ★★★
Best vintages: 1981, 1983, 1986

Named after an Irish family from Galway, Kirwan has belonged since 1925 to the *négociant* house of Schröder & Schyler. Not highly reputed in the 1960s and 1970s, this *cru*, placed at the head of the third growths in 1855, has been making a comeback as the vineyards replanted in the late 1960s have matured. The *encépagement* is curiously low in Cabernet Sauvignon but high in Petit Verdot, a variety Yann Schyler considers vitally important for structure. With a high proportion of Merlot this is one of the softer Margaux, but recent vintages have shown a good balance.

The 1983 has an interesting minty, blackcurrant nose (a Margaux hallmark) and is full and firm on the palate. The 1986 shows the influence of an increased proportion of new oak (up to 50 per cent) and is concentrated and powerful on the palate. This is probably the biggest Kirwan for some years.

CHÂTEAU LAFITE-ROTHSCHILD

Pauillac, *premier cru classé*

Vineyard: 250 acres (70 per cent Cabernet Sauvignon, 15 per cent Merlot, 12 per cent Cabernet Franc, 3 per cent Petit Verdot)

Production: 300,000 bottles

Second wine: Moulin des Carruades

Quality: 🍇🍇🍇🍇🍇   Price: ★★★★★

Best vintages: 1985, 1986, 1988

Lafite has tended to have the edge over the other first growths, projecting a certain mysterious allure, implying that it is *primus inter pares*. Recently, iconoclastic critics have dared to question this pre-eminence.

It is certainly not the most powerful of them, but it does have, with Margaux, the most exquisite bouquet. You might say that Lafite is a wine for sniffers more than swallowers: it is seldom very full-bodied and in lesser vintages can be disappointingly light. I do think that at its best it has a harmony and balance which can elude more powerful, swaggering wines like Latour and Mouton.

How often is it at its best? Both the atmosphere and the wine-making at Lafite are strikingly old-fashioned. Nothing wrong with fermentation in oak *cuves* (though a new battery of stainless steel fermenters has been introduced) and in-house cooperage (for 100 per cent new oak every year), but the chain of command does appear to have a near-feudal stratification. Baron Eric de Rothschild is the charming head of the organization, but he is very seldom at Lafite. One gets the impression of a marked change of style between the beautifully balanced, fresh 1985 and the massively powerful, tannic 1986.

Ricardo Bofill's circular underground *chai*, like the inside of an Egyptian pyramid, is one of the architectural sights of the Médoc.

CHÂTEAU LAFON-ROCHET

St Estèphe, *quatrième cru classé*

Vineyard: 110 acres (64 per cent Cabernet Sauvignon, 30 per cent Merlot, 6 per cent Cabernet Franc)

Production: 180,000 bottles

Second wine: Numéro 2 de Lafon-Rochet

Quality: 🍇   Price: ★★★★

Best vintages: 1985, 1986, 1988

There is a ghostly, impersonal feel about the château at Lafon-Rochet, apparently an eighteenth-century *chartreuse* but in fact built in 1970. The wine itself, despite undoubted commitment to quality on the part of the owner, Guy Tesseron, also seems to lack a certain identity. Produced from well-sited vineyards in the south of the commune, opposite Château Lafite, it is certainly not an earthy St Estèphe of the Montrose type. Increased planting of Cabernet Sauvignon has resulted in a firm, tannic wine, which tends to be closed and to lack charm when young but which can age impressively.

CHÂTEAU LAGRANGE

St Julien, *troisième cru classé*

Vineyard: 279 acres (66 per cent Cabernet Sauvignon, 27 per cent Merlot, 7 per cent Petit Verdot)

Production: 240,000 bottles

Second wine: Les Fiefs de Lagrange

Quality: 🍇🍇🍇🍇   Price: ★★★★

Best vintages: 1982, 1983, 1985, 1986, 1988

There has never been, perhaps, so dramatic a rehabilitation of a *cru classé* as that conducted at Lagrange since it was bought by the Suntory company of Japan in December 1984. Suntory had promised the French government, as a condition of purchase, that they would invest at least 20 million francs; in fact, their renovation programme has cost 150 million. In 1983 there were 140 acres under vines, of which 45 per cent were Merlot. Suntory have doubled the area under vine and greatly increased the percentage of Cabernet Sauvignon. Now not even the first growths can match Lagrange as a model estate, with its immense *barrique chais* and new *cuvier* containing fifty-six stainless steel *cuves*, each surrounded by six individually controlled heating and cooling bands. 'That is the sort of fermenting-room I have always dreamed of!' exclaimed Professor Peynaud, consultant to Suntory on the Lagrange project, when he first saw them.

One can be dazzled by such wealth and splendour. It is not worth anything unless the men in charge know what they are doing. It looks as though Suntory made a shrewd choice in appointing Marcel Ducasse as director. His determined leadership and refined palate have ensured that the reality of recent vintages of Lagrange lives up to the magnificent appearance. The 1985 is a really splendid wine, with an immensely deep colour and a terrific depth of red-fruit ripeness on the nose. In the mouth it is opulent, voluptuous, possessing great power but no hardness of tannin. Even the 1985 Fiefs de Lagrange is a delicious wine. The 1986 *grand vin* is much more backward, with a deep blackcurrant or blackberry fruit on the nose; this is a ripe and powerful wine but it lacks the fleshy allure of the 1985 at present. The 1988 will not be as big; it has attractive toasty oak on the nose (a minimum 50 per cent new oak is used for maturation) and is surprisingly approachable on the palate.

CHÂTEAU LA LAGUNE

Haut-Médoc, *troisième cru classé*

Vineyard: 173 acres (55 per cent Cabernet Sauvignon, 20 per cent Cabernet Franc, 20 per cent Merlot, 5 per cent Petit Verdot)

Production: 300,000 bottles

Quality: 🍷🍷🍷🍷🍷   Price: ★★★★

Best vintages: 1981, 1982, 1983, 1984, 1985, 1986, 1988

If I had to award the palm for consistency to any Médoc château, I would give it to this immaculate property, the southernmost of all the classed growths, owned by Champagne Ayala. La Lagune has a very distinctive style – rich and chocolatey, yet endowed with the tannic structure to last two decades. A high proportion of new oak (up to 80 per cent) has always been used, yet I do not find the wine excessively oaky; it has a robust enough constitution to digest the flavour of the wood.

La Lagune is especially good in off-vintages, and the 1984, which the *régisseuse* Mme Desvergnes considers '*trop boisé*' (over-oaked), is outstanding, with remarkable power, length and ripeness. But the 1980s show an almost uninterrupted string of successes for the château. The 1982 is extremely rich yet has the balance many châteaux lack in this vintage, while the 1983 is roasted, rich and ripe. The 1985 is superb, with exceptional ripeness and balance – much more immediately appealing than the vast, brooding 1986, which with its deep black-fruit nose should develop into an outstanding bottle. The 1988, tasted from cask, had a ravishing floral aroma and tasted full of fruit – another outstanding success.

CHÂTEAU LALANDE-BORIE

St Julien, *cru bourgeois*

Vineyard: 44 acres (65 per cent Cabernet Sauvignon, 25 per cent Merlot, 10 per cent Cabernet Franc)

Production: 75,000 bottles

Quality: 🍇🍇🍇   Price: ★★★★

Best vintages: 1982, 1983, 1985, 1986, 1988

Lalande-Borie is not, as many people think, the second wine of Ducru-Beaucaillou, but a separate vineyard, originally part of Lagrange, bought and planted by the Bories in 1970. It is, therefore, more like a mini-Gloria. The quality of vintages since 1982 suggests that standards can match or even surpass those of M. Martin. The 1982 is an opulent, full-bodied, deep-coloured wine, ready to drink by 1989 but definitely of *cru classé* quality. The 1988 is silky and elegant, rather than powerful, tending towards Margaux in style. With a fine *terroir* and one of the Médoc's most skilled wine-growing dynasties at the helm, this is a property to watch, and indeed to buy while it remains quite inexpensive.

CHÂTEAU LANESSAN

Haut-Médoc, *cru bourgeois*

> Vineyard: 100 acres (75 per cent Cabernet Sauvignon, 20 per cent Merlot, 3 per cent Cabernet Franc, 2 per cent Petit Verdot)
>
> Production: 200,000 bottles
>
> Second wine: Domaine de Ste Gemme
>
> Quality: 🍇🍇🍇 Price: ★★★
>
> Best vintages: 1983, 1985, 1986

Lanessan, situated just to the south of Gruaud-Larose in the commune of Cussac-Fort-Médoc, has the airs and accoutrements of a *cru classé*. The Scottish baronial château, built in 1878, stands at the end of an extremely long drive, and there is a splendid set of Victorian *chais* and stables. The wine itself is usually of *cru classé* standard. In fact, the story is that Louis Delbos, who owned the property at the time, refused to submit a sample to the Bordeaux Chamber of Commerce for the classification of 1855. His descendants, the Bouteiller family, who own the estate today, must rue that decision, but it is good news for the consumer, who can buy a distinguished wine at a reasonable price.

The style of the wine is classically Médocain, as one might expect from the high proportion of Cabernet Sauvignon in the vineyard: hard when young, but revealing a splendid bouquet and considerable finesse as it ages. Among recent vintages, 1983 and 1985 are both particularly ripe (Lanessan can be mean in lesser vintages), the former with a roasted, caramelly nose, the latter with vivid ripe fruit. The 1986 is even better, with a plummy nose, a powerful long flavour and the depth of a good *cru classé* at the finish.

CHÂTEAU LANGOA-BARTON

St Julien, *troisième cru classé*

> Vineyard: 50 acres (70 per cent Cabernet Sauvignon, 15 per cent Merlot, 8 per cent Petit Verdot, 7 per cent Cabernet Franc)
>
> Production: 100,000 bottles
>
> Quality: 🍇🍇🍇   Price: ★★★★
>
> Best vintages: 1981, 1982, 1983, 1985, 1986, 1988

This is the first of the two estates bought by the Irishman Hugh Barton in the 1820s, the other being Léoville-Barton. Still owned by the Bartons today, they represent the longest tradition of unchanged ownership in the Médoc. The Barton connection with Bordeaux goes back a further century, to the arrival of 'French Tom' Barton in the 1720s. Langoa is the name of the château (formerly called Pontet-Langlois), for me the most beautiful *chartreuse* in the Médoc. The main block is constructed above an extensive cellar; another striking feature is the parterre leading down to a swan-haunted lake.

The wine is made by exactly the same, rather traditional, methods as its big brother. The wine-making has been tactfully refined and modernized by Anthony Barton since he took over in 1982 from his celebrated uncle Ronald, one of the great chatelains of twentieth-century Bordeaux. The result has been a sustained and quite dramatic improvement in the wine, which could in the past be excessively dry and dusty. Fermentation takes place in a splendid battery of wooden *cuves*; afterwards, the wine spends up to two years in *barriques*, one-third new, in the cool, dark *chai*. The difference between Langoa and Léoville, always quite marked, must be put down to variations in the soil and the exposure of the blocks of vineyards, since the *encépagement* is identical. Langoa is almost always lighter and more forward than Léoville. It can have more charm, at least at an early stage; this is the case with the sweet, cedary 1985. The 1986 is very deep-coloured, with some fleshy ripeness on the nose. The 1988 has a charming raspberry freshness on the nose, and recalls the 1985 in style.

CHÂTEAU LARRIVET HAUT-BRION

AC Pessac-Léognan

> 33850 Léognan
>
> Vineyard: 37 acres, with a further 44 being planted (55 per cent Cabernet Sauvignon, 45 per cent Merlot)
>
> Production: 80,000 bottles
>
> Second wine: Domaine de Larrivet
>
> Quality: 🍇🍇🍇   Price: ★★
>
> Best vintages: 1987, 1988

This small property near Haut-Bailly has been involved for a century with Château Haut-Brion in a lawsuit over its use of the famous name. Larrivet may not have much in common with the top Graves château either geographically or stylistically, but it is producing a well-coloured, rounded red wine up to decent *cru classé* standard.

Considerable investments have been made following the property's purchase by a jam company in 1987. The full, deep, 1988 vintage was matured in 80 per cent new *barriques*. The 1987 is also a success for the vintage.

CHÂTEAU LASCOMBES

Margaux, *deuxième cru classé*

> Vineyard: 227 acres (65 per cent Cabernet Sauvignon, 32 per cent Merlot, 2 per cent Petit Verdot, 1 per cent Malbec)
>
> Production: 400,000 bottles
>
> Second wine: Château Segonnes

Quality: 🍇🍇🍇   Price: ★★★★
Best vintages: 1981, 1986, 1988

A map in the office of the *régisseur*, M. Gobinot, shows the one hundred or so different parcels of vineyard which go to make up what is one of the largest and probably the most fragmented *cru* in the entire Médoc. No one doubts the potential of Lascombes to make very fine wine, and the owners, the big British brewers Bass Charrington, have certainly not skimped on investment in the property: the new *cuvier*, all stainless steel, is particularly impressive. All the same, exciting, rather than merely reliable, quality has proved elusive. The 1982 is a big wine with a creamy, vanilla nose, but no great structure or complexity. Rather finer, though still on the soft side, is the 1983; but this is not one of the better wines of a great Margaux vintage. Considerably more encouraging are the 1986, with a deep, port-like nose, dense and concentrated on the palate, and the 1988, the most attractive Lascombes for many years, with a lovely flowery nose, forward sweet first flavour and tannic finish.

CHÂTEAU LATOUR

Pauillac, *premier cru classé*

Vineyard: 116 acres (80 per cent Cabernet Sauvignon, 15 per cent Merlot, 3 per cent Cabernet Franc, 2 per cent Petit Verdot)

Production: 200,000 bottles

Second wine: Les Forts de Latour

Quality: 🍇🍇🍇🍇🍇   Price: ★★★★★

Best vintages: 1981, 1982, 1983, 1984, 1985, 1986, 1988

People are always surprised to learn that the vineyard of Latour, the most powerful of the Pauillac growths, is situated on the St Julien border in the south, whereas that of elegant Lafite is at the other end of the commune bordering St

Estèphe. Latour's is without doubt a privileged *terroir*: the proximity of the Gironde, reflecting light and storing heat, protects it from frost and may help to explain why Latour is so good in off-vintages. The tower is a rather curious round one, dating from 1620, stuck out in the vineyards. It is a good deal more interesting than the modest Victorian château building.

For a long time the English seem to have had a predilection for Latour. It was controlled by the Pearson Group from 1963, then in May 1989 Pearsons sold out to Allied-Lyons. The descendants of the original owners, the de Beaumont family, retain a 10 per cent share. Perhaps the style of the wine, its frank power and its purity of fruit, particularly appeals to English taste.

Latour has a high proportion of Cabernet Sauvignon, which is immediately noticeable. It is probably the most tannic of the first growths, but the fruit is so rich that it does not seem harsh or austere. Lesser years, as I have said, are outstanding – the 1980 and 1984 both powerful, complex wines. The top years last for ever and are often not to be approached before their twentieth birthday.

The second wine, Les Forts de Latour, which comes from a separate parcel of vineyard, has the quality of a good second growth, and much the same bold, powerful style as the *grand vin*. Unusually, it is released by the château when it is considered mature: the 1975 came out in 1989.

CHÂTEAU LÉOVILLE-BARTON

St Julien, *deuxième cru classé*

Vineyard: 100 acres (70 per cent Cabernet Sauvignon, 15 per cent Merlot, 8 per cent Cabernet Franc, 7 per cent Petit Verdot)

Production: 140,000 bottles

Quality: 🍇🍇🍇🍇   Price: ★★★★

Best vintages: 1981, 1982, 1983, 1985, 1986, 1988

This smallest portion of what was once the great Léoville estate of the Marquis de Las Cases was bought by Hugh Barton in 1826. There is no château and the wine continues to be made, as it has for over 160 years, at Langoa. The achievement of the genial, humorous, but not-to-be-underestimated Anthony Barton in the years since he took over the reins from his uncle Ronald has been to bring Léoville-Barton within spitting distance of the quality of Léoville-Las Cases, while keeping it at roughly half the price. 'Wine-making is just a whole lot of small details,' says Barton modestly. By paying strict attention to such matters as control of temperature during fermentation, pumping-over, quality of barrels and, perhaps above all, selection, he has made Léoville-Barton an exciting, rather than merely a reliable, second growth.

The style of the wine is quite powerful and meaty, rather less austere than Léoville-Las Cases, but less supple and forward than Léoville-Poyferré. In time, Léoville-Barton develops the classic cedary quality of St Julien. A notable feature of recent vintages has been an intense purity of fruit. Among them, the 1986 is exceptionally successful – well coloured, meaty and intense. The 1985 is quite a big and backward wine for the vintage, less charming than the Langoa but more powerful and tannic. The 1988 is complex, meaty and backward, showing some new oak – roughly half the barrels are now replaced each year. The Barton succession looks secure in the hands of Anthony's daughter Lilian.

CHÂTEAU LÉOVILLE-LAS CASES

St Julien, *deuxième cru classé*

Vineyard: 240 acres (64 per cent Cabernet Sauvignon, 23 per cent Merlot, 10 per cent Cabernet Franc, 3 per cent Petit Verdot)

Production: 250,000 bottles

Second wine: Clos du Marquis

Quality: 🐓🐓🐓🐓🐓 Price: ★★★★★
Best vintages: 1981, 1982, 1983, 1985, 1986

This, the major part of the original vast estate of the Marquis de Las Cases, comprises one of the Médoc's finest vineyards, stretching between Château Latour and the village of St Julien and surrounded by a high stone wall. In the perfectionist hands of Paul Delon and his son Michel, this estate has sought not only pre-eminence among the three Léovilles, but also comparison with the first growths. It has only one rival for the position of top wine of St Julien – Ducru-Beaucaillou; for the position of most expensive wine of the commune it has no rival.

There can be no more immaculate or efficiently run working château in the Médoc. There are three *cuviers*, one in wood, one in cement and one in stainless steel, representing three generations of Bordeaux wine-making. Of the three, incidentally, M. Delon says he prefers the cement. The immensely long *chais*, with *barriques* only one storey high, are most impressive, and as for the marble-floored bottling hall, it has become something of a legend. Fermentation is at relatively low temperature – no more than 27 °C – in order to preserve aromatic freshness.

M. Delon, a clever, tough man, who commands respect if not always affection in the Médoc, produces a notably reserved, backward wine at Las Cases, which combines power and finesse but which takes at least a decade to begin to open up. Since 1979, M. Delon has been conducting micro-vinifications of each of the four grape varieties used at Las Cases; a ten-year vertical-by-horizontal tasting was a most educative experience. Cabernet Sauvignon on its own is often long and complex, but tends to be a little bony; Merlot adds fleshy richness. Cabernet Franc is the most subtle variety – aromatic and fine but short. Petit Verdot is variable, but in good years has deep colour, ripeness and alcoholic weight. In almost every case the assemblage is superior to any of the varieties on their own.

The 1981 is a splendid marriage of Merlot flesh with Cabernet structure, but needs time. The 1982 is still closed, but promises great things with Cabernet power and Merlot richness. The 1983 is dominated by fine, cedary Cabernet, but is far from ready, while the 1986 combines toasty oak and floral scents on the nose, and has a great power and complexity on the palate. This is one of the best wines of a classic vintage, and it is a tribute to M. Delon's pursuit of perfection that only 43 per cent of the crop was selected for the *grand vin*.

CHÂTEAU LÉOVILLE-POYFERRÉ

St Julien, *deuxième cru classé*

Vineyard: 200 acres (65 per cent Cabernet Sauvignon, 25 per cent Merlot, 8 per cent Petit Verdot, 2 per cent Cabernet Franc)

Production: 300,000 bottles

Second wine: Château Moulin-Riche

Quality: 🍇🍇🍇🍇   Price: ★★★★

Best vintages: 1982, 1983, 1984, 1985, 1986, 1987, 1988

Soon after the Cuvelier family purchased this final portion of the Léoville estate in 1920, Poyferré became the most sought-after of the three Léoville wines, with the 1929 being considered perhaps the finest wine of that great vintage in all Bordeaux. A decline followed, which was only arrested when young, enterprising Didier Cuvelier succeeded in interesting his family in the property once more in the 1970s. The area under vine has increased from 120 acres a decade ago to the current figure of 200, and much money has been invested in the *cuvier* and *chais*. The result has been an uninterrupted string of successes since 1982, which means that all three Léovilles are now performing to full potential.

Poyferré is the softest and most supple of the Léovilles. Past vintages may have lacked depth and concentration, but since 1982 there has been an excellent marriage of power and finesse. Didier Cuvelier has increased the percentage of Petit Verdot to give the wine more backbone. The 1982 is a plush, velvety wine of great richness and concentration. The 1983 is a contrast – deep-coloured with tight, compact Cabernet fruit, a success for the vintage. The 1984 is another, more surprising success, well knit with ripe blackcurrant fruit, not at all green. The 1985, with good youthful colour, is already quite developed on the nose, with warm, leathery tones – a sweet ripe wine, beautifully balanced, almost drinkable. The 1986 is a little like the 1983, only bigger – massive colour, great plummy depth on the nose, massive black-cherry fruit. The 1987 is attractively rounded and ripe-tasting, with a touch of spiciness from the oak (65 per cent new oak is now used, as opposed to 25 per cent eight years ago). The 1988 is aromatic and full of fruit, without the power of 1986.

CHÂTEAU LA LOUVIÈRE

AC Pessac-Léognan

> 33850 Léognan
>
> Vineyard: 100 acres (70 per cent Cabernet Sauvignon, 20 per cent Merlot, 10 per cent Cabernet Franc)
>
> Production: 200,000 bottles
>
> Second wine: Château Coucheroy
>
> Quality: 🍇🍇🍇🍇   Price: ★★★
>
> Best vintages: 1982, 1983, 1985, 1986

The beautiful eighteenth-century château, with an Ionic portico in front and a lake behind, together with a vineyard excellently sited between Carbonnieux and Haut-Bailly, were bought in a run-down state in 1965 by the dynamic M. André Lurton. Now, La Louvière is the flagship of his extensive fleet of vineyards, making wine which, almost everybody agrees, is on a par with the better *crus classés* of the Graves. Wine-making is in the classic Bordelais manner, with temperature-controlled fermentation and a year's ageing in *barriques*, of which one-third are new. The result is a wine which combines rich, supple fruit and the tannic structure necessary for ageing. The 1982 has all the sweetness of aroma of that vintage; on the palate it is rich and chocolatey, seemingly quite mature by 1989. The 1979, tasted at the same time, had an excellent long flavour and tasted fresher and livelier. Recent vintages may surpass these, if the 1986, deep in colour, with a wonderful nose combining jammy fruit and spicy oak, is anything to go by.

M. Lurton also owns Château Rochemorin, just south of Smith-Haut-Lafitte, and Château Cruzeau, near La Tour-Martillac, both of which produce excellent, typical Cabernet-based red Graves.

CHÂTEAU LYNCH-BAGES

Pauillac, *cinquième cru classé*

> Vineyard: 205 acres (70 per cent Cabernet Sauvignon, 15 per cent Merlot, 12 per cent Cabernet Franc, 2 per cent Petit Verdot, 1 per cent Malbec)
>
> Production: 420,000 bottles
>
> Second wine: Château Haut-Bages-Avérous
>
> Quality: 🍇🍇🍇🍇   Price: ★★★★
>
> Best vintages: 1982, 1985, 1986, 1987, 1988

Pauillac may have nothing between a second and a fifth growth, apart from the solitary fourth-growth Duhart-Milon, but it has one or two fifth growths which would not look out of place among the seconds. Lynch-Bages has been described as the poor man's Latour or Mouton: it is certainly a very full, plummy, typically Cabernet Pauillac. It may not have the finesse of the Pichons, but its richness of fruit and denseness of texture make it a formidable wine, impressive even in lesser years. The new *cuvier* installed in 1975 seems to be computer-controlled at every point – perhaps it is also programmed to provide the cellar-workers with cups of coffee. Fermentation is at a controlled temperature, with frequent pumping-over to ensure maximum concentration. A special system of pipes transfers the wine from the *cuves* to the *barriques* (50 per cent new each year) where it spends about fifteen months.

A varietal tasting of the 1987 was most interesting, with the Cabernet Franc (lively, forward fruit) and Petit Verdot (deep, rich and solid) especially, and perhaps surprisingly, impressive.

CHÂTEAU LYNCH-MOUSSAS

Pauillac, *cinquième cru classé*

Vineyard: 110 acres (72 per cent Cabernet Sauvignon, 28 per cent Merlot)

Production: 150,000 bottles

Quality: 🍇   Price: ★★

Best vintage: 1986

This is the second Pauillac *cru* belonging to M. Emile Castéja of Batailley, and M. Castéja himself would admit that it has been somewhat neglected in the past. It tended to produce a light, not very concentrated claret for early drinking, not up to *cru classé* standard. Recently M. Castéja has been able to invest some money in the vineyard, and the 1986 is a well-coloured wine, with an attractive ripe nose, considerable concentration and tannin on the palate.

CHÂTEAU MALARTIC-LAGRAVIÈRE

Pessac-Léognan, *cru classé de Graves*

33850 Léognan

Vineyard: 35 acres (50 per cent Cabernet Sauvignon, 25 per cent Merlot, 25 per cent Cabernet Franc)

Production: 80,000–90,000 bottles

Quality: 🍇🍇🍇   Price: ★★★★
Best vintages: 1982, 1988

This admirable property has been in the hands of the Ridoret and Marly families for 140 years – the patriarch Jacques Marly is not far short of a century himself – but because of divided inheritance among his ten children it is now, sadly, up for sale. The vineyard, situated on a fine gravel ridge, is now surrounded by the suburban outgrowth of Léognan. Malartic red does not enjoy quite the renown of the white (which sells for 40 per cent more), but it certainly deserves a place in the first division. It tends to be tough when young, but has a particularly good bouquet and considerable staying power.

Wine-making, supervised by Bruno Marly, youngest son of Jacques, is traditional: long *cuvaison* (twenty-one days on average), followed by twenty months in *barriques*, of which 50–60 per cent are new each year.

Among recent vintages the 1987 is light and pleasantly fruity; the 1988 is very deep-coloured and rich with considerable tannin; the 1982 is quite developed but still lively, unlike some, and has a very distinctive medicinal nose.

CHÂTEAU MALESCOT-ST-EXUPÉRY

Margaux, *troisième cru classé*

Vineyard: 74 acres (50 per cent Cabernet Sauvignon, 35 per cent Merlot, 10 per cent Cabernet Franc, 5 per cent Petit Verdot)
Production: 168,000 bottles
Second wine: Château de Loyac
Quality: 🍇🍇🍇   Price: ★★★
Best vintages: 1982, 1983, 1985, 1986, 1988

The Zuger family have been in charge at Malescot since 1938, and the current owner, M. Roger Zuger, has made this into one of the best-maintained and most quality-conscious of the Margaux *crus*. The vineyard now consists of five parcels, regrouped from no less than sixty, all within the commune of Margaux.

I must confess that I have not always found the Malescot style easy to like: the wines often seem both light and astringent, at least when young. Careful tasting at the château has prompted me to revise my opinion. Malescot, like some other Margaux *crus*, can actually gain colour with age, and the magnificent, rich, 1970 vintage and the remarkably fresh 1958 convinced me that this wine has an almost unlimited ageing potential.

There have been some notable successes in recent vintages. The 1982 has a warm, leathery nose and is full and rounded with a lovely silky texture; it will make a voluptuous bottle for the mid-1990s. The 1983 is surprisingly developed but has good ripeness and length. Unusually, the 1985 is tighter (*'plus stricte'*) than the full, perfumed 1986. The 1988 is extremely aromatic, but very tannic also.

CHÂTEAU DE MARBUZET

St Estèphe, *cru bourgeois*

Production: 60,000 bottles

Quality: 🍇🍇🍇   Price: ★★★

Best vintages: 1982, 1983, 1984, 1985, 1986

The vineyard surrounding the ravishing Louis XVI château which is the country home of the Prats family was classified as a *cru bourgeois exceptionnel* in 1966. Now, however, the wine it produces is mixed with the reject vats of Cos d'Estournel to make an excellent second wine. The proportion of Merlot is usually quite high, so that the wine tends to show, to a more pronounced degree, the leathery, animal aromas you can also find in Cos. Marbuzet has been almost as consistent as Cos itself during the 1980s, producing above-average wines in the lesser years 1984 and 1987, a splendidly rich 1982 and an attractive, elegant and forward 1983. This is something of a bargain.

CHÂTEAU MARGAUX

Margaux, *premier cru classé*

Vineyard: 185 acres (75 per cent Cabernet Sauvignon, 20 per cent Merlot, 3 per cent Petit Verdot, 2 per cent Cabernet Franc)

Production: 250,000 bottles

Second wine: Pavillon Rouge de Château Margaux

Quality: 🍇🍇🍇🍇🍇   Price: ★★★★★

Best vintages: 1981, 1983, 1985, 1986, 1987, 1988

In old classifications often placed at the head of all the wines of Bordeaux, Margaux has triumphantly resumed its rightful place since its purchase in 1977 by André Mentzelopoulos. The splendid Palladian mansion (which I must admit I find a trifle top-heavy) and the extensive *chais* make this perhaps the most impressive physically of all the first growths. The wine has always been considered 'feminine' in character, but recent vintages show what the talented young general manager, Paul Pontallier, aptly describes as the perfect marriage between finesse and power.

Fermentation takes place in broad-beamed wooden *cuves*, whose advantage, says M. Pontallier, is that they allow greater contact between the cap of skins and pips and the juice. The wine is fermented in mostly new oak barrels, made by Margaux's resident cooper. The second wine, Pavillon Rouge, has become notable in its own right; aged in the barrels which have housed the *grand vin*, it has the class and style of a second growth.

Among recent vintages, the 1983 – a wine of perfect

harmony, with subtle fruit on the nose, a suave elegant first flavour and compact, long finish – is superior to the ripe, jammy 1982, somewhat lacking in structure. The 1985 is ravishingly pretty and harmonious, while the 1986, with a massive aroma of ripe black-fruits, great velvety depth and length, is a classic for long keeping. The 1987 is flowery on the nose and extremely elegant, with surprising length – perhaps the best wine of the vintage. The 1988 has a blackcurranty Cabernet Sauvignon nose and combines depth, length and elegance in the manner that Margaux has once more made its own.

CHÂTEAU MARQUIS D'ALESME-BECKER

Margaux, *troisième cru classé*

Vineyard: 23 acres (30 per cent Cabernet Sauvignon, 30 per cent Cabernet Franc, 30 per cent Merlot, 10 per cent Petit Verdot), increasing to 40 acres by 1995

Production: 53,000 bottles

Quality: 🍇 Price: ★★★

Best vintages: 1985, 1986, 1988

The grand name is better suited to the massive Victorian château (formerly Château Desmirail), than to the quality of the wine, which until recently has been one of the hardest and least charming in Margaux. Under the present owner, Jean-Claude Zuger (younger brother of Roger of Malescot), there are signs of improvement. There is a new *cuvier*, and the wine now spends only a year in *barriques* (one-sixth new) to preserve fruit.

The 1982 and 1983 were both very hard, but the 1985 is more attractive, with a ripe nose but a certain roughness on the palate. The 1986 is very hard, but lively, and should be good one day. The 1988 may be the best vintage of recent years, with depth and perfume on the nose.

CHÂTEAU MARQUIS DE TERME

Margaux, *quatrième cru classé*

> Vineyard: 94 acres (60 per cent Cabernet Sauvignon, 30 per cent Merlot, 7 per cent Petit Verdot, 3 per cent Cabernet Franc)
>
> Production: 150,000 bottles
>
> Second wine: Château des Gondats
>
> Quality: 🍇🍇🍇🍇   Price: ★★★★
>
> Best vintages: 1983, 1985, 1986, 1988

The policy of the Séneclauze family, wine merchants from Marseilles and proprietors since 1936, has been to sell most of the production on the home market. That policy is now changing, and the export markets, which are beginning to see this Margaux fourth growth, may be surprised by its quality. There have been big investments here in the 1980s, with the proportion of new oak rising as high as 50 per cent. What used to be known as one of the hardest Margaux *crus* has gained richness and appeal; it is now one of the leaders of the appellation.

The 1983 has an attractive cedary nose and good concentration, but still needs time. The 1985 has an immediately appealing aroma of red-fruits, with new oak, and is a very charming wine, ripe and round. The 1986 is, predictably, powerful and concentrated, long and tannic. The 1988, on the other hand, shows a more delicate style, with good texture and ripeness.

CHÂTEAU MAUCAILLOU

Moulis, *cru bourgeois*

> Vineyard: 150 acres (58 per cent Cabernet Sauvignon, 33 per cent Merlot, 7 per cent Petit Verdot, 2 per cent Cabernet Franc)

Production: 400,000 bottles

Second wine: Cap de Haut-Maucaillou

Quality: 🍇🍇🍇   Price: ★★★

Best vintages: 1982, 1983, 1985, 1986, 1987, 1988

M. Philippe Dourthe, whose family bought Maucaillou in 1929, formidably combines the skills of an energetic businessman, a born communicator and a skilled technician. Various *négociant* and bottling businesses, carried on from the château, testify to the first; a well-designed wine museum and somewhat schizophrenic promotional video (in which footage from a rehearsal of Berlioz's *Symphonie Fantastique* is intercut with a tour of the château), to the second; and the very individual style of the wine – lighter and more supple than most Moulis – to the third. One secret of the style lies in the temperature of vinification, which at 21–22 °C is much cooler than that for most Bordeaux reds. As a result, Maucaillou remains remarkably fresh, even in hot vintages like 1982.

The 1983 is a powerful, tannic wine, long and complex – probably the biggest Maucaillou in recent years. The 1985 has very attractive red-fruit ripeness, whereas the 1986, deep in colour, is strongly marked by oak (70 per cent new for that vintage). The 1988 is characteristically fruity, with better-adjusted new oak character. Maucaillou is approachable when young but has, too, the structure and freshness to last for a decade.

CHÂTEAU MEYNEY

St Estèphe, *cru bourgeois*

Vineyard: 123 acres (70 per cent Cabernet Sauvignon, 24 per cent Merlot, 4 per cent Cabernet Franc, 2 per cent Petit Verdot)

Production: 300,000 bottles

Second wine: Prieur de Meyney

Quality: 🍇🍇🍇   Price: ★★

Best vintages: 1982, 1984, 1985, 1986

The vineyard of Meyney is beautifully sited just north of Montrose and very close to the Gironde. Domaines Cordier, who have owned the estate since 1919, have, in their character-istic way, immaculately maintained the long, low *chai* buildings which used to be part of a convent. There are no reproaches to be made on the wine-making side either: Meyney is one of the most reliable wines in the Médoc and one of the best below *cru classé* level. It is typical St Estèphe in style – big, dark and chewy – but usually with enough ripe fruit to balance the tannin. The 1986 is certainly unapproachably tannic at present, but the 1985 has an attractive, ripe gamy character, and the 1984 a cedary elegance which makes it one of the successes of the vintage. The 1962 was a marvellous wine.

CHÂTEAU LA MISSION HAUT-BRION

Pessac-Léognan, *cru classé de Graves*

33600 Pessac

Vineyard: 50 acres (60 per cent Cabernet Sauvignon, 20 per cent Merlot, 20 per cent Cabernet Franc)

Production: 84,000 bottles

Quality: 🍇🍇🍇🍇🍇   Price: ★★★★★

Best vintages: 1981, 1982, 1986

Situated just across the road from Haut-Brion (and thus in the commune of Talence), the second wine of the Graves has been, since 1983, in the same hands. The large following which this château built up under the years of Woltner ownership can be reassured that there seems to be no intention of changing the

highly distinctive style. La Mission continues to be big, powerful, tough and tannic, with a pronounced earthiness at times,
where Haut-Brion is suave and civilized.

The immaculate vineyard is flat and has the same suburban
surroundings as Haut-Brion. The main difference between the
two soils, according to M. Delmas, is that the gravel at La
Mission is more tightly packed.

An avant-garde new *cuverie*, designed by M. Delmas and
featuring two-part *cuves* for both alcoholic and malolactic
fermentations, was installed in 1987. The *cuvaison* lasts from
two to three weeks. The proportion of new *barriques* has been
raised dramatically, from 10 to 60 per cent. This is notable on
the 1988 La Mission, which has an oaky richness. The 1986 has
a marked Cabernet blackcurrant flavour, is stern and concentrated, and very long in the mouth. La Mission has consistently made excellent wines in lesser vintages.

CHÂTEAU MONTROSE

St Estèphe, *deuxième cru classé*

Vineyard: 168 acres (65 per cent Cabernet Sauvignon, 25 per
  cent Merlot, 10 per cent Cabernet Franc)

Production: 325,000 bottles

Second wine: La Dame de Montrose

Quality: 🍇🍇🍇   Price: ★★★★

Best vintages: 1979, 1982, 1985, 1986

If Cos is an exception among the wines of St Estèphe, being
rounder and more elegant than the norm, Montrose could be
regarded as the archetype of the commune, a big chunky earthy
wine, whose defect is clumsiness. The vineyard, mainly gravel
with some black sand, is to the north of the hamlet of Marbuzet, very close to the Gironde. According to the hospitable
proprietor, M. Charmolue (Montrose has been in his family

since 1896), this gives the vineyard an advantage in off-years and means it is little affected by frost.

Fermentation is in beautifully maintained wooden *cuves*, with strong pumping-over to ensure maximum extraction. Afterwards the wine spends up to two years in *barriques*, of which between a third and a half are new. Some writers have claimed to detect a change towards a more supple, early-maturing style in recent years: the 1985 is surprisingly supple, but the 1986 seems to me a classic, opaque, dense Montrose, with a brambly nose like a Californian mountain Cabernet and enough tannin to ensure life for several decades. The question, as always with Montrose, is whether the softening of the tannins will synchronize with the development of the fruit and make a harmonious wine.

CHÂTEAU MOUTON-BARONNE-PHILIPPE

Pauillac, *cinquième cru classé*

Vineyard: 100 acres (65 per cent Cabernet Sauvignon, 20 per cent Merlot, 15 per cent Cabernet Franc)

Production: 180,000 bottles

Quality: 🍇🍇🍇   Price: ★★★

Best vintages: 1982, 1986, 1988

The property, then named Mouton d'Armailhacq, adjoining Mouton-Rothschild, was bought by Baron Philippe de Rothschild in 1931. He changed the name to Mouton-Baron-Philippe in 1956, and then in 1975, in memory of his late wife, to Mouton-Baronne-Philippe. In April 1991 the name was changed again, to d'Armailhac. Although not officially the second wine of Mouton, coming from a separate vineyard, Mouton-Baronne-Philippe often seems like a paler, lighter shadow of the great first growth. In really top years, like 1961, it can be superbly stylish, but it is not to be recommended in lighter years: it can taste rather diluted. Mouton-Baronne-Philippe is made with all the care of its big brother, and spends twenty months in *barriques*, of which 25–30 per cent are new.

CHÂTEAU MOUTON-ROTHSCHILD

Pauillac, *premier cru classé*

Vineyard: 185 acres (85 per cent Cabernet Sauvignon, 10 per cent Cabernet Franc, 5 per cent Merlot)

Production: 240,000 bottles

Quality: 🍇🍇🍇🍇🍇 Price: ★★★★★

Best vintages: 1981, 1982, 1983, 1985, 1986

Always considered the best of the second growths, and often on a par with the firsts, Mouton was finally elevated to the peerage, after decades of tireless public relations work by Baron Philippe de Rothschild, in 1973. It is the only change yet made to the sacrosanct 1855 classification, and few would challenge its fairness. Under Baron Philippe's imaginative direction, Mouton became the most stylish and flamboyant château in Bordeaux. This is not just a question of the theatrically designed *chais*, the splendid museum of wine or the brilliant idea of commissioning paintings for labels from leading artists. The flair and style are also to be found in the wine itself. The very high proportion of Cabernet Sauvignon gives a blackcurranty depth to the fruit, but there is also the distinctive lead-pencil aroma. Mouton is perhaps not as consistent as Latour in lesser vintages, which can be light, but in top years (1982, 1986) it is superb. Great emphasis is given to picking the grapes at optimum ripeness: once or twice this has led to disaster (as in 1964, when rain set in half-way through the vintage), but on the whole it helps to give the wine its richness and suavity of texture. Fermentation, as at Lafite, is in wooden *cuves*, and afterwards the wine spends between twenty months and two years in 100 per cent new *barriques*.

CHÂTEAU OLIVIER

Pessac-Léognan, *cru classé de Graves*

> 33850 Léognan
>
> Vineyard: 57 acres (70 per cent Cabernet Sauvignon, 30 per cent Merlot)
>
> Production: 130,000 bottles
>
> Quality: 🍇🍇🍇   Price: ★★★
>
> Best vintages: 1985, 1986, 1988

The moated château, built in the twelfth and fourteenth centuries, with a round corner turret and a splendid Gothic hall, is the most beautiful in the region. It has a mysterious, remote feel, insulated from the outskirts of Léognan by 500 acres of pine forest. The proprietor, since 1945, is M. de Bethmann, whose main interests are in the north of France.

The wine of Olivier has not always matched the beauty of its surroundings, but excellent vintages, with a rich, plummy character, have been produced since 1985. The 1985 is a very complete wine, with a tobaccoey nose and rounded, plummy depth on the palate. The 1986 is most impressive on the nose, showing both cedary spice and depth; it is backward and closed on the palate, but promising. So too is the 1988, full of brambly fruit, concentrated and tannic. At the moment the quality of Olivier may be better than its reputation.

CHÂTEAU LES ORMES DE PEZ

St Estèphe, *cru bourgeois*

> Vineyard: 74 acres (55 per cent Cabernet Sauvignon, 35 per cent Merlot, 10 per cent Cabernet Franc)
>
> Production: 180,000 bottles
>
> Quality: 🍇🍇   Price: ★★★
>
> Best vintages: 1982, 1985, 1986

As you would expect from one of the properties of Jean-Michel Cazes, whose father Jean-Charles bought it in 1940, this is a well-run estate which reliably produces fine wine. Vinification is done in the slick, ultra-modern facilities at Lynch-Bages; the wine spends twelve to fifteen months in *barriques*.

Les Ormes tends towards a rounded, chunky style (not surprising, perhaps, from a stablemate of Lynch-Bages). With a lower percentage of Cabernet it does not have quite the classic profile of its neighbour de Pez, but it is a good, typical, solid St Estèphe, with all the commune's good points and occasionally its defect, clumsiness. Clumsiness of another sort may have been responsible for the fire of 2 October 1989 in which the *chai* containing the 1988 vintage burned down: the candles used for racking had been left unsnuffed.

CHÂTEAU PALMER

Margaux, *troisième cru classé*

> Vineyard: 110 acres (55 per cent Cabernet Sauvignon, 40 per cent Merlot, 3 per cent Cabernet Franc, 2 per cent Petit Verdot)
>
> Production: 180,000 bottles
>
> Second wine: Réserve du Général
>
> Quality: 🍷🍷🍷🍷🍷   Price: ★★★★★
>
> Best vintages: 1983, 1985, 1986, 1987, 1988

General Palmer's Victorian château in the village of Cantenac flies three flags – British, French and Dutch – from the iron roof-railings between its elegant turrets, symbolizing the complex ownership of the estate. The largest share of 34 per cent is held by the Sichel family, 22 per cent belongs to the Mähler-Besse family, with the remaining 44 per cent being split among four shareholders, including the Bouteiller family of Château Lanessan. Bertrand Bouteiller acts as general manager, while wine-making is supervised by Peter A. Sichel.

Palmer was established as a 'super-second' before Las Cases, Ducru, Pichon-Lalande and Cos, and still maintains a position somewhere between them and the first growths. In certain vintages (1961, 1966) it is as good as any wine in Bordeaux, with a wonderfully voluptuous scent and a combination of richness and delicacy which is unique. It is perhaps the closest in style of any Médoc to the great right-bank wines of Pomerol and St Emilion. Palmer is certainly the number two wine in the commune after Château Margaux; the only criticism sometimes levelled against it is a lack of consistency.

Wine-making at Palmer is distinctly old-fashioned – hardly surprising since the *régisseur*, M. Chardon, represents the third generation of his family to have worked at Palmer since 1870. Fermentation is in wooden *cuves*, and crushing and destemming was done by hand until 1982. The proportion of new wood varies from a third to a half.

Among recent vintages the 1983 is a very good wine, with a soft, flowery nose, and a ripe, rich flavour with enough structure to last fifteen years. It is markedly superior to the somewhat disappointing 1982 which lacks a certain concentration in the middle palate. The 1985 is a lovely ripe, elegant wine, more alluring than the more backward but well-constituted 1986. The 1988 has a splendid plummy richness on the nose but is not hugely concentrated on the palate.

CHÂTEAU PAPE-CLÉMENT

Pessac-Léognan, *cru classé de Graves*

33600 Pessac

Vineyard: 74 acres (60 per cent Cabernet Sauvignon, 40 per cent Merlot)

Production: 130,000 bottles

Second wine: Clémentin

Quality: 🍷🍷🍷🍷 (since 1985)   Price: ★★★★

Best vintages: 1985, 1986, 1988

Pape-Clément has probably the oldest documented history of any Bordeaux vineyard, having been planted in 1300 by Bertrand de Goth, who became Pope Clement V. For a long time it did not live up to its glorious past, but since the arrival of the new *régisseur*, M. Pujol, in 1984, its fortunes have risen steadily. The owner since 1939 has been M. Montagne.

I think of Pape-Clément as approaching the suave, silky style of Haut-Brion; M. Pujol finds more of the earthiness of La Mission. The wine is now made with a classic *cuvaison* of eighteen to twenty-one days in small, temperature-controlled *cuves* and spends eighteen months in *barriques*. Eighty-five per cent new wood was used in 1988.

The 1985 has a strong leathery, gamy nose and a most attractive long, open flavour. The 1986 is more closed but has impressive intensity of flavour. The 1988, rich and tannic, may turn out the best of the three.

CHÂTEAU PÉDESCLAUX

Pauillac, *cinquième cru classé*

> Vineyard: 44 acres (65 per cent Cabernet Sauvignon, 25 per cent Merlot, 8 per cent Cabernet Franc, 2 per cent Petit Verdot)
>
> Production: 90,000 bottles
>
> Second wine: Château Bellerose
>
> Quality: 🍇   Price: ★★★
>
> Best vintages: 1982, 1986, 1988

There is nothing pretentious either about the 'château' – some farm buildings adjoining a modest villa in the hamlet of Pouyalet – or about M. Bernard Jugla, who administers the property on behalf of his family. Jugla is a corruption of *jongleur*, so M. Jugla reckons his ancestors, who have lived in the neighbourhood since the fifteenth century, were troubadours. The vineyards are divided into three blocks, all well situated, one around the château, one between Mouton and Pontet-Canet and one near Lynch-Bages. One has to say that greater things could be achieved with this material, for Pédesclaux, while a good, solid, typical Pauillac, rarely scales the heights.

The 1986 is a medium-weight wine, quite elegant for the vintage. The 1988 is notably aromatic, with an unusual floral scent.

CHÂTEAU DE PEZ

St Estèphe, *cru bourgeois*

Vineyard: 57 acres (70 per cent Cabernet Sauvignon, 20 per cent Merlot, 9 per cent Cabernet Franc, 1 per cent Petit Verdot)

Production: 160,000 bottles

Quality: 🍇🍇🍇   Price: ★★★

Best vintages: 1980, 1981, 1982, 1983, 1986, 1988

De Pez considers itself too grand to be a *cru bourgeois*, and with some reason: this fine property, situated just west of St Estèphe, produces one of the most reliable wines of the Médoc, at least as good as some fifth growths. If you wanted to see a demonstration of traditional wine-making methods, well executed, this might be the château to visit. Fermentation is in wooden *cuves*, with the temperature kept to 29 °C; afterwards the wine spends eighteen to twenty-two months in *barriques*, of which a quarter are new. The wine is racked from barrel to barrel with a candle every three months, and fining is done using whites of egg. 'We try to avoid moving the wine around with pumps,' said the *chef de cave*, M. Faugère.

De Pez always has a good, bright, deep colour, even in lesser years; there is ample fruit on the nose, together with spicy oakiness. On the palate this is a robust wine with considerable tannin but not too much harshness.

CHÂTEAU PICHON-LONGUEVILLE (BARON)

Pauillac, *deuxième cru classé*

> Vineyard: 124 acres (75 per cent Cabernet Sauvignon, 24 per cent Merlot, 1 per cent Petit Verdot)
>
> Production: 200,000 bottles
>
> Quality: 🍷🍷🍷🍷 (since 1986)   Price: ★★★★
>
> Best vintages: 1983, 1986, 1988

The Bouteiller family, who consistently make good wine at Château Lanessan, were never able to inject the necessary cash to allow this splendid property to perform to its full potential. Both the wine and the fairy-tale turreted château had a neglected feel until their purchase in 1987 by Jean-Michel Cazes's Axa-Millésimes. The turn-around has been dramatic. It is already noticeable on the 1986 vintage, whose maturation has been conducted under the expert guidance of Daniel Llose and which shows a deeper colour and more vivid, fresh fruit than any vintage for many years. M. Cazes explained to me that the racking system had been changed; some earlier vintages have had a prematurely brown colour and a lack of freshness.

Pichon-Baron, as it is commonly called, has always been a more classic Pauillac than its sister château – firmer, deeper and more tannic. In the recent vintages I find a near-perfect balance of classic structure and velvety finesse. This is potentially one of the greatest wines in Bordeaux, first growths included.

CHÂTEAU PICHON-LONGUEVILLE-COMTESSE-DE-LALANDE

Pauillac, *deuxième cru classé*

> Vineyard: 185 acres (45 per cent Cabernet Sauvignon, 35 per cent Merlot, 12 per cent Cabernet Franc, 8 per cent Petit Verdot)

Production: 350,000 bottles

Second wine: Réserve de la Comtesse

Quality: 🍇🍇🍇🍇🍇 Price: ★★★★

Best vintages: 1981, 1982, 1983, 1985, 1986, 1988

This is the larger of the two parts of what used to be the single property of Pichon-Longueville, but it has not always been considered the better. In fact, most people in the Médoc say that the *terroir* of Pichon-Baron is superior. What is indisputable is that under the inspired and dynamic direction (since 1978) of Mme Hervé de Lencquesaing, Pichon-Lalande (or Pichon-Comtesse as it is known in Bordeaux) has been a conspicuous over-achiever, regularly producing wines as perfumed, silky, sensuous and delicious as any in Bordeaux. If Pichon-Lalande is not a typical Pauillac (big, firm, tannic), one can point to two obvious explanations: 20 per cent of the vineyard is in fact in the commune of St Julien (until the 1950s a separate St Julien *cuvée* had to be produced), and the percentage of Merlot is unusually high.

Under the keen eye of the able *régisseur*, M. Godin, the wine is fermented at a controlled temperature in a brand-new battery of stainless steel *cuves*, and then passes into *barriques* (50 per cent new) where it matures for twenty months. Recent vintages present a fascinating range of voluptuous flavours: the 1985 fragrant with cedar, red-fruits and a hint of tobacco, supple, full of finesse and elegance on the palate; the 1986 dark and closed, but with a rich velvety texture; the 1988 showing a wonderful bouquet of violet and blackberry. The second wine has considerable class.

CHÂTEAU PONTET-CANET

Pauillac, *cinquième cru classé*

Vineyard: 163 acres (70 per cent Cabernet Sauvignon, 26 per cent Merlot, 4 per cent Cabernet Franc)

Production: 240,000 bottles

Second wine: Château Les Hauts de Pontet

Quality: 🍇 Price: ★★★★

Best vintages: 1985, 1988

With its imposing creeper-covered château, its impressive *chais* and *cuvier* (rather like a Victorian railway station), this is one of the grandest properties in the Médoc. It also used to be one of the most highly regarded, but its reputation had been in decline for decades when the Cruse family sold it to Guy Tesseron in 1975. The fact that a good deal of Pontet-Canet was sold on the French railways perhaps did not help.

There is no doubt about the Tesserons' preparedness to invest and their will to improve matters (the creation of a second label in 1982 has enabled stricter selection), but so far results have been disappointing. The wine tends to be hard and lacking in charm. The 1986 I find surprisingly forward, broad and plummy, but the 1988, which shows an attractive touch of new oak, is deep-coloured, concentrated, tannic and unapproachable. There must be the potential to make very fine wine on these vineyards, which border those of Mouton-Rothschild; the Tesserons are, I am sure, determined to realize it.

CHÂTEAU POUJEAUX

Moulis, *cru bourgeois*

Vineyard: 128 acres (50 per cent Cabernet Sauvignon, 30 per cent Merlot, 10 per cent Cabernet Franc, 10 per cent Petit Verdot)

Production: 250,000 bottles

Second wine: La Salle de Poujeaux

Quality: 🍇🍇🍇 Price: ★★★

Best vintages: 1982, 1983, 1985, 1986

The diminutive Philippe Theil, who with his brother François runs the property bought in stages by his grandfather from 1921, is very proud of Poujeaux. He likes to tell the story of the dinner at the Elysée when Baron Elie de Rothschild refused to believe that the Poujeaux served in a decanter was not Lafite. This pride is well founded, for a very fine wine, with a magnificent, almost burgundian bouquet, is produced in most vintages. A special feature of the vinification at Poujeaux is extremely long *cuvaison* – up to six weeks in some years, which puts it in the Barolo class.

The 1982 does not suffer from the excessive fatness of some wines of the vintage; it is deep-coloured, big and complex, and still tannic. The 1983 has a lovely creamy texture and good length. The 1985 is lighter, with an attractively herbaceous nose – good, but no match for the splendidly perfumed 1986 with its dense concentration of blackberry fruit.

CHÂTEAU POUGET

Margaux, *quatrième cru classé*

Vineyard: 25 acres (66 per cent Cabernet Sauvignon, 30 per cent Merlot, 4 per cent Cabernet Franc)

Production: 53,000 bottles

Quality: 🍷🍷🍷🍷   Price: ★★★★

Best vintages: 1982, 1986

The quality of this rather obscure and lowly growth, owned by Pierre Guillemet of Boyd-Cantenac, is one of Bordeaux's best-kept secrets. The combination of old vines and M. Guillemet's scrupulous, old-fashioned methods produces a wine of greater softness and richness than Boyd, and I am tempted to call it the Pomerol of Margaux. The 1982 is a wine of opaque colour, great plush depth on the nose and impressive power and concentration. M. Guillemet claims that Pouget is more tannic than Boyd, but it does not taste so. The 1986 Pouget is similar to the 1982, with a rich velvety nose and long, concentrated flavour. What a shame the production is so limited!

CHÂTEAU PRIEURÉ-LICHINE

Margaux, *quatrième cru classé*

> Vineyard: 150 acres (58 per cent Cabernet Sauvignon, 34 per cent Merlot, 4 per cent Petit Verdot, 4 per cent Cabernet Franc)
>
> Production: 300,000 bottles
>
> Second wine: Château Clairefont
>
> Quality: 🍇   Price: ★★★★
>
> Best vintage: 1983

Alexis Lichine, who died in 1989, was certainly one of the great characters of post-war Bordeaux. The *cru* he reconstituted from 1951 and named after himself has probably done more for Bordeaux's public relations than any other. The attractive creeper-covered château is open every day of the year and is much visited by Americans. I wish I could be more enthusiastic about the wine. It is certainly made with great care (eighteen months in *barriques*, of which a half to two-thirds are new), but most vintages I have tasted belong to the hard, charmless, austere school of Margaux. An exception is the 1983, which has a perfumed nose with a firm structure but good depth on the palate.

CHÂTEAU RAUSAN-SÉGLA

Margaux, *deuxième cru classé*

> Vineyard: 104 acres (70 per cent Cabernet Sauvignon, 30 per cent Merlot)
>
> Production: 170,000 bottles

Second wine: Chateau Lamouroux

Quality: 🍇🍇🍇🍇 (since 1985)   Price: ★★★★

Best vintages: 1985, 1986, 1988

Placed at the head of the second growths in 1855, but for most of the 1960s and 1970s a spectacular under-performer, Rausan-Ségla has undergone a remarkable recovery. The English shipping firm of John Holt bought the property in 1960, but it was in the early 1980s that they began to invest very heavily in a bid to bring the growth up to its classified level. The proportion of Cabernet Sauvignon in the vineyard was dramatically increased, and a spanking new *cuvier* was built in 1986. The 1985 is the first vintage, in my view, to show the benefits of this investment. It has an attractive cedary nose, and combines ripeness with complexity and a long finish. The 1986 is in another class altogether: this is a massively concentrated wine, with a considerable dose of new oak which I am sure it will digest in time, whose great tannic structure is matched by plummy ripeness. The 1988 combines fragrance with power, tannin with ripeness. No major changes are planned by the new owners, the leisure group Brent Walker.

CHÂTEAU RAUZAN-GASSIES

Margaux, *deuxième cru classé*

Vineyard: 75 acres (60 per cent Cabernet Sauvignon, 35 per cent Merlot, 5 per cent Cabernet Franc)

Production: 130,000 bottles

Second wine: Le Mayne de Jeannet

Quality: 🍇🍇   Price: ★★★★

Best vintages: 1983, 1985, 1988

Much vilified, often with reason, this *cru* (originally part of the same estate as Rausan-Ségla) is showing signs of a return – if

not to top second-growth quality, then at least to respectable
cru classé level. The proprietor, Jean-Michel Quié, who also
owns Croizet-Bages, is undoubtedly serious about the pursuit
of quality, but the style of the wine seems obstinately coarse and
even rough. The 1983, though, is excellent, with ripe, roasted
aromas and a velvety texture. I also like the 1985, a complete,
balanced wine, much more approachable at this stage than the
1986. The 1988, with an attractive spicy nose showing the
influence of new oak, is relatively soft and round.

CHÂTEAU ST PIERRE

St Julien, *quatrième cru classé*

Vineyard: 44 acres (70 per cent Cabernet Sauvignon, 20 per
cent Merlot, 10 per cent Cabernet Franc)

Production: 50,000 bottles

Quality: 🍇🍇 Price: ★★★

Best vintages: 1986, 1988

Not only the smallest but also without doubt the most obscure
of the St Julien *crus classés*, St Pierre is a very old vineyard with a
history of divisions. Henri Martin of Château Gloria finally
regrouped the two remaining portions, Sevaistre and Bontemps
du Barry, in 1982, at which time the two vineyards, the *chais* and
the château all belonged to different people. St Pierre may now
be very much reduced from its original size (ironically M.
Martin himself cannibalized part of the vineyard to create
Gloria), but it is in safe and good hands. Recent vintages show a
property returning to form after some inconsistent years
(though 1970 and 1978 were both successes).

St Pierre is now matured in 50–75 per cent new wood; as
with Gloria (the same *cuvier* is used for both wines), part of the
wine is kept in large wooden *foudres* to preserve fruit and freshness. The style is quite powerful and tannic, perhaps contrast-
ing deliberately with the open, voluptuous Gloria style – more

in the Léoville-Las Cases or Barton than the Beychevelle mould. The wine acquires a classic cedary quality as it matures. Among recent vintages the 1986 is deep-coloured; there is toasty oak on the nose and considerable depth and concentration on the palate. The 1988 has depth and power and is unusually backward and tannic for the vintage.

CHÂTEAU SIRAN

Margaux, *cru bourgeois*

> Vineyard: 69 acres (50 per cent Cabernet Sauvignon, 25 per cent Merlot, 15 per cent Petit Verdot, 10 per cent Cabernet Franc)
>
> Production: 100,000 bottles
>
> Second wine: Château Bellegarde
>
> Quality: 🍇🍇🍇 Price: ★★★
>
> Best vintages: 1983, 1984, 1985, 1986

M. Alain Miailhe, whose ancestor bought this charming eighteenth-century property in 1848 from the parents of the artist Henri Toulouse-Lautrec, is a man of taste, style and humour. So at least I deduce (not having met him) from the *trompe-l'œil* frescoes on the *chai* windows, the piped Mozart piano concerto which accompanied my visit, the nuclear bunker named Chernobyl which M. Miailhe has stocked with old vintages of Siran – and the quality of the wine itself. Siran has the softness of the other Labarde wines, but also considerable structure and staying power (attributable partly no doubt to the high proportion of Petit Verdot). An English-bottled 1966 Siran was at its peak in 1987 – beautifully structured, ripe yet firm. The 1983 is a classic, elegant wine, with the Siran combination of firm structure and ripeness, while the 1984 is soft and delicate with a lovely core of fruit. The 1985 is very full-bodied, atypically powerful for a 1985. The 1986 has a sweet, vanilla nose which comes from new oak (70 per cent was used), but has characteristic ripeness and tannin. Should be a *cru classé*!

CHÂTEAU SMITH-HAUT-LAFITTE

Pessac-Léognan, *cru classé de Graves*

Martillac, 33650 Labrède

Vineyard: 125 acres (65 per cent Cabernet Sauvignon, 25 per cent Merlot, 10 per cent Cabernet Franc)

Production: 270,000 bottles

Second wine: Les Hauts de Smith-Haut-Lafitte

Quality: 🍇   Price: ★★★★

Best vintages: 1982, 1983, 1988

This property, superbly situated on a gravel ridge to the east of Haut-Bailly, belonged for many years to the shipping firm of Louis Eschenauer. Since 1990 its owners have been the Cathiard family. In 1974 Eschenauer built a vast new underground *chai*, and impressive wine-making facilities (modernized again in 1986) were installed. All the same, the wine (like the new buildings) has tended to lack personality.

I was surprised by how little difference of quality there was between the oaky 1987 and the 1986, which showed a typically minerally Graves character on the nose. The 1988 does seem more individual – deep in colour and blackcurrant-scented. That this wine can age magnificently was shown by the 1962, tasted in 1989, which paraded a beautiful colour, ripe nose and fine balance.

CHÂTEAU SOCIANDO-MALLET

Haut-Médoc, *cru bourgeois*

St-Seurin-de-Cadourne, 33250 Pauillac

Vineyard: 100 acres (60 per cent Cabernet Sauvignon, 30 per cent Merlot, 10 per cent Cabernet Franc)

Production: 200,000 bottles

Second wine: Lartigue de Brochon (will be Demoiselle de Sociando)

Quality: 🍇🍇🍇🍇   Price: ★★★

Best vintages: 1982, 1983, 1985, 1986

M. Jean Gautreau is one of the Médoc's greatest individualists. He bought this property in a run-down state in 1969, and has turned it into one of the very best *crus* below classified status. In fact, Sociando-Mallet regularly outclasses more highly placed châteaux in comparative tastings. He gives most of the credit to his *terroir*: 'I have a superb *terroir*, which I want to express in the wine. I try to make a classic Médoc for long keeping.' M. Gautreau opts for very long *cuvaison* – up to six weeks in all. He also uses new oak – 100 per cent in good vintages, slightly less in lesser – but keeps the wine for not more than a year in *barriques* to preserve the character of the fruit.

It is the rich powerful fruit, spiced but not dominated by oak, which is immediately apparent in the wine. The 1982 has a porty richness on the nose and is extremely dense and concentrated on the palate; it clearly needs time. The 1983 is a warm, rich, powerful wine. The 1985 is well-constituted wine and unusually tannic for the vintage, almost rough. The 1986 is opaque in colour and entirely closed, though clearly endowed with massive concentration. Somewhat lighter, though still inky black in colour, is the violet-scented 1988. M. Gautreau was so proud of his 1989 in the November after the vintage that he had me taste every one of fourteen vats. They promised another wine of massive concentration.

CHÂTEAU TALBOT

St Julien, *quatrième cru classé*

Vineyard: 240 acres (70 per cent Cabernet Sauvignon, 20 per cent Merlot, 5 per cent Cabernet Franc, 5 per cent Petit Verdot)

Production: 450,000 bottles

Second wine: Connétable-Talbot

Quality: 🍇🍇🍇🍇 Price: ★★★★

Best vintages: 1980, 1981, 1982, 1983, 1985, 1986, 1988

The second of the Cordier *crus classés*, in rank but not size, is named after Connétable (Constable) Talbot, English warrior and governor of Guienne in the middle of the fifteenth century. Beautifully kept up, like all Cordier properties, it produces a fine and typical St Julien, a little lighter and quicker to mature than Gruaud-Larose, but very consistent and often just as good as its higher-ranking brother. A feature of the cellar-work, conducted under the meticulous supervision of oenologist Georges Pauli, is that part of the wine's maturation takes place in large oak *foudres*. For most of its twenty-month maturation period, however, Talbot is kept in *barriques*, which are renewed in thirds.

A feature of Talbot is how well it performs in supposedly off-vintages. The 1980 was one of the best wines of the vintage, full-bodied and substantial, and similar successes have been scored in 1984 (typical cedary nose, attractive roundness) and, to a slightly lesser extent, 1987 (extremely fruity). The 1985 and 1986 are both excellent, deep-coloured wines with complex aromas and the tannic structure to age. The 1988 is very concentrated and aromatic, and should make an exceptional bottle. Another feature of Talbot, and all the Cordier Médoc properties, is the second wine, Connétable-Talbot, which provides almost as consistent enjoyment as the *grand vin*, at a much lower price.

CHÂTEAU DU TERTRE

Margaux, *cinquième cru classé*

Vineyard: 110 acres (85 per cent Cabernet Sauvignon, 10 per cent Merlot, 5 per cent Cabernet Franc)

Production: 200,000 bottles

Quality: 🍇🍇🍇🍇   Price: ★★★★

Best vintages: 1983, 1984, 1986, 1988

Philippe Gasqueton of Calon-Ségur is the owner of this strangely little-known *cru*, one of the most underrated in the Médoc. The vineyards are situated in the commune of Arsac. Recent vintages have been marked by a lovely violety scent, piercing blackcurrant or raspberry fruit (note the unusually high proportion of Cabernet Sauvignon) and a soft, velvety texture – textbook Margaux, in other words, and better value than many more highly ranking but under-performing Margaux *crus*.

The 1984 is most attractive for the vintage, with vivid raspberry fruit. The 1985 has a herbaceous nose, with notes of green pepper. The 1986 is subtle and refined, with a touch of new oak (25 per cent is used) apparent on the nose, and elegant, almost delicate, on the palate. Best of all recent vintages, though, looks like being the 1988 – deep in colour, with splendid blackcurrant depth on the nose, and soft with velvety tannins in the mouth.

CHÂTEAU LA TOUR-CARNET

Haut-Médoc, *quatrième cru classé*

Vineyard: 96 acres (53 per cent Cabernet Sauvignon, 33 per cent Merlot, 10 per cent Cabernet Franc, 4 per cent Petit Verdot)

Production: 100,000 bottles

Second wine: Le Sire de Camin

Quality: 🍇🍇   Price: ★★★

Best vintages: 1982, 1985, 1986

Mme Pélégrin has bravely shouldered the burden of running

this beautiful property, with its thirteenth-century tower surrounded by a moat, since the tragic death of her husband Guy-François, publisher turned wine-maker, in a cellar accident in 1988. The energetic work of the Pélégrins has certainly restored some lustre to the badly tarnished reputation of this St Laurent growth, but there is still a certain lack of consistency in the wine. This problem can probably be traced to the vineyard, which is divided between one very fine block of well-exposed gravel near the château and a much less favourably situated block nearer St Laurent.

The style is relatively open and easy-going, lighter in colour and character than that of most classified growths, but with attractive cherry fruit. An indication of the potential of this property was given by the 1979 vintage of the second wine, Le Sire de Camin, which was remarkably rich and ripe, yet youthfully fresh.

CHÂTEAU LA TOUR HAUT-BRION

Pessac-Léognan, *cru classé de Graves*

> 33400 Pessac
>
> Vineyard: 15 acres (70 per cent Cabernet Sauvignon, 15 per cent Merlot, 15 per cent Cabernet Franc)
>
> Production: 18,000 bottles
>
> Quality: 🍇🍇🍇   Price: ★★★★
>
> Best vintages: 1982, 1986

Although classified as a separate *cru* in 1953, La Tour Haut-Brion had become in effect the second wine of La Mission when Etats Dillon bought the latter. Under the new ownership, the original vineyard, across the railway line at the back of La Mission, has been restored to independent production.

La Tour Haut-Brion has tended to be a big, tannic, Cabernet-dominated wine (under the Woltner regime it contained a good deal of the press wine), sometimes a little coarse, and recent vintages seem to be following the same line. The 1986 is in fact softer and more developed than the La Mission, but the 1988 is big, very Cabernet (reminiscent of a New World varietal) and tannic. No new oak was used on this vintage. La Tour Haut-Brion is a wine which ages extremely well, and in certain vintages (1978, 1982) has proved the equal of its big brother.

CHÂTEAU LA TOUR-MARTILLAC

Pessac-Léognan, *cru classé de Graves*

Martillac, 33650 Labrède

Vineyard: 44 acres (60 per cent Cabernet Sauvignon, 25 per cent Merlot, 6 per cent Cabernet Franc, 5 per cent Malbec, 4 per cent Petit Verdot)

Production: 120,000 bottles

Second wine: La Grave-Martillac

Quality: 🍇🍇🍇   Price: ★★★

Best vintages: 1982, 1985, 1988

This is an attractive property, named after the small circular twelfth-century tower which sits on a grass knoll in the driveway, flanked by gracious eighteenth-century buildings in the *chartreuse* style. It has belonged to the wine-shipping family of Kressmann since 1930 and the current owner is Jean Kressmann, a most cultured historian and pianist, whose two sons manage the estate. Everything is beautifully maintained, and methods are on the whole traditional. But the younger generation has certainly brought a breath of fresh air to the winemaking, which used to result in tough tannic wines lacking charm. Though wooden *cuves* are still used for fermentation, the most recent vintages have a liveliness and class I do not recall from tastings a decade ago. Selection (over 30 per cent rejected in 1987) is also probably stricter than it used to be.

La Tour-Martillac spends the usual eighteen to twenty-two months in *barriques*, of which one-third are new. Tristan Kressmann is experimenting with different coopers and degrees of toast, which is perhaps one reason for the added spice in the wine of late. This is certainly a rising estate, worth watching.

DOMAINE DE CHEVALIER

Pessac-Léognan, *cru classé de Graves*

> 33850 Léognan
>
> Vineyard: 64 acres (65 per cent Cabernet Sauvignon, 30 per cent Merlot, 5 per cent Cabernet Franc)
>
> Production: 60,000–70,000 bottles
>
> Quality: 🍇🍇🍇🍇🍇   Price: ★★★★★
>
> Best vintages: 1981, 1984, 1985, 1986

Domaine de Chevalier is one of the most modest and unlikely of the great wines of Bordeaux – the vineyard is a forest clearing, the château a sort of hunting bungalow. But a great wine it is, on a level with the best second growths of the Médoc. The property, long in the hands of the Ricard family, was bought in 1983 by the young Olivier Bernard. Claude Ricard, pianist and perfectionist, remains in charge, however, during an eight-year handing-over process. The length of this regency, surely unprecedented, testifies to the reputation Ricard has built up and the care with which Olivier Bernard is treating his acquisition.

Domaine de Chevalier is a civilized, complete, harmonious claret, particularly noted for its ability to shine in off-vintages. The secret is simply care at all stages of the wine-making process – 10 per cent of grapes are rejected in the vineyards. There is a long *cuvaison*, with fermentation at relatively high temperature for maximum extraction, before the wine goes into *barriques* (half of them new), where it spends the customary twenty months.

Among recent vintages the 1985 is outstanding – charming, cedary, with beautiful texture. The 1986 is much tougher and more austere. A surprise success is the big, powerful 1984.

Corsica

There are now 400 acres of Cabernet Sauvignon in Corsica, and the variety thrives on this rugged island. Most is planted on the plain south of Bastia in the north-east. At the moment Cabernet Sauvignon is not permitted in any of the island's appellations, but it is used for the romantic-sounding Vin de Pays de l'Ile de Beauté. A pure Cabernet Sauvignon *cuvée* from the Bastia co-operative I sampled had the authentic Cabernet dusty nose, and rich, if slightly blunt, fruit.

Loire

Though the vineyards of the Loire region have nearly 4,000 acres planted to Cabernet Sauvignon, it is the Cabernet Franc which, unusually, is the senior partner. In the Touraine red wine appellations of Chinon, Bourgueil and St-Nicolas-de-Bourgueil, Cabernet Sauvignon is permitted up to a maximum of 10 per cent. The biggest plantings of Cabernet Sauvignon in the Loire are in Anjou. Straight Anjou, both red and rosé, can contain a proportion of Cabernet Sauvignon, though that is usually insignificant. Cabernet Sauvignon can play a more important part in the Cabernet d'Anjou and Cabernet de Saumur rosé appellations, though it is rare for Cabernet Sauvignon to predominate in these pale-pink, usually medium-sweet rosés. Saumur-Champigny, the best red wine appellation in Anjou, can contain a proportion of Cabernet Sauvignon, which adds backbone to the blend.

Well to the south of the traditional Loire wine regions, in the departments of Charente and Charente-Maritime, best known for Cognac, over 1,000 acres of Cabernet Sauvignon have been planted, for inclusion in the red Vin de Pays Charentais, first seen in 1981.

Midi

The vast vineyards of Languedoc-Roussillon have been known for the quantity rather than the quality of their wine. Cabernet Sauvignon is not a traditional grape in these regions, and is not to be found in the better-known appellations, such as Fitou, Corbières and Minervois. However, a great deal has been planted in recent years to improve the quality of the local *vin de table*, *vin de pays* and certain *vins délimités de qualité supérieure*, such as Cabardès and Côtes de la Malapère. The most famous Cabernet-based wine in the Midi, Mas de Daumas Gassac, is a simple Vin de Pays de l'Hérault. The 1988 figures for the three departments of Aude, Gard and Hérault show dramatic increases in the planting of Cabernet Sauvignon since 1979 (see Table). In 1968 there was no Cabernet Sauvignon at all in these regions.

Table: Area planted to Cabernet Sauvignon in the Aude, Gard and Hérault, 1979–88 (acres)

Department	1979	1988	Percentage increase
Aude	1,360	3,640	168
Gard	1,380	4,490	225
Hérault	695	3,300	375

The largest single plantings of Cabernet Sauvignon in the Midi, and indeed in the whole of France, are those in the Rhône delta belonging to the salt company Les Salins du Midi. Their wines, which carry the designation Vin de Pays des Sables du Golfe du Lion, carry the Listel label; the Cabernet Sauvignon is a sound commercial wine.

MAS DE DAUMAS GASSAC

Vin de Pays de l'Hérault

34150 Aniane

Vineyard: 37 acres

Production: 75,000 bottles

Quality: ♚♚♚♚   Price: ★★★

Best vintages: 1982, 1984, 1985

Aimé Guibert is a tireless ambassador for the remarkable wine he has created in the hills west of Montpellier. Whether you believe everything he says about the effects of the unique Günzian soil and the way the scents of the wild *garrigue* scrub are transferred to the wine, you cannot deny that this is one of the most powerful, concentrated and tannic Cabernets pro-duced anywhere. Low yields and care in selection have certainly contributed to the consistently high quality of the wine since the first vintage in 1978. The microclimate of the valley at the foot of the Larzac plateau where the vineyard is planted (with non-selected vines on a north-facing slope) may be relatively cool for this hot corner of southern France, but in years like 1982 and 1985 there are hot baked aromas to go with the pepper, spice and black fruits. You may not go quite as far as M. Guibert in claiming that this is the world's most complex bouquet: it is something special none the less. As well as the *terroir* of which M. Guibert is so proud, there is an unusual mix of grape varieties: 70 per cent Cabernet Sauvignon, then around 5 per cent each of Syrah, Merlot, Cabernet Franc,

Malbec, Pinot Noir and Tannat. On the palate the wine has great attack and chewy density (*matière* is one of M. Guibert's favourite terms), but it is hardly elegant. One wonders whether vintages like the 1982 will ever lose their tannic finish. The wine spends eighteen months in Allier oak *barriques*, of which 10 per cent are new: M. Guibert believes that wine should dominate oak and not vice versa. It is not filtered – appropriately for a natural product which, according to M. Guibert, represents a 'kind of museum of the French vineyard before the technical explosion of the 1960s, which led to disastrous standardization in many fields'.

Provence

There has been more emphasis on straight Cabernet Sauvignon and, especially, Cabernet-based blends in Provence than in Languedoc-Roussillon. The large cover-all appellations of Côtes de Provence and Coteaux d'Aix-en-Provence both permit Cabernet Sauvignon: up to 30 per cent of the blend in Côtes de Provence, but with no restriction in Coteaux d'Aix-en-Provence where Cabernet Sauvignon is one of a list of permitted grape varieties which also includes Carignan, Cinsault, Counoise, Grenache, Mourvèdre and Syrah. Both Georges Brunet at Château Vignelaure and Eloi Durrbach at Domaine de Trevallon have shown how well a blend of Cabernet and Syrah, originally recommended by Dr Guyot in 1865, can work in Provence. Cabernet Sauvignon is not included in the small, historic appellations of Bandol, Palette and Bellet, but the Bunan family of the Mas de la Rouvière estate, in Bandol, make an excellent non-appellation Cabernet Sauvignon called Mont Caume.

DOMAINE DE TRÉVALLON

Coteaux d'Aix-en-Provence

13150 St-Etienne-du-Grès

Vineyard: 30 acres

Production: 70,000 bottles

Quality: 🍇🍇🍇🍇 Price: ★★★

Best vintages: 1984, 1985, 1986, 1987

The wine made by Eloi Durrbach among the strange white bauxite rocks of the northern slopes of the Alpilles was inspired by Château Vignelaure, where Durrbach worked for a while before producing his first vintage in 1978. It re-creates the 'hermitaged' claret of the nineteenth century with its blend of 60 per cent Cabernet Sauvignon and 40 per cent Syrah. The other comparison that suggests itself is with the Cabernet–Shiraz blends of Australia. The style of Trevallon is rich, chocolatey, complex and above all elegant – no mean achievement in the modest appellation of Coteaux d'Aix-en-Provence. Most of the wine spends eighteen months in small oak *foudres*, though a proportion is aged for eight months in new *barriques*. M. Durrbach is a serious, skilled producer of one of the finest Cabernet-based wines made outside Bordeaux.

CHÂTEAU VIGNELAURE

Coteaux d'Aix-en-Provence

83560 Rians

Vineyard: 80 acres

Production: 300,000 bottles

Quality: 🍇🍇🍇 Price: ★★★

Best vintages: 1982, 1983, 1985

Georges Brunet sold the third growth Château La Lagune in Bordeaux (after an impressive effort of renovation) in 1966, and bought this property in the Haut Var twenty miles from Aix-en-Provence. The property was sold in 1987 to an American firm and then sold on again in 1990 to its present owner, Sonu Shivdasani. The appellation is Coteaux d'Aix-en-Provence. The wine Brunet created, from 45 per cent Cabernet Sauvignon, 40 per cent Syrah and 15 per cent Grenache (all grown organically), has been mistaken for *cru classé* claret. It has rather less tannin, and is approachable younger, but the essential qualities of elegance and balance are there. Vignelaure, which spends between sixteen and thirty months in large Hungarian oak vats, will age for at least a decade in good vintages.

South-west

Cabernet Sauvignon forms a significant part of the red blend in the Bordeaux satellite appellations of Bergerac (including the superior enclave of Pécharmant), Buzet, Côtes de Duras and Côtes du Marmandais. At Nick Ryman's Bergerac estate of Château de la Jaubertie, the proportion of Cabernet Sauvignon for the red wine is 25 per cent. At Château Tiregand, in Pécharmant, the proportion is 30 per cent. Côtes de Duras, perhaps the most Bordeaux-like of all these wines, generally contains around 60 per cent Cabernet Sauvignon. However, these are mostly wines for everyday drinking, and little oak is used. Buzet is very similar, producing attractive blackcurranty reds; the local co-operative handles 95 per cent of the production and ages its top blend, Cuvée Napoléon, in oak. Only a small proportion of Cabernet Sauvignon is used in the Côtes du Marmandais VDQS in the Garonne Valley: the permitted grape varieties are a maximum of 75 per cent Merlot, Cabernet Franc and Cabernet Sauvignon, and a maximum of 50 per cent Côt, Fer Savadou, Gamay, Syrah and Abouriou.

Moving further inland, the main varieties used for the sappy, herbaceous, red Gaillac are the local Duras, Fer Savadou and Negrette, together with Syrah and Gamay; up to 40 per cent of Cabernet Franc, Cabernet Sauvignon and Merlot is permitted. The dark-coloured, soft red wine of Côtes du Frontonnais outside Toulouse is made mainly from Negrette, but up to 25 per cent Cabernet Sauvignon, Cabernet Franc and Fer Savadou is also allowed. In the Côtes de Gascogne region, best known for its fruity whites, there have been recent plantings of Cabernet Sauvignon, together with Merlot, Cabernet Franc and Tannat.

GREECE

The Greek mainland and islands, once the source of exquisite vintages celebrated in the poetry of Homer and Sappho, are now best known for retsina. Most Greek table wine is ordinary indeed. A few outposts of quality exist, of which the most notable is probably the Côtes du Meliton appellation where Château Carras is produced. There is another Cabernet Sauvignon enclave at Metsova in the wild but comparatively well-watered Pindus mountains.

DOMAINE PORTO-CARRAS

N. Marmaras, Sithonia, Chalkidiki

Vineyard: 350 acres

Production: 200,000 bottles

Labels: Domaine Carras, Château Carras, Cava Carras

Quality: 🍇🍇🍇   Price: ★ – ★★

Best vintages: 1977, 1981

The Domaine Porto-Carras, which belonged, until his death in 1989, to the shipping millionaire John Carras, covers 4,500 acres of land on Sithonia, the middle prong of the Chalkidiki peninsula in north-eastern Greece. These west-facing slopes, very close to the Aegean, have proved extremely amenable to the classic Bordeaux grape varieties. Domaine Carras is a blend of Cabernet Sauvignon and the Greek variety Limnio. Considerably more refined is Château Carras, a blend of 70 per cent Cabernet Sauvignon, 20 per cent Cabernet Franc and 10 per cent Merlot, made under the guidance of Professor Peynaud and aged eighteen to twenty months in Limousin and Nevers oak *barriques*. With its warm, velvety nose, authentic dusty, cedary Cabernet flavour, subtle oak and classic structure, it could be mistaken for a good-quality Bordeaux – though it is closer to Pomerol than Pauillac. In exceptional years a 100 per cent Cabernet Sauvignon wine called Cava Carras is produced; so far only the 1977 has been released.

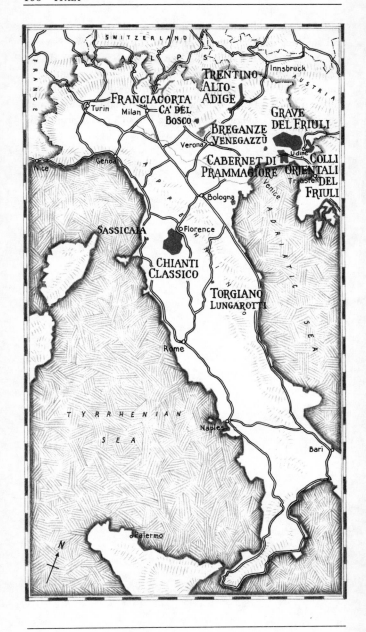

ITALY

| Total vineyard area: 2,800,000 acres

Cabernet Sauvignon has been around in Italy for a long time. According to Count Ugo Contini Bonacossi, Cabernet Sauvignon was among the grapes planted by the Francophile Medicis around their villa of Capezzana, in the Montalbano hills north-west of Florence, in the early eighteenth century. There is firm evidence that Count Sambuy introduced it on his estate near Alessandria in Piedmont in 1820.

These days, the largest plantations of Cabernet are in the north-eastern zones of Friuli-Venezia-Giulia, Veneto and Trentino-Alto-Adige. The main problem here is a reluctance to distinguish between Cabernet Sauvignon and Cabernet Franc. Very few of the many DOCs that sanction Cabernet specify which of the two they mean. Collio in Friuli, which specifies Cabernet Franc, is an exception. In practice, the wines are mainly Cabernet Franc, with small amounts of Cabernet Sauvignon blended in. Very few of these north-eastern Cabernets have the power, depth and complexity of classic Cabernet Sauvignon.

In Friuli-Venezia-Giulia, the more serious Cabernets tend to come from Colli Orientali del Friuli, Grave del Friuli and Isonzo. In the Veneto, Breganze stands out, partly because of the excellent producer Maculan, one of whose Cabernets, Fratta, is made from partially dried grapes. Decent Cabernets also come from Lison-Pramaggiore. The obscure DOC of Montello e Colli Asolani is worth mentioning because it is where the well-known non-DOC wine of Venegazzù orig-inates. Venegazzù belonged for centuries to the Loredan-Gasparini family who produced several doges; it may have been the first wine in Italy to include Cabernet. The Venegazzù

Riserva della Casa is a Bordeaux blend of Cabernet Sauvignon, Cabernet Franc, Merlot and Malbec, highly reputed in the past but somewhat declined of late.

I have never been particularly impressed by the light, grassy Cabernets from the twin northern provinces of Trentino and Alto-Adige. The type of Cabernet is seldom specified but the style is overwhelmingly Franc.

It is Tuscany, without any doubt, that produces the most successful Italian Cabernets, those which come closest to attaining the structure and complexity of Bordeaux, while possessing a distinctive, fuller, rounder character. Cabernet Sauvignon was introduced primarily as a blending component, notably by Antinori with Tignanello, in order to fill out the harsh and sometimes hollow flavour of Sangiovese. Now, most ambitious Chianti producers make a *barrique*-aged Sangiovese–Cabernet blend, on the lines of Tignanello. Less common and, according to many, less successful, are the wines that contain a preponderance of Cabernet Sauvignon. Incisa's eccentric, pioneering and consistently brilliant Sassicaia is still the touchstone. Villa Banfi's Tavernelle is an unusual example of 100 per cent Cabernet Sauvignon.

Though Cabernet Sauvignon plantings are still on the increase, there are signs of a return to native varieties, with producers such as Isole e Olena and Monte Vertini preferring to use Sangiovese (or the clone called Sangioveto) for their top-range 'super-Tuscans'.

Outside Tuscany there are notable Cabernet enclaves at Torgiano in Umbria (the fief of the Lungarotti family) and in the Colli Bolognesi in Emilia-Romagna, where Terre Rosse make a solid, highly acceptable version of what is very definitely Cabernet Sauvignon, not Franc. The big bulk-producing areas of the south and the islands have yet to come up with any exciting Cabernet-based wines, but the variety is increasingly being used as a *cépage améliorateur*.

ANTINORI, MARCHESI L. & I.

Palazzo Antinori, Piazza degli Antinori 3, 50123 Firenze
Labels: Tignanello, Solaia
Quality: 🍇🍇🍇🍇   Price: ★★★★
Best vintages: Tignanello, 1983, 1985, 1988; Solaia, 1982

Tignanello is the name of a vineyard on Antinori's Santa
Cristina estate in the heart of Chianti Classico, planted to
Cabernet Sauvignon in the late 1960s by Marchese Piero Antinori. The wine bearing that name, a blend of 20 per cent
Cabernet Sauvignon and 80 per cent Sangiovese aged for
eighteen months in *barriques*, caused an immediate stir when it
first appeared in 1971. Though some accused it of betraying
Italian tradition, it proved to be immensely influential. Soon,
barrique-aged blends of Sangiovese and Cabernet (only qualify-
ing as *vini da tavola* under the Italian wine laws) were appearing
all over Tuscany, as producers realized that they could charge
considerably more for them than for straight Chianti. For Marchese Piero Antinori, the purpose of blending in Cabernet was
to add elegance, and Tignanello (not really qualified to appear
in this book) is still one of the most elegant of the so-called
'super-Tuscans'. In exceptional years, Antinori release a reverse
blend of 80 per cent Cabernet Sauvignon and 20 per cent
Sangiovese called Solaia. Those lucky enough to have tasted it
consider it on a par with Sassicaia, with a slightly plummier
fruit character.

CA' DEL BOSCO

Via Case Sparse 11, 25030 Erbusco
Vineyard: 5 acres
Production: 15,000–25,000 bottles
Label: Maurizio Zanella

Quality: 🍇🍇🍇🍇   Price: ★★★★★

Best vintages: 1982, 1985, 1987

Maurizio Zanella's Ca' del Bosco, an estate set in the Francia-corta hills not far from Lake Iseo, specializes in sparkling wine and aims for the highest standards (and prices). Zanella's 'claret', a blend of 45–50 per cent Cabernet Sauvignon, 25–30 per cent Merlot and 20–25 per cent Cabernet Franc, is certainly one of the most stylish, elegant and French-tasting Cabernet blends made in Italy. Elegance and freshness, rather than power, are its hallmarks. It has a blue-purple, almost Beaujolais-like colour in its youth, a fresh herbaceous nose and cherry fruit on the palate. This sophisticated wine's high quality, though, is shown by a vintage like 1987, which has completely digested the new oak in which it was aged for a year. Signor Zanella obviously believes in the wine's staying power: he uses the longest corks I have ever seen.

CANTINE LUNGAROTTI

Torgiano, 06089 Perugia

Label: Cabernet Sauvignon di Miralduolo

Quality: 🍇🍇   Price: ★★★★

Best vintages: 1982, 1985

Dr Giorgio Lungarotti, creator of the well-known and success-ful Rubesco Torgiano (a Chianti-style wine from the gentle hills between Perugia and Assisi) planted Cabernet Sauvignon in his San Giorgio vineyard in 1970. San Giorgio is a successful blend of 75 per cent Sangiovese and Canaiolo (the Chianti grapes) and 25 per cent Cabernet Sauvignon, on the same lines as Antinori's Tignanello. As with that wine, the Cabernet serves to soften and add richness to the astringent native varieties. Markedly less successful is his 100 per cent Cabernet Sauvignon, which, while deep-coloured, dense and powerful, is clumsy and lacks balance.

CASTELLO DI RAMPOLLA

Panzano (Chianti)

Label: Sammarco

Quality: 🍷🍷🍷🍷   Price: ★★★★★

Best vintage: 1985

Alceo de Napoli, owner of this famous Chianti estate, is on record as saying that he believes passionately in Cabernet Sauvignon and detests Canaiolo. Certainly his 'super-Tuscan' Sammarco, though abominably expensive, supports his argument. This blend of 75 per cent Cabernet Sauvignon and 25 per cent Sangiovese is one of the very best Cabernet-based wines in Italy. It has the dusty, minerally nose of classy Cabernet, and masses of rich fruit on the palate backed by considerable tannin.

FRESCOBALDI, MARCHESI DI

Via S. Spirito 11, 50125 Firenze

Label: Mormoreto

Quality: 🍷🍷🍷🍷   Price: ★★★

Best vintages: 1983, 1985

Frescobaldi have had Cabernet Sauvignon planted on their great Nipozzano estate in the Rufina sub-region of Chianti for over a century. It was in 1983 that they brought out the first vintage of Mormoreto. It falls under the new system of *vini con predicato* developed by a group of larger producers including Antinori and Ruffino. Mormoreto carries the appellation Predicato di Biturica, which stipulates a minimum of 30 per cent Cabernet Sauvignon. The blend for Mormoreto is 85 per cent Cabernet Sauvignon, 10 per cent Sangiovese and 5 per cent Cabernet Franc. The first release in 1983 impressed me with its cigar-box Cabernet nose and its elegance and spiciness on the palate. While remaining unmistakably Cabernet, it had a clear family resemblance to other wines from the Nipozzano estate, with their special fragrance and combination of gentleness and power.

GAJA

> Barbaresco (Alba)
> Vineyard: 5 acres
> Production: 9,000 bottles
> Label: Darmagi
> Quality: 🍇🍇🍇   Price: ★★★★★
> Best vintages: 1983, 1985, 1986

When Angelo Gaja planted a fine vineyard in Barbaresco with Cabernet Sauvignon in 1978, his father's reaction was 'Darmagi!' – in Piedmontese dialect, 'What a pity!' Others' reactions have been more favourable, and Gaja has been able to sell his very limited production at his usual crazily high prices. Whether Darmagi is a classic Cabernet Sauvignon is another matter. I find it strongly marked by a *goût de terroir*, and closer in character to other Alba red wines, made from the Nebbiolo grape, than to other Cabernets – which is a tribute to the extremely strong character of this particular *terroir*. Darmagi is very deep in colour and has a mineral tone on the nose; on the palate it is big, rich and powerful, with highish acidity. In the case of the 1985, the elements are not yet in harmony.

MARCHESI DI FRESCOBALDI. See Frescobaldi, Marchesi di

MARCHESI L. & I. ANTINORI. See Antinori, Marchesi L. & I.

SASSICAIA

Tenuta San Guido, Bolgheri

Vineyard: 49 acres

Production: 80,000 bottles

Quality: 🍇🍇🍇🍇🍇   Price: ★★★★★

Best vintages: 1982, 1984, 1985

Sassicaia is the result of the vision and, one might add, stubbornness of one man, Mario Incisa della Rocchetta. Incisa, a Piedmontese aristocrat and distinguished horse-breeder, married Clarice della Gherardesca, scion of one of the great Tuscan families, in 1932. Part of Clarice's dowry was half of the vast estate of Bolgheri, near Cecina on the Tyrrhenian coast, which had belonged to the della Gherardescas for a thousand years. Bolgheri, eighty miles from the Chianti country, in a different landscape and with a different, maritime climate, had never been known for producing good wine. In fact, the reputation of Bolgheri wine was abysmal: 'Always salty, it had a different defect every year – fizzy, vinegary, oxidized,' wrote one Italian authority. Incisa was not deterred. Having always been a fan of great Bordeaux, especially Château Margaux, he decided in 1944 to plant the Bordeaux varieties 400 metres up at Castglion-cello, in the deep-green hills above Bolgheri. For a long time the production remained on a small scale and in the rustic mode, and early comments were not favourable. But Incisa persevered, and in 1964–5 planted another vineyard, only 50 metres above sea-level and much less exposed, in the stony ground called Sassicaia. Seven thousand bottles of the 1968 vintage were produced, and Incisa decided that they merited professional marketing. His first cousin Piero Antinori offered help on the commercial side; a bottle was sent to the influential wine critic Luigi Veronelli. He wrote a eulogistic column, and the wine's reputation was made. Antinori's 'wizard' wine-maker, Giacomo Tachis, was brought in to oversee production, as he still does today.

Now closely supervised by Mario Incisa's son Niccolo,

Sassicaia, I feel, fully deserves its reputation as an Italian 'first growth'. It may not be 'Italy's best wine' (Hugh Johnson), but it is consistently Italy's best Cabernet Sauvignon. A blend of 80 per cent Cabernet Sauvignon and 20 per cent Cabernet Franc, it really does fulfil Mario Incisa's ambition by tasting remarkably like a first-growth Bordeaux, though there is usually a touch of extra ripeness compared to the wines of the Médoc. With its cedary elegance, richness, ripeness, power and length, it is perhaps closest, of all clarets, to Château Haut-Brion. The French flavour has been enhanced in recent years by a marked shift away from Slovenian to French (mainly Tronçais) *barriques*, in which the wine spends twenty months to two years. Among recent vintages the 1984 is a surprise success, beautifully balanced and long, while the 1985 has immense power and plummy depth, and needs putting away for eight years. Very good wines were made also in 1986 and 1987.

The winery, a former bulb-storage shed, is neat, efficient and unshowy. Niccolo Incisa, who has now taken over the marketing of his wine from the Antinoris, does not wish to expand production, which fits the scale of the winery and enables him to exercise selection both at harvest and after fermentation.

TENUTA DI CAPEZZANA

Carmignano (Firenze)

Vineyard: 25 acres

Label: Ghiaie della Furba

Quality: 🍇🍇🍇🍇   Price: ★★★

Best vintages: 1985, 1987

Count Ugo Contini Bonacossi, godfather of the Carmignano DOC in the Montalbano hills north-west of Florence and owner of the ravishing Medici villa and estate of Capezzana, has discovered evidence that Cabernet was planted in the region in the eighteenth century. The grape disappeared during the trauma of phylloxera but was replanted by Count Ugo in the

1960s, using cuttings from Bordeaux (including some from Château Lafite). From 1967, 10 per cent of Cabernet Sauvignon was blended into the Capezzana Carmignano Riserva, for me one of Italy's best and most long-lived wines. It was a personal triumph for Count Ugo that, in 1975, Carmignano became the first Tuscan DOC to sanction a proportion of Cabernet. Ghiaie della Furba, named after the pebbles deposited by the Furba stream on its way down the Montalbano slopes, is a blend of roughly 40 per cent Cabernet Sauvignon, 30 per cent Cabernet Franc and 30 per cent Merlot. Unexpectedly, perhaps, Ghiaie is less tannic and quicker to come round than the rather stern, powerful Carmignano Riserva. The 1985 is quite a powerful, sturdy wine, blood-red in colour, with mulberry fruit and soft tannin. The 1987 was already drinking well in early 1990, with an almost Australian minty nose and seductively soft, ripe fruit.

VILLA BANFI

Montalcino (Siena)
Label: Tavernelle
Quality: 🍇🍇🍇   Price: ★★★
Best vintages: 1982, 1983, 1985, 1986, 1987

Villa Banfi, the largest importers of Italian wine into the USA, spent $100m on a vast new vineyard and winery complex outside Brunello di Montalcino from 1977 to 1984. Most unusually for Tuscany, they launched a 100 per cent Cabernet Sauvignon, aged in two-thirds new French oak. Tavernelle has excellent colour and a big, bold, blackcurrant-and-oak style which brings California to mind. At the moment the wine lacks something in finesse; this shortcoming may disappear as the vines age.

MIDDLE EAST AND NORTH AFRICA

Israel

As numerous references in the Bible demonstrate, from the drunkenness of Noah to the image of the cup in the Garden of Gethsemane, wine has been made in the Holy Land for more than three millennia. Modern Israeli wine comes mainly from the vineyards at Rishon-le-Zion south of Tel Aviv and Zichron-Yaacov some 50 km north, which Edmond de Rothschild presented as a gift to the nation. The Cabernet Sauvignons I have tasted under the Carmel label have been heavily oxidized and almost undrinkable. It is possible that perfectly decent wine was ruined in the wine-making process by being boiled to make it kosher. Carmel are now producing a supposedly superior Cabernet Sauvignon for export, mainly to the United States. I have not been able to taste it.

Entirely responsible for a move towards higher quality wine production in Israel is the Golan Heights winery, established in 1983. This well-managed operation has transformed the Israeli wine scene.

GOLAN HEIGHTS–YARDEN WINERY

Industry Area, Quatzrin, P O Box 183, 12900 Israel

Vineyard: 60 acres

Production: 150,000 bottles

Labels: Yarden, Gamla, Galil

Quality: 🍇🍇🍇   Price: ★ – ★★★
Best vintages: 1985, 1987

This is an admirably run winery, precariously situated near the town of Quatzrin in what is now Upper Galilee and was once Syria. One of the secrets is the high altitude (from 300–1,100 m) of the vineyards, which belong to eight kibbutzim and moshavim (communal farms) mainly on the lower slopes of Mount Hermon. Another is Californian expertise, in the form of consultant Peter Stern and wine-maker Jim Klein, and a determination not to compromise quality despite the special conditions of working in Israel. Kosher regulations mean that the wine can be handled only by orthodox Jews until it is in the bottle. Jim Klein is Jewish but not orthodox, so he must have his barrel samples drawn by orthodox cellar-workers.

This does not deter him from making excellent Cabernet Sauvignon wines. The Cabernet Sauvignon which carries the top-of-the-range Yarden label comes from one of the lower vineyards, Ramat Naftali, on the left bank of the Jordan (Yarden) River. A special microclimate produces a very deep-coloured wine of great fruit density and some complexity – rather in a Californian style, perhaps, but long, concentrated and not without elegance. It can be kept at least five years. The more straightforward Gamla Cabernet Sauvignon is powerful and deep-coloured, without the same complexity, and ready for drinking after two years.

Lebanon

Wine production in the Lebanon goes back to Roman times and almost certainly much earlier. Now one family obstinately continues to make one of the world's most unusual Cabernet Sauvignon-based wines in unpromising, and sometimes down-right dangerous conditions.

CHÂTEAU MUSAR

Ghazir, Lebanon
Production: 200,000 bottles
Quality: 🍇🍇🍇   Price: ★★
Best vintages: 1964, 1979, 1981, 1982

Château Musar was established in 1930 by Gaston Hochar, and continues to be run by his sons Serge and Ronald. The vineyards are situated in the Bekaa Valley at an altitude of about 1,000 m. As this area is controlled by Syrian troops, the Hochars have to rely on reports about when the grapes are ripe from the Bedouin tribesmen who work as pickers. The grapes must then be transported, through at least five checkpoints, to the winery in the hills to the north of Beirut. The wonder is that only two vintages, 1976 and 1984, have been very seriously interrupted.

The sensational nature of the Musar story should not distort appreciation of the wine. The blend of grapes varies from year to year, but is usually about 75 per cent Cabernet Sauvignon, 15–20 per cent Cinsault and the rest Syrah. The Rhône grapes give a special warmth and spiciness to the aroma (perhaps Musar's greatest glory). On the palate the impression is of a softer, riper, warmer claret than the Bordeaux standard. Musar is matured for up to two years in Nevers oak *barriques*, and released after seven years. Of the two current vintages, the 1981 is gamy and developed, the 1982 more concentrated and backward. Serge considers his wine only starts to be at its best after fifteen years; older vintages certainly hold up very well.

Other Regions

A certain amount of Cabernet Sauvignon is grown in Turkey and Cyprus. Cabernet Sauvignon also has a small presence among the large (though reduced) vineyards of Algeria and Morocco. I have not seen a single varietal from any of these countries, which are not at the forefront of quality wine production at the moment.

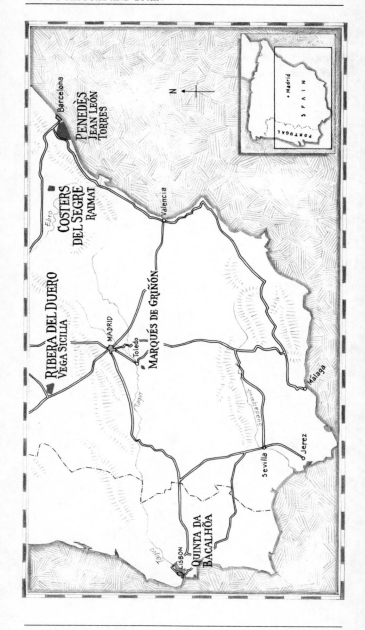

PORTUGAL AND SPAIN

Portugal

Portugal has one of the largest vineyard surfaces in the world, but remains overwhelmingly loyal to its native varieties, few of which are known anywhere else (and some of which, one feels, may not be known even to the people who grow them). There is certainly an exciting potential for good- to-exceptional quality Cabernet Sauvignon, as the one commercially available example shows. Cabernet Sauvignon can also be very effective in blends, as is proved by J. M. Fonseca Succrs.' remarkably claret-like Quinta de Camarate (50 per cent Castelão Frances, 25 per cent Espadeiro, 25 per cent Cabernet Sauvignon) from the Estremadura region north of Lisbon.

QUINTA DA BACALHÕA

c/o João Pires & Filhos, Pinhal Novo

Vineyard: 25 acres

Quality: 🍇🍇🍇   Price: ★★

Best vintages: 1982, 1983, 1985, 1986

This single estate on the middle slopes of Azeitão in the Setúbal peninsula south of Lisbon was planted to 90 per cent Cabernet Sauvignon and 10 per cent Merlot in 1974. The wine made from the estate by João Pires's Australian wine-maker Peter Bright is in the classic Bordeaux mould: blackcurrant-scented, with a considerable overlay of new oak when young (Bacalhõa is aged for twelve to fourteen months in new *barriques*), firmly structured and austerely tannic for several years.

Spain

| Total vineyard area: 3,996,460 acres

The first Cabernet Sauvignon vineyard in Spain was planted by the Marqués de Riscal at Elciego in the Rioja in 1860. There are still 123 acres planted to Cabernet Sauvignon and Merlot on the Riscal estate, included in the Riscal Rioja only by special dispensation in a region which, despite considerable Bordelais influence, stuck with its native varieties. The second Cabernet vineyard was most probably the one planted at Vega Sicilia in Ribera del Duero four years later. The exact proportions of grape varieties in the Vega Sicilia blends are kept secret, but once again it is the local version of Tempranillo, Tinto Fino, which reigns supreme in these vineyards.

Cabernet Sauvignon only found its way to the Penedès region of Catalonia, the part of Spain where it seems most at home, in the 1960s, when first Jean León and then Miguel A. Torres planted their vineyards, with notably successful results. Several other Penedès producers have followed in their footsteps, in particular Mont Marçal, Gran Caus, René Barbier and Masia Bach, and there is no doubt about the grape's suitability to this area. However, the nature of the Spanish market, much stronger in the middle and lower range than at the top, has militated against the appearance of other really outstanding, world-class Cabernets. The most exciting Cabernets from Catalonia, apart from those of Torres and León, are being produced on the huge Raimat estate near Lérida. A small amount of Cabernet Sauvignon is also to be found in the DO Priorato in southern Catalonia.

Outside Catalonia, one solitary Cabernet outpost of high quality has been established by the Marqués de Griñón on his Casadevacas estate near Toledo. The grape is increasingly being planted in such regions as La Mancha, Valdepeñas and Navarra, mainly as a *cépage améliorateur* for blending, though single varietals from these areas are beginning to appear on the market.

GRIÑÓN, MARQUÉS DE

Malpica de Tajo, Toledo

Vineyard: 35 acres

Production: 100,000 bottles

Quality: 🍇🍇🍇🍇   Price: ★★★

Best vintages: 1984, 1985

The wine produced by Carlos Falco, Marqués de Griñón, on his estate not far from Toledo, may be a parvenu compared to its aristocratic maker, but it has quickly established itself as one of the handful of Spanish Cabernet-based wines that deserve serious attention. The fairly hot climate produces a rich, chocolatey wine, not at all like the Cabernets of Penedès, but fermentation at controlled temperature and two years' maturation in *barriques*, all under the guidance of Professor Peynaud, ensure that the wine retains fruit and structure. The nose has the characteristic Cabernet dustiness, together with a hint of green pepper, and the palate is dominated by rich, ripe fruit. Some might find the style a trifle flat and lacking in acidity, but this is an admirably made wine.

LEÓN, JEAN

DO Penedès

Torrelavid, Pla del Penedès

Vineyard: 94 acres

Production: 180,000–200,000 bottles

Quality: 🍇🍇🍇🍇   Price: ★★★

Best vintages: 1978, 1980, 1981, 1983

Jean León was born in Santander in the late 1920s but by 1953 was driving a taxi in Los Angeles. He soon moved into the restaurant business (the uniforms were similar, he claims) and by 1956 was part-owner of the La Scala restaurant in Beverly

Hills. He quickly became one of the most famous restaurateurs in the Los Angeles area; film stars and presidents flocked to his tables. By 1962, having developed a keen interest in wine, he had decided to buy a vineyard. Chance took him to the Penedès region of Catalonia (he tried Napa and Vouvray first), where in 1963 he became landlord of 450 acres and 97 families. In 1964 he started bringing cuttings of Cabernet Sauvignon over from Bordeaux (he claims to have stolen some from Lafite). Trouble at the Spanish border meant that the vines had to be smuggled over the Pyrenees along paths used by the Republicans in the Civil War. By whatever means, they were planted, Jean León likes to insist, at least a year before the Torres experiments.

It is a commonplace, but still true, to say that Jean León's Cabernet Sauvignon has a Californian flavour. This is a big, powerful wine with what sometimes seems an excessive amount of tannin, requiring ten years to soften. In 1981 a decision was made, for commercial reasons, to lighten the style. Maceration after fermentation was shortened from ten days to four and, from 1980, a significant proportion of Cabernet Franc, now around 15 per cent, was added to the Cabernet Sauvignon, with softening effect. Though the former decision, at any rate, may sound like a move away from quality, the results have been beneficial. Whereas the 1978, though impressively deep and rich, seems slightly out of balance, the 1981, with little apparent loss in concentration, has a lovely cedary complexity and silky texture. The 1983 has depth and perfume on the nose, power, structure and length on the palate. Jean León Cabernet has always been aged in 100 per cent American oak; Jean León and his wine-maker, Jaime Rovira, like the touch of vanilla and spice it brings. There are plans to introduce a Gran Reserva, released only when it is ten years old.

RAIMAT

DO Costers del Segre

| Raimat, Lérida

Vineyard: 988 acres

Production: not released

Labels: Clos Abadía, Cabernet Sauvignon

Quality: 🍇🍇🍇🍇   Price: ★★

Best vintages: 1982, 1983

The vast Raimat estate of the Raventós family (owners also of the Codorníu empire) is one of the agricultural marvels of Spain. It is situated in an extremely dry area near Lérida, 160 km east of Barcelona, described in the press literature, with a certain poetic licence, as being 'very similar to the Sahara desert'. Certainly the combination of low rainfall, salty soil and extreme temperatures does not look favourable for the making of fine wines. However, irrigation by water brought in canals from the Pyrenees 150 km to the north, desalination of the soil using alfalfa and pine trees, and modern methods of vinification have wrought a minor miracle. Raimat grapes seem to give particularly intense fruit flavours and aroma, with excellent natural acid balance, surprising in a comparatively warm region.

Cabernet Sauvignon features in three of the Raimat reds. Clos Clamor, comprising 20 per cent Cabernet Sauvignon, 40 per cent Tempranillo and 40 per cent Garnacha, is an excellent and, I feel, underrated wine, in a more traditionally Spanish, rich mellow style than the other Raimat reds. Clos Abadía has just over 50 per cent Cabernet Sauvignon, with about 40 per cent Tempranillo and 10 per cent Garnacha. Though similar in composition to Torres' Gran Coronas, it spends rather less time in oak (American), and has a very different character – lighter and more elegant, though not lacking in depth. Some prefer this to the straight Cabernet Sauvignon (which is in fact blended with 10 per cent Merlot and 5 per cent Tempranillo), but I find the latter, though more reserved, has greater richness, length and depth.

*

TORRES, VINOS Y LICORES

DO Penedès

Comercio 22, Vilafranca del Penedès

Vineyard: Mas La Plana, 71 acres; other Cabernet vineyards at San Marti Sarroca, Milmanda, San Juan de Mediona

Labels: Gran Coronas, Mas La Plana (Gran Coronas Black Label)

Production: Gran Coronas, 600,000 bottles; Mas La Plana, 150,000 bottles

Quality: 🍷🍷🍷 – 🍷🍷🍷🍷🍷   Price: ★★ – ★★★★

Best vintages: Gran Coronas, 1982, 1983; Mas La Plana, 1981, 1982, 1983, 1985

The Catalan wine and brandy firm of Torres was founded in 1870, but it is in the last twenty years that its reputation as a world-class producer has been established. Thanks to the commercial shrewdness of Don Miguel Torres, the octogenarian patriarch who died in 1991, the firm moved steadily away from selling wine in bulk towards high-quality bottled wine production, with increasing emphasis on Reservas. It was the viticultural and oenological expertise of his son Miguel A. Torres that brought Torres international renown – and set an example which other Spanish wine producers have tried, with limited success, to follow. Miguel Jr, who trained at Dijon and Montpellier, began planting European grape varieties in the Penedès vineyards in the 1960s. He planted the first twenty-two acres of the hilltop site of Mas La Plana near Pacs del Penedès with Cabernet Sauvignon in 1966.

Gran Coronas, the excellent Reserva introduced by Don Miguel Sr in the 1970s, has gradually become more dominated by Cabernet Sauvignon. In the late 1970s it consisted of approximately half Cabernet Sauvignon and half Tempranillo (the Rioja grape known in Penedès as Ull de Llebre); since 1981 the proportion of Cabernet has been 75 per cent. Ninety-five per cent of the fruit comes from Torres's own vineyards. The rich, warm, mellow style of early releases (enhanced by twenty months ageing in American oak) has changed slightly, becoming slightly firmer and more tannic. The 1985 seems unusually light; I hope that subsequent vintages will see a return to the richer style of 1982 and 1983. Even Torres's basic red Coronas now contains a proportion, around 15 per cent, of Cabernet Sauvignon.

The wine which catapulted Torres into the élite group of world wine-producers was the single-vineyard Cabernet Sauvignon originally called Gran Coronas Black Label and now renamed after the vineyard, Mas La Plana, as part of Torres's *pago* (single vineyard) series. The very first commercial vintage, the 1970, released in 1978, caused a sensation when it won the 1979 Gault-Millau Olympiad, beating such Bordeaux luminaries as Château Latour 1970 and Château La Mission Haut-Brion 1961. The 1970 vintage consisted of 70 per cent Cabernet Sauvignon, 20 per cent Tempranillo and 10 per cent Monastrell. In its prime (which lasted at least until 1983 – by 1989 it was fading) it had a gamy, complex nose and delicious sweet fruit on the palate, with a cedary quality reminiscent of St Julien. The 1971 was rich and sweet also, if not quite so long-lived. In 1975 the composition changed to 90 per cent Cabernet Sauvignon, 10 per cent Cabernet Franc. The 1976 was still tasting well in 1990 – mature and gamy on the nose with a hint of green pepper, initially mellow on the palate but with a tannic finish. The 1978 (100 per cent Cabernet Sauvignon) seems lighter and has not aged so gracefully. With 1981 came a change to lower yields in the vineyard and longer fermentation time: the result is one of the best of all Black Labels, splendidly concentrated with ripe blackcurrant and plum aromas, hints of coffee and tobacco on the palate and a firm finish – a five-star wine. The 1982, with a superb, subtle, rooty nose and great velvety palate, and the classically structured 1983, with hints of redcurrant and cedar, are both excellent also. The oak regime has changed from 100 per cent American to a judicious mixture of American and French.

SOUTH AFRICA

Vineyard area: 247,000 acres
Area planted to Cabernet Sauvignon: 6,916 acres

South African viticulture has a long and at times distinguished history; the one South African wine to have achieved world renown (in the eighteenth century) was the sweet Constantia, made from various types of Muscat. It is possible that Cabernet Sauvignon, together with other classic French varieties, was introduced as early as the late seventeenth century by the French Huguenots, but authorities such as Hugh Johnson have been unable to prove this.

The modern history of Cabernet Sauvignon in South Africa dates back to the 1920s. There are now a considerable number of estates, mainly in the Paarl and Stellenbosch regions not far from Cape Town, making straight Cabernet Sauvignon and Bordeaux-type blends. The South African style of Cabernet Sauvignon tends to be lean, austere, high in acidity and sometimes hollow. More sophisticated wine-making techniques and greater use of new oak are beginning to make themselves felt, but at the moment considerable natural potential is not being fully realized.

SOUTH AMERICA

Argentina

Total vineyard area: 795,340 acres
Area planted to Cabernet Sauvignon: 7,410 acres

One might expect Argentinian Cabernet Sauvignon to be very similar to that grown in Chile on the other side of the Andes. The distance between Santiago in Chile and Mendoza, by far the largest wine region of Argentina, is only 150 miles as the condor flies. Ninety per cent of Argentina's vines, like those of Chile, are ungrafted. However, whether because of climatic differences (Mendoza is hotter than the Central Valley of Chile) or lack of ambition in the winery, Argentinian Cabernet Sauvignon never reaches the standard of the best from Chile. The French oenologist Michel Rolland, who consults for Bodegas Etchart, admitted to me that he did not think very highly of Cabernet Sauvignon from Argentina, which he found marked by a vegetal character. I find most Argentinian Cabernet Sauvignon – as well as vegetal – bland, soft and unstructured. Strangely, Malbec, almost forgotten in Bordeaux, seems to perform better than Cabernet Sauvignon in Argentina.

Chile

Total vineyard area: 287,000 acres
Area planted to Cabernet Sauvignon: 64,000 acres

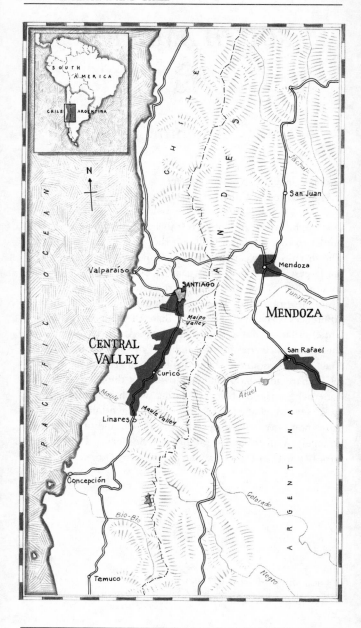

The first vintage was recorded in Chile in 1551, but the first three centuries of Chilean viticulture, under the influence of Spain and the Catholic Church, need not detain us. The missionaries planted the variety called País, related to the Californian Mission, which did not produce wine of world-beating quality.

The most significant date in the history of Chilean wine is 1851, the year Don Silvestre Ochagavía employed a French wine-maker to plant a number of European varieties, including Cabernet Sauvignon, on his farm outside Santiago. His example was quite quickly followed by others, for example the Cousiño family at Macul around 1860 and Errázuriz Panquehue in 1870.

In the Central Valley area of Chile, according to several authorities, Cabernet Sauvignon found the land most perfectly suited to it anywhere in the world. Cool winters, dry warm summers, clear skies and lack of spring frost combine to make the climate close to ideal. The only problem is shortage of rainfall (15 inches around Santiago), but glacial water from the Andes is used for irrigation. Another, much touted, advantage, is freedom from pests. Phylloxera, deterred by the great barrier of the Andes, has never been known in Chile, so all wine is made from ungrafted vines. The advantage for quality is the much greater longevity of these vines, but average ages of between fifteen and twenty-five years, quoted to me by a number of Chilean producers, do not compare favourably with those of good-quality Bordeaux châteaux. Certainly, however, the quality of much Chilean fruit – ripe, aromatic, full of fruit yet possessing natural structure and balance – is the envy of wine-makers in many regions of the world.

Magnificent natural resources have not been matched by advanced technology in the winery. Until recently, Chilean wine-makers were generally content to use old-fashioned methods, whose main drawback was inconsistency between bottlings caused by ancient, unreliable barrels. The last fifteen years have seen considerable investment in modern equipment such as stainless steel tanks. The general standard of wine-making has certainly improved, though it lags far behind that of Australia or California. It was thus most unfortunate that Chile should have been tainted by a wine scandal in 1990, when considerable quantities of Sorbitol, a harmless but illegal additive which occurs naturally in grapes and apples, were found in a number of Chilean wines.

Chilean Cabernet Sauvignon has been called, by Hugh Johnson, 'one of the great natural resources of the planet'. There is certainly the potential in Chile for producing Cabernet Sauvignon that combines the ripeness of California or parts of Australia with the aromatic complexity and balance of Bordeaux. It is to be hoped, under the new, at least semi-democratic system (in a country that until recently enjoyed a long democratic tradition), that that potential will finally be realized. Small proportions of Cabernet Franc and Merlot are often added to Cabernet Sauvignon in Chile.

COUSIÑO MACUL

Huerfanos 979, Santiago

Vineyard: 381 acres

Labels: Cabernet Sauvignon, Cabernet Sauvignon Antiguas Reservas

Quality: 🍇🍇🍇 (Antiguas Reservas, 🍇🍇🍇🍇)   Price: ★ – ★★

Best vintages: 1979, 1981, 1982

In 1856, Don Matias Cousiño bought the historic Macul *hacienda* (estate) in the Maipo Valley. Macul, which means 'right hand' in Quechua, the Inca language, had been settled by Juan Jufré, lieutenant of the *conquistador* Pedro de Valdivia, in 1546. Grapevines were flourishing on the *hacienda* by 1554. Thus Cousiño Macul, one of the grandest and oldest wine firms in Chile, can claim an astonishingly long unbroken history of viticulture. Don Luis Cousiño, son of Matias, who had been educated in Paris, returned to France in 1860 to acquire cuttings of the noble French varieties, including Cabernet Sauvignon. The impressive winery buildings at Macul were constructed by Don Luis in the 1870s, as was the splendid park.

The pride of Cousiño Macul is their Antiguas Reservas Cabernet Sauvignon. This comes from a vineyard planted in 1937 and is aged for three years in American oak – half of that time in very large vats, the other half in small barrels. Good bottles of Antiguas Reservas are probably the best red wines made in South America, with the cigar-box complexity of fine Bordeaux combined with riper, richer fruit, and the structure to age for a decade. Unfortunately, I have found over the years that not all bottles of the same vintage taste the same. Some are considerably lighter than others. The lesser quality Cabernet Sauvignon Don Luis, also estate-grown, has attractive cedar-and-tobacco complexity, but is lighter and looser-knit than Antiguas Reservas.

TORRES, MIGUEL

Panamerica Sur, Km 195, Curicó

Vineyard: 100 acres

Labels: Santa Digna, Manso de Velasco Reserve

Quality: 🍇🍇🍇   Price: ★★

Best vintages: 1986, 1987

The Torres family, from Vilafranca del Penedès in north-east Spain, pioneered the recent spate of foreign investment in Chile. In 1979 Torres bought a winery near Curicó, well to the south of Santiago, and then proceeded to modernize it along the lines of their ultra-modern winery at Pacs del Penedès. Stainless steel tanks, allowing temperature-controlled fermentation, and new 300-litre oak barrels were the first seen in Chile for decades. The operation is now supervised by Miguel Agustín Torres, who visits Chile three times a year during his peregrinations across three continents.

The light, fresh style of Torres Cabernet Sauvignon owes something both to the southerly position of the vineyards and to relatively cool fermentation. This is 'new-style' Cabernet

Sauvignon, and very well done in its way, though I feel that Torres's Chilean reds are less outstanding than the excellent whites, which have less competition. The Reserve Cabernet Sauvignon, from a seven-acre plot of eighty-year-old vines, has not yet been released, but promises to be exciting.

VIÑA CALITERRA

PO Box 2346, Santiago
Quality: 🍇🍇🍇   Price: ★
Best vintage: 1986

Caliterra, one of the most exciting new ventures in Chilean wine, is a partnership between the Chilean bodega Errázuriz Panquehue and the Franciscan Winery in the Napa Valley, California. The winery is outside Curicó in the Maule Valley, well to the south of Maipo. The influence of the cooler climate is apparent in the fresh, herbaceous, well-structured Cabernet Sauvignon, which apparently spends one year in American oak, though it shows little oak character.

VIÑA CARMEN

Gertrudis Echenique 49, Santiago
Quality: 🍇🍇🍇   Price: ★ – ★★
Best vintage: 1986

One of the first wineries established in Chile, in 1850, Carmen was in a state of neglect when it was purchased by Santa Rita in 1988. However, these are some of the most elegant Cabernets from Chile: the 1986 shows the influence of new oak, together with gentle blackcurrant fruit.

VIÑA CONCHA Y TORO

Fernando Lazcano 1220, San Miguel, Santiago

Labels: Cabernet Sauvignon, Casillero del Diablo, Marqués de Casa Concha, Don Melchor

Quality: 🍇🍇🍇   Price: ★

Best vintages: 1985, 1986

This is one of the largest and best known of the Chilean bodegas, named after Don Melchor de Concha y Toro, the Marqués de Casa Concha, who was the son-in-law of the founder. I have always found Concha y Toro's straight Cabernet Sauvignon – very full, deep-coloured and fruity – to be excellent value. The Casillero del Diablo is still big and rich, but shows more oak influence. Heavily oaked, to my taste, is the top-of-the-range Marqués de Casa Concha. The 1982 had dried out and lost suppleness by 1990. The excellent Don Melchor is aged in French oak.

VIÑA SANTA EMILIANA

Fernando Lazcano 1220, Santiago

Labels: Cabernet Sauvignon Maipo Region, Cabernet Sauvignon Reserva Especial

Quality: 🍇🍇🍇   Price: ★

Best vintages: 1983, 1987

This bodega, established as recently as 1986 and owned by Concha y Toro, is currently making some of the best Cabernets in Chile. The Cabernet Sauvignon Maipo Region is relatively light and loose-knit, with an attractive tobacco character. The Reserva Especial has a fragrant cedary nose, velvety texture and impressive length – a wine of some class.

★

VIÑA SANTA RITA

Gertrudis Echeñique 49, Santiago

Vineyard: 370 acres

Production: 6 million bottles

Labels: '120' Cabernet Sauvignon, Reserva Cabernet Sauvignon, Medalla Real

Quality: 🍇🍇🍇   Price: ★ – ★★

Best vintages: 1985, 1986

Santa Rita was founded in 1880 by the politician Don Domingo Fernández Concha; the original vineyards at Buín in the Maipo Valley still provide the basis for the wine today. Santa Rita, now owned by a consortium of businessmen, has been at the forefront of the move towards new technology and aggressive export marketing. The vaulted red-brick cellar, in which the liberator Bernardo O'Higgins hid with 120 of his men from the Spanish in 1814, and which now houses over 4,000 *barriques* and puncheons, provides a link with the past (and the source of the '120' label).

Both the Reserva (aged in American oak) and Medalla Real (aged in French oak) are among Chile's best Cabernets, combining rich fruit with cedary finesse. I found the 1986 Medalla Real beautifully fragrant on the nose, yet marked by uncomfortably high acidity. The '120' spends very little time in oak, and is blended with a proportion of Merlot to make an attractive wine of easy-going, uncomplicated fruit character. Several Santa Rita wines were found to contain Sorbitol in 1990.

VIÑA UNDURRAGA

Lota No. 2305, Santiago

Vineyard: 173 acres

Production: 900,000 bottles

Labels: Cabernet Sauvignon, Cabernet Sauvignon Special Selection

Quality: 🍇   Price: ★
Best vintage: 1987

Still family-owned, Undurraga appeared until recently to be a traditional winery, producing rather old-fashioned, heavy, over-oaked wines. The company seems to have been galvanized by a new approach, if the 1987 Cabernet Sauvignon (blended with 15 per cent Merlot) is anything to go by. This is very much a 'new-style', light, fragrant, forward, fruity, unoaked Cabernet, completely in contrast to the heavy, soupy style of the Special Selection, which spends four years in Bosnian oak.

Other Regions

There are small plantings of Cabernet Sauvignon in Brazil, Uruguay and Peru. The quality of the wine made from the Tacama vineyards in Ica Province in Peru is surprisingly good.

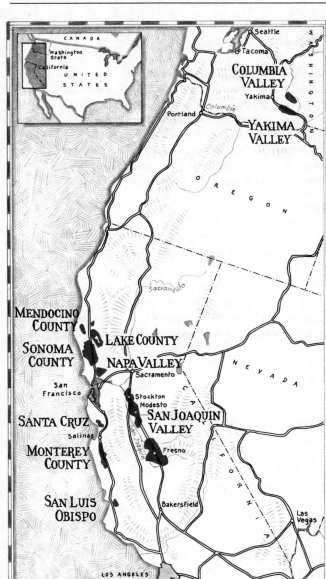

USA

California produces the bulk of the United States' Cabernet Sauvignon, and dominates discussion of the subject. However, Cabernet Sauvignon is also produced in two other areas of the vast country: in very small quantities in New York State in the north-east, and in more significant quantities in Washington State in the north-west. There is also a little Cabernet Sauvignon, of potentially exciting quality, in the neighbouring state of Idaho.

California

Total vineyard area: 324,000 acres

Area planted to Cabernet Sauvignon: 26,404 acres

California, and especially the Napa Valley, has established itself as the most prominent stronghold of Cabernet Sauvignon in the world outside Bordeaux. A cynic might say this had more to do with marketing, promotion, hype and PR than with the quality of the wine. I would argue that the climate in most parts of California is too hot to produce Cabernet Sauvignons of elegance and finesse. Washington State, the cooler corners of South Australia, Victoria and Western Australia, the middle Penedès and parts of Tuscany are all more naturally suited to making great Cabernet Sauvignon than the Napa Valley. However, this valley, together with Sonoma and a few other enclaves of coastal California, does produce many magnificent Cabernet Sauvignons. The sensational blind tastings in which

California Cabernet Sauvignons wipe the floor with the best Bordeaux *crus* do not prove that the California wines are better – though they are certainly larger, riper and more vivid. What they do prove is that two generations of gifted and technically very well-equipped California wine-makers have brought their wines up to top international standards.

There are two problems with California Cabernet Sauvignon. The first relates to the dynamic, restless, unstructured and manically innovative state of the California wine industry. The rabbit-like propagation of small 'boutique' wineries means vast numbers of new labels every year. You might think this was entirely desirable, but the promise of extended consumer choice is deceptive; far too many of these wines are almost indistinguishable in taste. Secondly, most are competing at the premium end of the market, which means swarms of unknown Cabernet Sauvignons costing fifteen to eighteen dollars, and not enough good solid wine at around ten dollars. The second problem is more fundamental. I have tasted large numbers of California Cabernet Sauvignons and often been impressed by their power, weight and vividness of flavour. But how many are actually drinkable? How many form a harmonious partnership with food? These are the questions which always preoccupied André Tchelistcheff, and which are now exercising an increasing number of the more far-sighted producers.

History

Wine production in California was started by Spanish–Mexican missionaries in the late eighteenth century. Their main concern was with sacramental wine and not with the nuances of flavour to be derived from different grape varieties. The variety they planted, Mission, still exists in largish quantities but gives dull wine.

A wide range of European varieties was introduced in the mid nineteenth century by the Hungarian Count Agosthon Haraszthy, founder of the Buena Vista winery in Sonoma. In 1857 the Frenchman Charles Lefranc was planting Cabernet

Sauvignon at his Almaden winery in Santa Clara County. Charles Krug, in the 1880s, mentions Cabernet Sauvignon among a list of varieties planted in the Napa Valley (including Miller Burgundy and Crabb Burgundy), which will, he says, 'improve the character of our clarets wonderfully'.

It was only after Prohibition came to an end in 1933 that the making of varietal wines began. A handful of wineries, such as Beaulieu (where André Tchelistcheff started working in 1935), Inglenook, Louis Martini and Charles Krug, produced fine Cabernet Sauvignons in the 1930s, '40s and '50s. It was in the 1960s that the modern, dynamic California wine industry, of which Robert Mondavi is the living embodiment, was born. Cabernet Sauvignon quite quickly established itself as the premium red wine grape – much more quickly than Chardonnay as the premium white grape. It was heavily planted in Napa, somewhat less so in Sonoma, in considerable quantities in Monterey and the Central Valley and in smaller quantities in Mendocino and Lake Counties to the north.

Regions and sub-regions v. intrastate blending

California used to take a New World pride in being untrammelled by the hierarchies and the petty concerns with geographical minutiae which bedevil the Old World, especially France. Soil in particular was treated with minimal reverence: 'soil is dirt', as Bill Jekel of Monterey put it. A California Cabernet Sauvignon can still be made with grapes which come from anywhere in the state, so long as 75 per cent of them are Cabernet Sauvignon. Recently, however, a greater concern for individual locality has been evident, most notably in the establishment of the AVAs, or Approved Viticultural Areas, by the Board of Alcohol, Tobacco and Firearms. AVAs are not to be confused with French appellations, since they do not control yields, grape varieties or methods of viticulture. They are simply geographical designations of origin: 85 per cent of the grapes must come from the named area.

Some AVAs cover a whole California county, such as Monterey. Areas such as Napa and Sonoma are subdivided into a number of AVAs (Carneros, Howell Mountain, Alexander Valley, Russian River Valley, Knight's Valley, for example) with others in the process of legitimation (Stag's Leap, Rutherford-Oakville, Spring Mountain, Mount Veeder).

The acreages of Cabernet Sauvignon in the leading California counties are as follows:

Napa	7,910
Sonoma	5,641
Monterey	3,026
San Joaquin	1,746
San Luis Obispo	1,586
Mendocino	1,055
Lake	966

Napa Cabernet Sauvignons tend to be full-bodied, robust and tannic, often marked by scents of mint and eucalyptus. The wines of the Rutherford Bench, the foothill slope on the west side of the valley between Rutherford and Oakville, are marked by a special dusty character known (not very revealingly) as Rutherford dust. The Stag's Leap district to the south-east of the Napa Valley gives more elegant, supple wines, while the wines of the hillside vineyards of Spring Mountain and Howell Mountain tend to have a brambly tone on the nose and to be robust and peppery on the palate.

The leading area of Sonoma for Cabernet Sauvignon is the Alexander Valley, which gives smooth, mellow wines which mature more quickly than those of Napa. The Dry Creek district can give firm, long-lasting wines, as can isolated parts of Sonoma Valley and Sonoma Mountain. The best Cabernet Sauvignons of Sonoma certainly challenge those of Napa in quality, and tend to be considerably cheaper.

Monterey County, which looks hot and dusty, is in fact one of the coolest parts of California. Cabernet Sauvignon can have difficulty ripening and the wines tend to be marked by a very strong vegetal tone, sometimes suggesting asparagus.

Mendocino and Lake Counties produce some very decent Cabernet Sauvignons, which tend to be somewhat lighter and looser-knit than the best from Napa and Sonoma. So far none has scaled the heights.

Vineyard siting

A major difference between the California wine industry before and after Prohibition is the move of vineyards from the hillsides to the valley floors. The Napa Valley, formerly planted with cereals while vines hugged the slopes, now an almost unbroken carpet of vines hemmed in by wooded hillsides, is the most dramatic example. The vast plantations in the Central Valley, and smaller ones in the Salinas Valley, are also on the flat. However, a move back to hillside planting has been underway for some years and is gathering momentum. With lower yields and higher production costs, hillside Cabernet Sauvignons will always be rather expensive, but the quality, as shown by Dunn, Mayacamas, Newton and others, can be exciting.

100 per cent Cabernet Sauvignon v. Bordeaux blends

In most Californian conditions, Cabernet Sauvignon has no difficulty in ripening to 12 or 12.5° potential alcohol (practically unheard of in the Médoc). A number of outstanding California Cabernet Sauvignons, such as BV Private Reserve and Heitz Martha's Vineyard, continue to be made from 100 per cent Cabernet Sauvignon. These show that the grape, in the Napa Valley as never in Bordeaux, can achieve the ripeness to stand on its own as a balanced wine – though one with a much richer, more robust character than the elegant growths of Bordeaux.

Increasingly, however, the tendency is to blend in small amounts of Merlot, Cabernet Franc and even Petit Verdot (planted in tiny but increasing quantities), with the aim of producing a more balanced, elegant blend. Whether the result can be called a Bordeaux blend is debatable. Merlot in California can be bigger, more deeply coloured and tannic than Cabernet Sauvignon – very different from Merlot in the Médoc. Sometimes I feel that the rationale behind such blends has more to do with the marketing, and the desire to charge a higher price, than with the aim of making better wine. I am suspicious of the new term Meritage, used to describe 'Bordeaux blends' which may contain less than 75 per cent Cabernet Sauvignon; it seems both an ugly coinage and a blatant attempt to charge more for what is not necessarily better.

Stylistic developments

Recent years have seen a move away from the big, tannic, massively alcoholic Cabernet Sauvignons which were prevalent in the 1970s and had an element of John Wayne, Wild West machismo. Buzz-words are now elegance, balance and harmony. Yet there had always been (since the 1930s at least) a tradition of Cabernet Sauvignon wines which combined elegance and suppleness with power – this is the hallmark of the wines made by André Tchelistcheff at BV and this is the tradition that now dominates. The influence of Tchelistcheff, who remains amazingly active on the brink of his nineties, can be compared to that of Emile Peynaud.

Tchelistcheff has never favoured the technique of prolonged *cuvaison*, traditional in Bordeaux, with which many winemakers in Napa and Sonoma are experimenting. Some claim that the effect of macerating the wine on the skins for anything up to three weeks after fermentation is to produce softer, smoother tannins. Paul Draper of Ridge asserts that there are no such things as soft tannins. Of such controversies is the world of California wine composed.

The search for elegance can go too far. A number of the new-style, 'elegant' Cabernet Sauvignons seem weedy and etiolated, lacking individual character. California Cabernet Sauvignon will always be a bigger, chunkier wine than a Médoc *cru*, and should, in my view, rejoice in its individuality. French oak is now *de rigueur* in most ambitious wineries, despite costing four times as much as native American oak. I find this surprising, since a number of the best California Cabernet Sauvignons, including BV Private Reserve, Ridge Monte Bello and Jordan, are matured either largely or wholly in American oak.

Vintage guide

1990. A successful vintage in most Californian areas.

1989. The wonder year in Europe was a near-disaster in California, with heavy rain during the vintage and widespread rot (not to mention an earthquake). Still, some fine Cabernet Sauvignons were made: selection will be especially important. Drink 1993–8.

1988. Somewhat lighter than the previous years, but some excellent wines – Dunn's Howell Mountain was exceptional. Drink 1992–8.

1987. Initially not thought as good as the previous trio, but looking promising. Drink 1992–2000.

1986. The grapes ripened very quickly as harvest approached; some picked grapes with high sugar levels, but green tannins to avoid making alcoholic blockbusters. Still, the best are superb, majestically ripe and full-flavoured. Drink 1991–2010.

1985. A year of consummate balance, generally not as big and powerful as either 1984 or 1986 and, with its red-berry fragrance, strangely reminiscent of 1985 Bordeaux. Drink 1991–2010.

1984. Classic California Cabernet Sauvignon – big, ripe and chunky. Some lack the balance of 1985. Drink 1991–2010.

1983. Rather hard and charmless, in spite of favourable conditions. Some will develop well. Drink 1991–5.

1982. Very attractive, supple, ripe wines from a warm year. Most need drinking.

1981. A very hot harvest led to doubts about balance, but some Napa wines have turned out very fine. Drink now.

1980. A vintage which has never lived up to expectations.

BEAULIEU VINEYARD

Napa Valley

> 1960 St Helena Highway, Rutherford, CA 94573
>
> Vineyards: 387 acres owned; 212 contracted in Rutherford
>
> Total Cabernet Production: 2,640,000 bottles (figures for Private Reserve not released)
>
> Labels: Georges de Latour Private Reserve Cabernet Sauvignon, Rutherford Cabernet Sauvignon, Beau Tour Cabernet Sauvignon
>
> PRIVATE RESERVE
>
> Quality: 🍇🍇🍇🍇🍇   Price: ★★★★★
>
> RUTHERFORD
>
> Quality: 🍇🍇🍇   Price: ★★★
>
> Best vintages (Private Reserve): 1966, 1968, 1970, 1973, 1976, 1982

Founded by the Frenchman Georges de Latour in 1900, BV, as it is known, has become something of a legend for consistency and durability in the California wine scene. The feeling it transmits to the visitor, with its octagonal, chapel-like reception area and reverential PR personnel, is more that of a shrine or institution than an enterprise. De Latour has also given his name to what is perhaps California's most famous Cabernet. The style of the Private Reserve – rich and intense yet supple; not excessively tannic, though capable of extremely long ageing – owes much to the guru of California Cabernet, André Tchelistcheff, who began working at BV in the 1930s. The list of wine-makers who have followed Tchelistcheff is pretty impressive: Joe Heitz, Mike Grgich, Richard Peterson of Atlas Peak and Tom Selfridge, now the winery's president.

The wine-making for the Private Reserve involves quite short *cuvaison* with frequent pumping-over, a period of maturation in large redwood tanks and up to thirty months in American oak *barriques*. The American oak gives a sweet, vanilla quality, and the redwood perhaps a touch of resin, but the real secret of Private Reserve is in the purity and concentration of the fruit, which comes from BV's famous vineyards on the Rutherford Bench. Acidity has always been considered as important as tannin here.

I was lucky enough to taste several vintages from the 1960s and 1970s, and found both the 1966 and 1968 beautifully preserved, sweet and full. The winery now belongs to the British Grand Metropolitan group; after some murmurings of uneven quality (though I find the 1982 highly impressive and typical of the house style) the 1984 has won plaudits from many wine critics. I found it velvety but surprisingly evolved, from what was perhaps a faulty bottle.

The Rutherford Cabernet Sauvignon tends to be overlooked, but is a very attractive Cabernet in its own right, somewhat lighter but possessing much of the fruit purity of Private Reserve. It also has surprising ageing potential: twenty years on, a 1970 was still alive, sweet and dusty, if a little maderized on the nose.

BERINGER VINEYARDS

Napa and Sonoma Valleys

2000 Main St, St Helena, CA 94574

Vineyards (for Private Reserve): St Helena, 40 acres; State Lane, 15 acres; Chabot, 33 acres

Production: not released

Labels: Napa Valley Private Reserve Cabernet Sauvignon, Knight's Valley Cabernet Sauvignon

PRIVATE RESERVE

Quality: �🌿🌿🌿🌿   Price: ★★★★

KNIGHT'S VALLEY

Quality: 🌿🌿🌿   Price: ★★

Best vintages (Private Reserve): 1982, 1984, 1985

Beringer was founded in 1876 by two German immigrant brothers, who left their mark in the form of the Rhine House, a spectacular Gothic monstrosity which goes down well with the 350,000 visitors the winery receives each year. Now owned by Nestlé, it is one of the largest producers in the Napa Valley but, under the skilful wine-making direction of Ed Sbragia, turns out some very high-quality wine under its premium labels.

The two main Cabernet labels are the Napa Valley Private Reserve and the Knight's Valley from eastern Sonoma County. The Private Reserve, which spends twenty-seven months in new French oak *barriques*, is a dark, powerful, masculine, mouth-filling wine, sometimes with a mint-and-eucalyptus character on the nose. The mintiness may come from the hill-side Chabot vineyard, which is sometimes bottled separately. Beringer Private Reserve is currently one of the very best Cabernets in California.

Although the Knight's Valley Cabernet, from higher vineyards with warmer days and cooler nights than Napa, is lighter, with red-cherry fruit and herbaceous tones on the nose, it has considerable tannic structure and can easily age ten years.

CARMENET

Sonoma County

1700 Moon Mountain Drive, Sonoma, CA 95476

Vineyards: Cabernet Sauvignon, 40 acres; Cabernet Franc, 8 acres; Merlot, 5 acres

Production: 120,000 bottles

Quality: 🍇🍇🍇   Price: ★★★★

Best vintages: 1984, 1985, 1986

Way up in the red volcanic hills that straddle the Napa–Sonoma border on the appropriately named Moon Mountain Drive, Carmenet is one of the most spectacularly sited and remote wineries in California. The parent company,

Chalone, has a liking for such places – its own winery is in the John Wayne country of Pinnacles National Monument, Monterey.

The name Carmenet is intended to suggest the Bordeaux blend of grape varieties; as it happens, Cabernet Franc thrives better in the mountain vineyard than Merlot, and usually forms 15 per cent of the blend. Carmenet is certainly one of the most Bordeaux-like of California Cabernets. Closed and austere when young, it has undoubted complexity and can even develop the lead-pencil aroma I associate with Mouton-Rothschild. As Jeff Baker, the reserved wine-maker who seems to enjoy the solitude of his surroundings, points out, 'the excitement of a mountain vineyard is the complexity within the vineyard'. Fifteen to twenty lots are kept separate until the summer after the vintage. The 1986 is the most accessible Carmenet I have tasted – velvety and subtle, with a long, fine, fruit intensity. The wine's vanilla oakiness may have something to do with the *barriques* from Château Lafite, which are now used as a result of Chalone's 20 per cent share swap with Lafite.

CAYMUS

Napa Valley

8700 Conn Creek Road, Rutherford, CA 94573

Vineyard: 73 acres

Production: 240,000 bottles

Labels: Special Selection Cabernet Sauvignon, Estate Bottled Cabernet Sauvignon, Napa Valley Cuvée Cabernet Sauvignon

Quality: 🍇🍇🍇   Price: ★★★★

Best vintages: 1985

Caymus, a smallish winery owned by the Wagner family, has always had a very high reputation for its Cabernets. The style that wine-maker Chuck Wagner aims for is 'lush, rich, with medium tannin and medium oak'. He adds, disarmingly, 'It should taste good!' Well, the deep-coloured Napa Valley Cuvée 1985, with an interesting resin-and-eucalyptus nose, is full and lush, as he says, but not exceptionally characterful. The 1983 Special Selection Cabernet is considerably more oaky, but has intense fruit too. Good but not great is my verdict.

CHÂTEAU MONTELENA

Napa Valley

> 1429 Tubbs Lane, Calistoga, CA 94515
>
> Vineyard: 70 acres around winery
>
> Production: 144,000 bottles
>
> Quality: 🍇🍇🍇🍇   Price: ★★★★
>
> Best vintages: 1982, 1984, 1985

It was the 1973 Château Montelena Chardonnay that created the sensation by beating the French at Steven Spurrier's notorious 1976 Paris tasting. Now the winery is best known for its powerful, long-lived Cabernet Sauvignons. Sometimes referred to as the Latour of Napa, Château Montelena, with its handsome castellated stone winery and its unexpected, beautiful Chinese water-garden, sits at the head of the valley beneath the imposing volcanic bulk of Mount St Helena. According to wine-maker Beau Barrett, the volcanic soil is the key to the highly distinctive, earthy, dry, long-lasting style of the Cabernet Sauvignon, made from 100 per cent estate grapes. 'This is a power district,' says Barrett, a swashbuckling southerner. 'You can smell the dirt in the wines.'

The 1982 Cabernet Sauvignon has a clarety, gamy nose, a dusty ripeness and an earthy tannic finish. The 1984 is lusher, with a deep, dark, violet aroma, rich and full and chocolatey on the palate, but still possessing backbone. The 1985 is particularly well balanced, but you can smell the minerals and taste the earth. These highly individual Cabernets will probably divide opinion, but for aficionados (including myself) they are among the top half-dozen in California. A small percentage (3–5 per cent) of Cabernet Franc is added to make the wine more aromatic when young.

CLOS DU BOIS

Sonoma County

> 5 Fitch Street, Healdsburg, CA 95448
>
> Vineyards: 100 acres in Dry Creek and Alexander Valleys
>
> Production: 240,000 bottles
>
> Labels: Briarcrest Cabernet Sauvignon, Marlstone Vineyard
>
> Quality: 🍇🍇🍇🍇   Price: ★★★
>
> Best vintages: Briarcrest, 1981, 1984; Marlstone, 1985

Clos du Bois was founded when Frank Woods and a group of friends bought a 500-acre prune ranch in the Russian River Valley in 1969. Their original intention was to build condominiums, but the land, subject to flooding, was more amenable to grape-growing. Initially, Woods and partners sold the grapes to other wineries, but in 1977 they launched their first range of varietals. Clos du Bois was sold in July 1988 to Hiram-Walker (part of Allied-Lyons).

With its unshowy winery – a kind of all-purpose hangar – in the centre of the little town of Healdsburg, Clos du Bois has an engagingly down-to-earth air. If the PR profile is refreshingly low, the quality of the wines, and above all the quality/price ratio, is exceptional. The Cabernets from the Briarcrest vineyard in the Alexander Valley are deep-coloured, with ripe brambly fruit; on the palate they are rich and silky, with notably soft tannins. The Marlstone vineyard is a Bordeaux blend of 68 per cent Cabernet Sauvignon, 22 per cent Merlot, 7 per cent Cabernet Franc and 3 per cent Malbec. It is softer and more elegant, though not as intense, as the Briarcrest. A little American oak is used.

CLOS DU VAL

Napa Valley

> 5330 Silverado Trail, Napa, CA 94558
>
> Vineyards: 265 acres, including 90 acres in Stag's Leap
>
> Production: 300,000 bottles
>
> Labels: Cabernet Sauvignon, Gran Val, Jolival
>
> Quality: 🍇🍇🍇🍇   Price: ★★★
>
> Best vintages: 1982, 1984, 1985, 1986

In 1972, the millionaire John Goelet hired Bernard Portet, son of the *régisseur* of Château Lafite, to find the best location for a vineyard and winery in California. Portet, in whom Goelet obviously has total confidence, chose the Stag's Leap district in the south-east of Napa because he noticed that the evenings were cooler than in the centre of the valley. At that time, no Cabernet was planted south of the Fay vineyard in Oakville.

Few wineries in California are so much the creation of one individual as Clos du Val is Portet's. A dapper, young-looking, sharp-eyed man, unmistakably French in manner, Portet has always sought, and achieved, a French restraint and elegance in his Cabernets. Merlot has been blended in to achieve greater softness, but Portet says he is using less Merlot as the Cabernet vines mature and produce softer wine. 'I try to produce wines which go well with food – not powerful in the mouth but long in the finish.' The velvety 1985 is a fine example of Portet's art – a long, beautifully balanced wine which has considerable ageing potential. The 1984 is a bigger wine, generous and chocolatey, though it has a heavily tannic structure. With older vintages, Portet can wax lyrical: the 1980, with its fat nose, he described as 'like a Buddha'. Jolival is a second label for a lighter Cabernet, made from a blend of estate and bought-in grapes, introduced with the 1986 vintage.

*

CLOS PEGASE

Napa Valley

> 1060 Dunaweal Lane, Calistoga, CA 94515
> Production: 90,000 bottles
> Quality: 🍇🍇   Price: ★★★★

The post-modern winery founded by the millionaire art collector Jan Schrem in 1985 is at present more notable for its architecture than its wine. The winery building, in terracotta (to symbolize the red earth), beige (the colour of the burnt Napa grass) and blue (the sky), stands at the head of the valley opposite Sterling like some latter-day Egyptian temple. The Cabernet, made in consultation with André Tchelistcheff from Mount Veeder, Stag's Leap and Rutherford fruit, is very much in the modern, elegant style. The 1985 has a relatively light colour, attractive redcurrant and red-cherry fruit and light tannin, but good acidity. This is a pleasant lunch wine, no more.

CONN CREEK

Napa Valley

> 8711 Silverado Trail, St Helena, CA 94574
> Vineyards: various, including Collins north of St Helena
> Production: 130,000 bottles
> Labels: Napa Valley Barrel Select, Private Reserve
> NAPA VALLEY
> Quality: 🍇🍇🍇   Price: ★★★
> PRIVATE RESERVE
> Quality: 🍇🍇🍇   Price: ★★★★
> Best vintages: 1984, 1985

Founded by Bill Collins in 1974, Conn Creek now belongs to
the Stimson Lane company which owns Château Ste Michelle
and Columbia Crest, both in Washington State. It has always
been known for its Cabernets, blended from different vineyards
in Napa, which achieve consistently good quality without the
last ounce of individuality. The Napa Valley is elegant, with a
lot of spice (cloves, vanilla) on the nose, and a lively balance on
the palate. The Private Reserve, often based on fruit from the
Collins family vineyard, is much deeper, bigger, denser and
more tannic. It can have a distinctive tarriness on the nose. The
goal, according to wine-maker Jeff Booth, is to achieve complexity through blending, and not to emphasize oak. Only
French *barriques* are used, of which one-third are new.

CUVAISON

Napa Valley

4550 Silverado Trail, Calistoga, CA 94515

Vineyard: Cabernet grapes currently bought from Rutherford–Oakville area

Production: 70,000 bottles

Quality: 🍇🍇🍇🍇   Price: ★★★★

Best vintages: 1985, 1986

It is surprising to find Cuvaison tucked away at the narrow
north end of the Napa Valley since the winery owns 270 acres
in Carneros, way to the south, where it grows mainly Chardonnay. Though Cuvaison makes six times as much Chardonnay as
Cabernet, it has a deservedly high reputation for its reds, meti-
culously made by wine-master John Thacher. The emphasis,
logically in a winery which regards control of the vineyards as
crucial for quality, is on intense purity of fruit. The style is lean,
not for hedonists, but the 1986 has superb length and structure.
John Thacher now believes that each vintage has an intrinsic
character, which he can guide along but not fundamentally
change. Only French oak barrels are used.

DIAMOND CREEK

Napa Valley

> 1500 Diamond Mountain Road, Calistoga, CA 94515
>
> Vineyards: Red Rock Terrace, 7 acres; Volcanic Hill, 8 acres; Gravelly Meadow, 5 acres
>
> Production: 36,000 bottles
>
> Labels: Red Rock Terrace, Volcanic Hill, Gravelly Meadow

One of California's smallest and most dedicated specialist wineries, Diamond Creek was founded in 1968 by Al Brounstein with the aim of making top-class single-vineyard Cabernets in tiny quantities. The wines are fermented in redwood tanks and matured in French oak *barriques*. Unfortunately I have not been able to taste any of the wines. The Red Rock Terrace is said to be the most accessible, the Volcanic Hill the most austere and long-lasting, with the Gravelly Hill somewhere in between.

DUCKHORN

Napa Valley

> 3027 Silverado Trail, St Helena, CA 94574
>
> Vineyards: none owned; grapes bought on contract from Howell Mountain, Spring Mountain, Dry Creek
>
> Production: 50,000 bottles
>
> Labels: Cabernet Sauvignon
>
> Quality: 🍇🍇🍇🍇   Price: ★★★★
>
> Best vintage: 1986

The Duckhorn winery was founded in 1978 by a group of ten families, including Dan and Margaret Duckhorn who manage it today. Despite having worked for a bench-grafting company, the Duckhorns do not own vineyards (or do not yet – they are scouring the valley for suitable land), but oversee the growing and harvesting of the grapes they buy very closely. The sturdy, strong look of the winery, with its rough-hewn stone arches, reflects the character of the wines. Wine-maker Tom Rinaldi makes very intense, deep-coloured Cabernet from mainly mountain fruit – quite chewy and tannic when young but exceptionally concentrated and characterful. The deep, tarry, brambly 1986 promises to be one of the best wines of the vintage. This is an impressive winery, whose rating may need to be revised upwards before long. Duckhorn's Merlot is one of the most sought-after in California.

DUNN

Napa Valley

805 White Cottage Road, Angwin, CA 94508

Vineyards: 5 acres owned on Howell Mountain; grapes also bought from vineyards on Howell Mountain and in Napa Valley

Production: 48,000 bottles

Labels: Howell Mountain Cabernet Sauvignon, Napa Valley Cabernet Sauvignon

Quality: 🍇🍇🍇🍇   Price: ★★★★

Best vintages: 1985, 1986

Laconic, ginger-bearded, a latter-day frontiersman, Randy Dunn seems absolutely in his element in his timber ranch on Howell Mountain, 2,000 feet above the floor of the Napa Valley. Dunn is a passionate proponent of mountain Cabernet. 'The chances of succeeding are ten times better in the hills than on the valley floor,' he says, reminding you that before Prohibition there were over 1,000 acres of vines planted in the red soil of Howell Mountain.

Dunn's star wine is his Howell Mountain Cabernet – typically intense in colour, with a nose that combines bramble and blackcurrant fruit with tar, and sturdy and peppery on the palate. This is not an elegant Cabernet, and reminds me more of Cornas than claret, but it is certainly one of the most characterful Cabernets in California. Both 1987 and 1988 are successes, following the excellent 1986. Dunn produces 2,000 cases of Howell Mountain and a further 2,000 of Napa Valley Cabernet, which is intense, powerful and concentrated. He uses only French oak: 'People who think they can make world-class wine with American oak are just kidding themselves,' he states with unanswerable conviction.

FREEMARK ABBEY

Napa Valley

3022 St Helena Highway North, St Helena, CA 94574

Vineyards: various, including Bosché and Sycamore

Production: Heritage, 84,000 bottles; Bosché, 48,000 bottles; Sycamore, 36,000 bottles

Labels: Heritage Cabernet Sauvignon, Cabernet Sauvignon Bosché, Cabernet Sauvignon Sycamore

Quality: 🍇🍇🍇🍇   Price: ★★★★

Best vintages: 1984, 1985

Wine-making started at this site in 1886; the solid-stone winery building dates from 1900. Freemark Abbey, which belongs to five general partners, was reborn in its present form in 1967. It is best known for its single-vineyard Cabernets from the Bosché vineyard on the Rutherford Bench. These are among the firmest and most austere of California Cabernets when young; they develop complexity with age. The 1985, blended with 15 per cent Merlot, is notable for its intensity of red-fruit flavour and quite astringent finish. In 1984 the single-vineyard Sycamore Cabernet was launched. The 1985, with 5 per cent

Cabernet Franc, is a richer, more voluptuous wine than the Bosché, with some mint on the nose, though it still finishes firm. The Heritage Cabernet, which contains up to 20 per cent Merlot, has an attractive minty, dusty nose, sweet fruit in the middle palate, then the characteristic dry finish.

FROG'S LEAP

Napa Valley

3358 St Helena Highway, St Helena, CA 94574

Vineyards: 5 acres in Napa, and others

Production: 36,000 bottles

Quality: 🍇🍇🍇🍇   Price: ★★★

Best vintages: 1984, 1985, 1986

If one wanted a word to describe John Williams's and Larry Turley's minuscule winery on the site of a former frog farm outside St Helena, it would have to be 'wacky'. The timber house dating from 1850 took a leap itself: Williams and Turley had it moved from across the street in 1981. When Turley, a tall bearded figure who as well as part-owning the winery is a full-time doctor and former aerospace engineer, wanted to build a bathroom extension, there was an evergreen oak in the way. The solution was typical of the man: he built the extension round the tree. 'When there's a high wind we have surf in the bath,' he explained.

The great mistake, though, would be to assume that just because Frog's Leap has a sense of humour, it is all a joke. In fact, the wines made by John Williams are consistently excellent, combining rich fruit with elegance. The Cabernets are typical of the Rutherford–Oakville part of Napa. Sometimes possessing a tobaccoey, dusty quality on the nose, they have a velvety richness and depth. The Frog's Leap style does not favour austerity and hard tannin: the wines are drinkable after three or four years.

GRGICH HILLS

Napa Valley

> 1829 St Helena Highway, Rutherford, CA 94573
>
> Vineyards: 70-acre Austin Hills vineyard in Rutherford, and others
>
> Production: 120,000 bottles
>
> Quality: 🍇🍇   Price: ★★★★
>
> Best vintages: 1981, 1984

Miljenko (Mike) Grgich is one of the great characters of the California wine industry. Formerly assistant to André Tchelistcheff at BV, and wine-maker at Château Montelena, he started up this winery in partnership with grape-grower Austin Hills in 1977. Grgich is perhaps better known for his rich, oaky Chardonnays than for Cabernets, which he started making in 1980. The 1980 Cabernet is a lightish red-berry wine with a hint of chocolate, made from Sonoma fruit. This seems to be an odd one out among Grgich Hills Cabernets: the 1984, with an excellent colour, minty, dusty nose, velvety mouth-feel and considerable oak character, is truer to the big, rich style Grgich is seeking to maintain. The wine, which contains 4 per cent each of Merlot and Cabernet Franc, spends two years in French *barriques* and is only released after three years' bottle ageing.

GUNDLACH-BUNDSCHU

Sonoma County

> 2000 Denmark St, Sonoma, CA 95476
>
> Vineyard: 38 acres in southern Sonoma Valley
>
> Production: 84,000 bottles
>
> Labels: Rhinefarm Cabernet Sauvignon, Cutler Cellar Batto Ranch Cabernet Sauvignon, Vintage Reserve Cabernet Sauvignon

Quality: 🍇🍇🍇🍇   Price: ★★★ – ★★★★
Best vintages: 1984, 1985

This unshowy winery outside Sonoma has one of the longest histories in California, having been started by two immigrant German families as long ago as 1858. Jim Gundlach, great-great-grandson of the founder, is now the owner. As often in Sonoma, the surroundings and equipment look rough-and-ready, but the quality of the wine surpasses the products of several of the tourist Meccas of Napa. There are three levels of Cabernet, but all share a house style which is big, lush and minty, and which I find extremely attractive. The 1985 Rhine-farm is deep in colour with a lovely black-cherry nose, and rich and voluptuous on the palate. The 1985 Cutler Cellar, named after the wine-maker, former teacher Lance Cutler, has a more lifted, mint-and-eucalyptus character on the nose and is somewhat less dense and more elegant.

HEITZ WINE CELLARS

Napa Valley

500 Taplin Road, St Helena, CA 94574

Vineyard: 50 acres on west side of Napa Valley

Production: 160,000 bottles

Labels: Napa Valley Cabernet Sauvignon, Martha's Vineyard Cabernet Sauvignon, Bella Oaks Cabernet Sauvignon

Quality: 🍇🍇🍇🍇🍇   Price: ★★★★★
Best vintages: 1982, 1984

If makers of great Cabernet Sauvignon tend to be individualists, frontiersmen who go their own way with little regard for others, Joe Heitz is their epitome. Now turned seventy, this blunt, outspoken son of an Illinois farmer is a legend in the world of California wine, and especially Cabernet Sauvignon. André Tchelistcheff has called him 'the best in California', and his Martha's Vineyard bottling is the most distinctive and, at auction, consistently the most highly priced of California Cabernets. Heitz Cellars started in 1961 and in 1964 moved to its present site in Spring Valley, a narrow fold in the hills on the east side of the Napa Valley. The speckled-grey, rough-hewn stone barn was built into the side of the hill by the Rossi family in 1898.

Rough-hewn, though not coarse, is not a bad description of the character of Heitz's Cabernets. Never blended with other varieties, they are aged for a year in large American oak tanks then two years in French oak *barriques*. The Napa Valley has a minty, resiny nose and is a good, big, sturdy wine with chocolatey richness and a tannic finish. But it is the single-vineyard bottlings which have made Heitz world-famous. Martha's (first vintage 1966), from a gravelly vineyard near Oakville belonging to Tom and Martha May, has the most immediately recognizable nose in California – pure eucalyptus and mint. This may have something to do with the fact that the vineyard is surrounded by eucalyptus trees. On the palate the 1984 has a lovely sweet, rich, chocolatey texture, leading to a silky finish. This is a wine which fills the mouth and whose flavour stays there. One of the secrets of Martha's is late picking: when I saw Joe Heitz the day after the California earthquake of 18 October 1989, he told me that Martha's had not yet been picked. Bella Oaks (first vintage 1976), near Rutherford, produces a rich silky wine, more voluptuous and less minty, more elegant than Martha's. The 1984 is also superb.

Sadly, a cautionary note must be added. On two separate occasions there has been an unpleasantly musty tone on the 1984 Napa Valley Cabernet, noticed by me and some of my colleagues. Whether this is a cork or barrel problem, it certainly means those bottles cannot be recommended – a crying shame, when the wine at its best is excellent.

THE HESS COLLECTION

Napa Valley

4411 Redwood Road, Napa, CA 94558

Vineyards: 285 acres on Mount Veeder

Production: not released

Labels: Cabernet Sauvignon, Cabernet Sauvignon Reserve

Quality: 🍇🍇🍇   Price: ★★★

Best vintages: 1984, 1985, 1986

Having made his millions out of mineral water, the Swiss businessman Donald Hess turned his attention to collecting modern art (he has significant pieces by Francis Bacon and Frank Stella, among others), and then to making wine. He seems to be doing it rather well. He now has over 900 acres of land on Mount Veeder, and has leased the old Mont la Salle winery building from Christian Brothers. The 1985 Cabernet Sauvignon is a rich, well-balanced wine, with subtle vanilla and red-fruit aromas, good length and structure but no hard tannin. Fine though it is, it cannot hold a candle to the superb 1986 Cabernet Sauvignon Reserve, with its fascinating, complex, tarry aroma and beautiful feel in the mouth. This looks a very promising winery.

INGLENOOK

Napa Valley

1991 St Helena Highway, Rutherford, CA 94573

Vineyards: various

Production: 200,000 bottles

Labels: Cabernet Sauvignon, Reserve Cask Cabernet Sauvignon, Reunion, Niebaum Claret

Quality: 🍇 – 🍇🍇🍇   Price: ★★★★
Best vintages: 1985, 1986

Inglenook, founded by the Finnish sea-captain Gustave
Niebaum in 1879, lays claim to being the first great claret estate
in the Napa Valley. Niebaum's nephew, John Daniel Jr, played
an important part in the rebuilding of the California wine
industry after Prohibition – indeed, the 1933 vintage Cabernet
Sauvignon became a symbol of that rebirth. Following a period
of decline, Inglenook, now owned by Heublein, a subsidiary of
Grand Metropolitan, is once more playing a leading part in the
California wine scene.

The 1985 Cabernet has a chocolatey, blackcurranty nose and
is relatively one-dimensional, with a tannic finish. In quite a
different league is the 1985 Reunion, a 100 per cent Cabernet
wine made with fruit from the three vineyards that made
Inglenook's fame in the 1930s – Inglenook itself, Napanook
and Coppola (now owned by the film director Francis Ford
Coppola). This has a rich, dark colour, is closed but deep on the
nose, and has a long velvety flavour leading to a tannic finish – a
wine which needs some time, but of very high class. Niebaum
Claret is a Bordeaux blend, usually containing slightly more
Merlot than Cabernet Sauvignon. The 1986, unusual in having
72 per cent Cabernet Sauvignon, is an aromatic wine in a much
lighter style, more or less ready to drink.

IRON HORSE

Sonoma County

9786 Ross Station Road, Sebastopol, CA 95472
Vineyards: 38 acres in Alexander Valley
Production: 42,000 bottles
Quality: 🍇🍇🍇   Price: ★★★
Best vintages: 1984, 1985, 1986

Situated in the wooded, hilly country of Sonoma's Green Valley (only 10 miles from the Pacific), Iron Horse is best known for its refined, elegant sparkling wines, California's closest approximation to champagne. The fruit for the Cabernets (Sauvignon and Franc) comes from the warmer Alexander Valley, 30 miles to the north-east, but the style Forrest Tancer seems to aim for is very much on the lean, structured side. Some Iron Horse Cabernets have seemed to me too green and stalky, but the 1985 (72 per cent Cabernet Sauvignon, 28 per cent Cabernet Franc) is impressive for its pure attack, sweet first flavour and long, concentrated finish.

JEKEL VINEYARD

Monterey County

40155 Walnut Avenue, Greenfield, CA 93927

Vineyard: 60 acres

Production: 96,000 bottles

Labels: Cabernet Sauvignon, Cabernet 'Proprietary', Private
Reserve Cabernet Sauvignon

Quality: 🍇 – 🍇🍇🍇🍇   Price: ★★★

Best vintage: 1983

The Arroyo Seco district of Monterey County, where Bill Jekel set up his vineyard in 1972 and his winery in 1978, has several curious climatic features. The area is a dry, dusty plain which receives only 8 inches of rain annually, making irrigation a necessity. But despite its hot appearance, the plain is actually one of the coolest wine-growing regions in California: the Cabernet harvest does not start until late October. The reason is the morning fogs which roll in from the Pacific, followed by maddeningly persistent cool afternoon winds. This is not an area one would want to live in, but it produces some interesting wines. The most consistent success at Jekel is the startlingly aromatic Riesling. The Cabernet can be extremely good but is dogged by variation of style. The biggest problem is a strong vegetal tone, sometimes suggesting green pepper but more often asparagus: much depends on individual tolerance of this particular flavour component. The 1983 Private Reserve Cabernet Sauvignon, on the other hand, has performed consistently well in my California Cabernet tastings. It is a lusciously rich chocolatey wine, with mint but no asparagus on the nose.

An intriguing feature of wine-making here is the use of hoops of French oak inserted into American oak barrels. The wine now spends less time in oak, but I do not see the benefit of this.

JORDAN VINEYARD AND WINERY

Sonoma County

1474 Alexander Valley Road, Healdsburg, CA 95448

Vineyard: 170 acres

Production: 540,000 bottles

Quality: 🍇🍇🍇   Price: ★★★★

Best vintages: 1981, 1982, 1983, 1985

The drive leading up to the immaculate wine-palace of Denver oil magnate Tom Jordan is alone worth more than some entire wineries. The building itself, surrounded by hundreds of acres of golden grass and dark-green oaks, is both discreet and imposing. A yellow-ochre 'château' with a tiled roof, rather French, it incorporates such un-French features as a dining-room looking on to varnished oak fermentation tanks and bedrooms leading into a *barrique chai*.

The wines, on which no expense has been spared, are also both French and un-French. The Cabernet, blended with 12–15 per cent Merlot and just a touch of Cabernet Franc, is notably elegant and aromatic, with a spicy vanilla nose and supple, mellow flavour. Some of this has to do with the charming, red-berry character of Alexander Valley fruit; there is also the influence (not surprising at a winery where André Tchelistcheff still consults once a week) of 60 per cent new small American oak barrels. Critics of Jordan Cabernet say it is lightweight and lacks ageing potential. The 1979, however, was still going strong at ten years old. Jordan Cabernets are notably consistent from vintage to vintage.

JOSEPH PHELPS. See Phelps, Joseph

MASSON (PAUL) VINEYARDS

Monterey County

800 South Alta Street, Gonzales, CA 93926
Production: 840,000 bottles
Quality: 🍇🍇🍇   Price: ★★
Best vintages: 1984, 1985

Paul Masson may be best known for carafe wines, more interesting, perhaps, for the actual carafes than their contents, but the Masson Vineyards range of varietals, introduced in 1987, is not to be scorned. The 1986 Cabernet, made from Monterey County fruit, has an appealing dusty berry nose and attractive fruit on the palate. The 1985 is a bigger, more powerful wine, with almost Bordeaux-like complexity. These Cabernets, which are good value for money, are aged in American oak.

MAYACAMAS

Napa (Mount Veeder)

1155 Lokoya Road, Napa, CA 94558
Vineyard: 14 acres
Production: 24,000 bottles

Quality: 🍷🍷🍷🍷🍷   Price: ★★★★

Best vintages: 1974, 1978, 1985

The black basalt cliffs of Mount Veeder are a beautiful but forbidding backdrop to what is perhaps California's most reactionary winery. The name is Indian for 'howl of the mountain lion'. Turkey vultures circle overhead, 'waiting for the day you don't make it back home', as the soft-spoken proprietor Bob Travers likes, grimly, to put it. Travers is an ex-stockbroker who is clearly much happier in his plaid shirt among the vines in this remote spot. (There used, in fact, to be several vineyards in these mountains, where there is less danger of spring frosts than on the valley floor.) The winery at Mayacamas dates back to 1889, but was in a dilapidated state when Travers arrived in 1968. From low yields of small mountain grapes, he makes probably the longest-living Cabernet in California, certainly the one which is least approachable when young, despite spending two years in American oak vats and one year in French oak *barriques*. A certain amount of Merlot (up to 15 per cent) and Cabernet Franc is added, but to increase complexity, not to make the wine softer. The 1985 is deep in colour and has a young-wine nose, with tones of tar and blackberries. On the palate you can discern complexity and balance, but the wine is far too young and tannic to drink. The splendid, Rhône-like 1978 is also considered by Travers to be 'by no means mature yet'. Even the big, long-flavoured 1974 will improve.

MONDAVI (ROBERT) WINERY

Napa Valley

7801 St Helena Highway, Oakville, CA 94508

Vineyards: 447 acres owned in Napa Valley

Production: not released

Labels: Woodbridge California Cabernet Sauvignon; Robert Mondavi Cabernet Sauvignon, Napa Valley; Robert Mondavi Cabernet Sauvignon Reserve; Opus One

Quality: 🍇🍇 – 🍇🍇🍇🍇🍇   Price: ★ – ★★★★★
Best vintages: 1984, 1985, 1986

Robert Mondavi is not just a man (though he is very much alive and active in his seventies) or a winery – it is a name that symbolizes the renascent California wine industry, and especially its quality end, based in the Napa Valley. The winery itself, a latter-day Mission with its distinctive low, wide arch, welcomes hundreds of thousands of visitors a year and has done more than any other to make the name of Napa world-famous. As for the wines, Mondavi has achieved the rare feat of combining large-scale commercial production with the very highest quality, in what remains a family operation. The Woodbridge label is drinkable, in a rather green, stalky, neo-Médocain style. The Napa Valley (only 75 per cent Cabernet Sauvignon) can be excellent, with pure fruit and some elegance. It is with the Reserve, however, aged in French oak *barriques*, that Mondavi bids for greatness. This has always (or since the early 1980s at least) been a notably elegant California Cabernet, aiming for balance and refinement rather than muscle-power. The 1986 (90 per cent Cabernet Sauvignon, with about 5 per cent each of Merlot and Cabernet Franc) is perhaps the best Mondavi Reserve yet – deep in colour, lifted and complex on the nose, with considerable concentration yet supple tannin ('soft as a baby's bottom', in the words of Mondavi himself). The 1987 Reserve, with a marked mint-and-eucalyptus character on the nose, deep, ripe and concentrated, looks highly promising also.

In 1979, Mondavi joined forces with Château Mouton-Rothschild to produce Opus One, a Cabernet Sauvignon from a single close-planted vineyard. The wine, aged in 100 per cent new French oak, is even more elegant and Gallic than the Reserve – also more closed when young. Whether it is worth its elevated price is another matter.

MONTEREY VINEYARD

Monterey

800 South Alta Street, Gonzales, CA 93926

Vineyard: 395 acres in San Lucas

Production: 490,000 bottles

Labels: Classic Cabernet Sauvignon (450,000 bottles), Limited Release Cabernet Sauvignon (36,000 bottles)

Quality: 🍇🍇 Price: ★★ – ★★★

Best vintages: 1985, 1986

Owned by Seagram, and sharing with Paul Masson a huge, airport-like complex on the outskirts of Gonzales, the Monterey Vineyard does a notably good job in what is called the 'fighting varietal' market. The 1985 Classic Cabernet, made from a combination of Monterey, San Luis Obispo and Sonoma fruit, has an attractive dusty, cherry-and-tobacco nose and is a good medium-weight, forward wine. The 1986 Limited Release has a delicate oakiness (100 per cent French oak is used) and a tight, well-knit structure, which needs time to open out.

MONTICELLO CELLARS

Napa Valley

4242 Big Ranch Road, Napa, CA 94558

Vineyard: 26 acres owned

Production: 140,000 bottles

Labels: Jefferson Cuvée Cabernet Sauvignon, Reserve Cabernet Sauvignon

Quality: 🍇🍇🍇 Price: ★★★

Best vintages: 1983, 1984, 1985, 1986

Monticello was founded by the Jeffersonian scholar and

Virginian Jay Corley and endowed by him with a building loosely modelled on Jefferson's Virginia house, after which the winery is named. Corley began by selling grapes, mainly Chardonnay, then in 1980 moved into making wines. Now two levels of Cabernet are produced. The Jefferson Cuvée, blended with about 15 per cent Merlot and 5 per cent Cabernet Franc, is designed to be relatively supple and approachable, an aim certainly achieved in the elegant, harmonious 1985. The Reserve, always 100 per cent Cabernet Sauvignon, is a much bigger wine, with more tannin, colour and extract. The 1986 is inky black in colour, with great fruit intensity on the nose, still backward on the palate and needing five years to reach its full potential.

NEWTON

Napa Valley (Spring Mountain)

2555 Madrona Avenue, St Helena, CA 94574

Vineyard: not released

Production: not released

Quality: 🍇🍇🍇🍇   Price: ★★★

Best vintages: 1984, 1985, 1986

Peter Newton's winery, a cross between a Buddhist shrine and an institute of contemporary art, is perched high up on Spring Mountain with breathtaking views over the Napa Valley. Oxonian, ex-Lex columnist on the *Financial Times* and founder of Sterling Vineyards in 1964, Newton is as passionate an advocate of mountain planting as Randy Dunn on the other side of the valley. His steeply terraced vineyards boast seven different types of volcanic soil, planted with the four Bordeaux varieties, Cabernet Sauvignon, Cabernet Franc, Merlot and, unusually in California, Petit Verdot. Whether it is due to the soils or the blend of grapes (or both), Newton Cabernets are some of the most satisfyingly complex in California. They tend to be pretty tannic when young, but 50 per cent new, heavily toasted oak imparts a chocolatey richness which gives them precocious charm. The 1986 is very good, if a trifle green still. The somewhat softer 1987 looks promising – soft and elegant, yet concentrated.

PAUL MASSON VINEYARDS. See Masson (Paul) Vineyards

PHELPS, JOSEPH

Napa Valley

> 200 Taplin Road, St Helena, CA 94574
>
> Vineyard: 80 acres
>
> Production: 300,000 bottles
>
> Labels: Cabernet Sauvignon, Eisele Vineyard Cabernet Sauvignon, Backus Vineyard Cabernet Sauvignon, Insignia
>
> Quality: 🍇🍇🍇🍇   Price: ★★★★
>
> Best vintages: 1984, 1985, 1986

Joe Phelps's training as a civil engineer shows in the trellis construction of the winery building, which commands a beautiful view over the Napa Valley. The Phelps winery is notable for its versatility – wines are made from no less than ten different grape varieties – but also for the quality of its Cabernets. These are big, rich, quintessentially California wines which tend to be fairly tannic and sometimes astringent. The 1985 'straight' Cabernet Sauvignon has an intense colour, a powerful minty nose, and lots of sweet, concentrated fruit leading to a tannic finish. Phelps buys grapes from the Eisele vineyard to make a massive, dark, tarry, chewy wine – one of California's most formidable and long-living Cabernets. The wine from the Backus vineyard has a distinctive mintiness on the nose. Top of the Phelps range is Insignia, a proprietary blend usually containing about two-thirds Cabernet. The 1985 Insignia (60 per cent Cabernet Sauvignon, 25 per cent Merlot, 15 per cent Cabernet Franc) has a very aromatic minty nose and develops attractively in the mouth with raspberry fruit, but still has some astringency at the finish. A certain amount of Merlot and, more recently, Cabernet Franc has always been added to Phelps Cabernets.

PINE RIDGE

Napa Valley

> 5901 Silverado Trail, Napa, CA 94558
>
> Vineyard: 120 acres
>
> Production: 200,000 bottles
>
> Labels: Cabernet Sauvignon, Cabernet Sauvignon Rutherford Cuvée, Cabernet Sauvignon Stag's Leap Cuvée, Andrus Reserve
>
> Quality: ♥♥♥♥   Price: ★★★★
>
> Best vintages: 1985, 1986

The owner of this winery on the fringes of Stag's Leap is the perfectionist Gary Andrus, an ex-Olympic skier and property developer. He believes that 100 per cent Cabernet Sauvignon is too masculine, and that 'you develop your house style by blending'. He also believes in the Napa sub-appellations, and makes two *cuvées* from Rutherford and Stag's Leap. The Stag's Leap is the softer of the two. The 1985 shows a sweet, lifted, black-cherry nose and ripe blackcurrant fruit on the palate, with highish acidity. The Rutherford 1985 (7 per cent Merlot, 6 per cent Cabernet Franc) is deeper and earthier, with a long, rich flavour. Top of the range is the Andrus Reserve. The 1985 (8 per cent Merlot, 6 per cent Cabernet Franc, 2 per cent Malbec) is deep in colour, subtle and complex on the nose and, on the palate, seems to combine the qualities of the other two *cuvées*. Andrus is meticulous in his selection of *barriques*; all come from French coopers, including François Frères whose heavy toast he likes for his red wines.

RIDGE

Santa Cruz

> 17100 Monte Bello Road, Cupertino, CA 95015
>
> Vineyard: Monte Bello Estate Vineyard, 50 acres
>
> Production: 200,000 bottles
>
> Labels: Monte Bello Cabernet Sauvignon, Santa Cruz Mountains Cabernet Sauvignon, York Creek Cabernet Sauvignon (Napa Valley)
>
> Quality: ♥♥♥♥♥   Price: ★★★★
>
> Best vintages: 1981, 1984, 1985, 1987

From the saddle of the steep Santa Cruz mountains, 2,300 feet up, Ridge looks down on one side over Silicon Valley and on the other over an idyllic-looking fold in the hills, through which runs the San Andreas fault. It was in these hills in the 1850s that French settlers planted what was probably the first Cabernet Sauvignon in California. The charming timber winery (which survived the 1989 quake) was built in 1885.

From the Monte Bello vineyard which surrounds the winery, Paul Draper, wine-maker and philosopher, makes one of California's finest, most complex and longest-living Cabernets. He believes in filtering his wines as little as possible, sometimes not at all, in order to retain maximum complexity and character. The 1972 Monte Bello was still tasting young in 1989, with a subtle, Bordeaux-like nose and firm structure on the palate – austere but satisfying. The 1981 seemed more open and less tannic at the same stage, with rich berry-fruit. The 1985 (blended with 7 per cent Merlot) has a strong cedary character on the nose, with lush fruit leading to a tannic finish. Draper uses 95 per cent air-dried American oak barrels, which impart a touch of sweetness to these sometimes austere wines. The York Creek Cabernet Sauvignon comes from a vineyard in the Napa Valley belonging to Fritz Maytag. This produces a lusher, softer wine with more obvious fruit character but less elegance and ageing potential than Monte Bello. The Santa Cruz Mountains

Cabernet Sauvignon is the second wine of Monte Bello and is somewhat lighter and more accessible. Ridge's Zinfandels are not to be missed either.

ROBERT MONDAVI WINERY. *See* Mondavi (Robert) Winery

SHAFER VINEYARDS

Napa Valley (Stag's Leap)

> 6154 Silverado Trail, Napa, CA 94558
>
> Vineyard: 30 acres
>
> Production: 78,000 bottles
>
> Labels: Napa Valley Cabernet Sauvignon, Hillside Select Cabernet Sauvignon
>
> Quality: 🍷🍷🍷🍷   Price: ★★★★
>
> Best vintages: 1982, 1984, 1985

The Shafer winery is dramatically sited beneath the rocky palisades of Stag's Leap, and in a decade of existence has established itself as one of the leaders of this Napa sub-appellation. Shafer Cabernets, made by Doug Shafer, the young and enthusiastic son of proprietor John Shafer, are immediately appealing – rich, vibrant and satiny in texure. The style has evolved somewhat since 1979, moving towards elegance and balance, and away from power. This might seem regrettable when tasting the 1979 Napa Valley Reserve, a magnificent, big, minty, long-flavoured wine with 14° alcohol. Recent vintages of Hillside Select Cabernet Sauvignon, made from quite steep vineyards surrounding the winery, have been excellent too. The 1984 is a lovely ripe wine, almost sweet-tasting but with lively acid balance. The 1985 has an open, appealing nose, with hints of ripe red berries, balanced fruit and satiny texture.

SILVER OAK CELLAR

Napa Valley

> PO Box 414, Oakville, CA 94562
>
> Vineyard: 200 acres
>
> Production: 300,000 bottles
>
> Labels: Cabernet Sauvignon Alexander Valley, Cabernet Sauvignon Napa Valley, Cabernet Sauvignon Bonny's Vineyard
>
> Quality: 🍇🍇🍇🍇   Price: ★★★★
>
> Best vintage: 1984

Justin Meyer's winery specializes in the production of Cabernet Sauvignon, from three locations: Alexander Valley in Sonoma (the largest part of his production), Napa Valley and Bonny's Vineyard, a small plot named after his wife. All the wines are aged for a longish period (around two and a half years) in American oak, 50 per cent new for the Alexander Valley, 100 per cent new for Bonny's. This oak-ageing gives the wines a distinctive softness and sweetness of aroma. The Alexander Valley 1983 is soft and round, and has lovely length and subtlety, but I find the Napa Valley 1983 less appealing, with a rubbery tone on the nose and a hard finish. The Alexander Valley 1984, though, is a seductive wine with sweet fruit at the core.

SIMI WINERY

Sonoma County

> 16275 Healdsburg Avenue, Healdsburg, CA 95448
>
> Vineyard: 99 acres in Alexander Valley
>
> Production: 400,000 bottles
>
> Labels: Cabernet Sauvignon, Cabernet Sauvignon Reserve

Quality: 🍷🍷🍷　　Price: ★★★★

Best vintages: 1985, 1986, 1987

Simi is one of the oldest wineries in California, having been founded in 1876. Now owned by the French Louis Vuitton-Moët-Hennessy combine, it is at the forefront of new research into clonal selection, trellising systems in the vineyard and wine-making techniques. The avowed aim with Cabernet is to achieve ripeness, complex aromas and satisfying mouth-feel. The 1986 Cabernet Sauvignon is deep-coloured, with a subtle nose in which oak is integrated; this is a medium-weight wine with a silky middle palate, quite hard but not bitter at the finish. The Cabernet Sauvignon Reserve 1986 (92 per cent Cabernet Sauvignon, 8 per cent Petit Verdot) is less developed, with a tarry quality on the nose and hard tannin at the finish – perhaps attributable to the Petit Verdot? The 1985 Cabernet Sauvignon Reserve (100 per cent Cabernet Sauvignon) has a ripe prune-like nose and is soft, rich and chocolatey on the palate. Best of the Reserves that I have tasted seems to be the 1987 (100 per cent Cabernet Sauvignon), which is deep-coloured, with long, intense fruit and a hint of mint, and excellent texture in the mouth. The overall impression of these Simi Cabernets is one of restless experimentation, leading to lack of consistency. Perhaps this 1987 will be the basis of a more reliable style.

STAG'S LEAP WINE CELLARS

Napa Valley (Stag's Leap)

5766 Silverado Trail, Napa, CA 94558

Vineyard: 50 acres

Production: not released

Labels: Stag's Leap Wine Cellars Cabernet Sauvignon, Stag's Leap Vineyard Cabernet Sauvignon, Stag's Leap Vineyard Cask 23 Cabernet Sauvignon, Hawk Crest Cabernet Sauvignon

Quality: ♦♦♦♦ – ♦♦♦♦♦   Price: ★★★ – ★★★★★
Best vintages: 1984, 1985

In 1964 Warren Winiarski resigned an academic job in Social Science at Chicago University to work in the cellars at Souverain in the Napa Valley. In 1970 he bought some land on the east side of the valley and called it Stag's Leap. The first release of his Stag's Leap Cabernet Sauvignon was the 1972 vintage; his second release, the 1973, created one of the biggest stirs in wine history by coming first in Steven Spurrier's 1976 France v. California tasting in Paris. With the 1974 vintage, Winiarski put aside the best lots of the Stag's Leap Vineyard as a reserve and called it Cask 23.

Cask 23 is, with BV Private Reserve, Heitz Martha's Vineyard, and Ridge Monte Bello, one of California's acknowledged 'first growths', and several critics would place it right at the top of the list. The key to its style is harmony and balance of parts. The 1984 combines voluptuous richness with firm structure; it is deep, subtle, complex and long, though some might find its restraint less exciting than the more obviously Californian style of Heitz or BV.

The 1985 Napa Valley Cabernet Sauvignon has a minty nose and is a big wine with a mineral solidity and complexity. The 1984 Stag's Leap Vineyard is quite alcoholic on the nose, and rich and rounded on the palate with a satisfying balance. Hawk Crest, Winiarski insists, is not a second label but a brand in its own right. The fruit comes from various locations in Sonoma, Mendocino and Lake Counties, and the wine is in an early-maturing style, quite dry but elegant and good value.

TREFETHEN

Napa Valley

1160 Oak Knoll Avenue, Napa, 94558 CA
Vineyard: 110 acres
Production: 120,000 bottles

Labels: Cabernet Sauvignon, Eshcol Red Wine
Quality: 🍇🍇🍇 Price: ★★★
Best vintages: 1981, 1982, 1984, 1985

The Trefethen winery, an impressive clapboard structure dating from 1886, is situated towards the southern end of the Napa valley. It is surrounded by 600 acres of vineyard, much of whose produce is sold as fruit to other wineries, though John and Janet Trefethen have increased the estate's production from 2,000 to 75,000 cases. The location is considered quite far south, and therefore cool, for Cabernet Sauvignon in the Napa Valley, and Trefethen Cabernets, which generally contain about 15 per cent Merlot, can have a strongly herbaceous tone. These are solid, reliable wines, and the 1984, minty on the nose, dense, powerful and concentrated on the palate, is one of the best Cabernets of the vintage.

Trefethen put away small quantities of wines from outstanding vintages as a Library Reserve: the 1981 Cabernet is concentrated and tannic, still tough; the 1979 is in a lighter style, with a ripe gamy nose, now fully mature. A word should be put in for the proprietary estate-blend Eshcol, made from 40 per cent Cabernet Sauvignon with Pinot Noir, Merlot and Zinfandel, and excellent value.

ZD WINES

Napa Valley

8383 Silverado Trail, Napa, CA 94558
Vineyard: 3 acres
Production: 15,000 bottles
Quality: 🍇🍇🍇 Price: ★★★★
Best vintage: 1985

Norman De Leuze concentrates on his unashamedly full-blown Chardonnay, which accounts for 85 per cent of the winery's production. His Cabernet, even if only a sideline, shares many of the attributes of the Chardonnay: it is big, rich, voluptuous, made from very ripe grapes. The 1985 is especially good: full, rich and concentrated, it lacks the harsh tannin of the 1984. The 1987 has splendidly intense fruit, like blackcurrant essence.

Washington State

This north-westernmost of the states is divided into two very different climatic zones by the lofty Cascade Mountains. West of the Cascades is the sodden, lush landscape of Seattle, Tacoma and the forests; east is a near-desert which, with irrigation from the Columbia River, can be turned into something of an agricultural and viticultural paradise. The latitude here in the Columbia and Yakima Valleys is 46° North, the same as Bordeaux. The climate is characterized by warm sunny days in summer with cool nights. The result is a style of Cabernet Sauvignon (only produced in significant quantities in the last twenty years) very different from that of California: leaner, with higher natural acidity, firmly structured but with striking fruit intensity. It is early days for the Washington wine industry, initially known for its white wines, especially Rieslings; many Washington Cabernets exhibit excessively vegetal, herbaceous characteristics. But there are some, not necessarily commercially biased, who would argue that the state's potential for producing top-quality Cabernet Sauvignon is greater than California's.

The vineyards of Washington State are divided into three main appellations, or AVAs: Columbia River is by far the largest in geographical extent, stretching several hundred miles from near Spokane in the north-east across the border into Oregon; Yakima Valley is situated along the Yakima River in south-west Washington State; and Walla Walla occupies an area to the east just above the Oregon border.

Other than those detailed here, recommended producers are **Hedges Cellars**, **Pintler Cellar**, **Quilceda Creek** and **Rose Creek**.

CHÂTEAU STE MICHELLE

Columbia River

> 1 Stimson Lane, Woodinville, WA 98072
>
> Production: 400,000 bottles
>
> Labels: Cabernet Sauvignon, Cabernet Sauvignon Reserve, Cold Creek Vineyard, River Ridge Vineyard
>
> Quality: 🍇🍇🍇   Price: ★★★
>
> Best vintages: 1985, 1986, 1987

Château Ste Michelle is by far the largest of Washington's wineries, controlling nearly half of the state's 10,000 acres of *vinifera* vines and producing over a million cases of wine a year. The winery was founded in the 1930s but only started to produce wines from classic European varieties in the late 60s, pioneering the vineyard development of the Columbia River Valley south-east of Seattle. Cabernet Sauvignon is produced in relatively small quantities compared to big lines such as Riesling (4 million bottles a year). However, it is a most successful wine, with solid depth of colour, an interesting, somewhat austere nose with a hint of clove, and a nice balance of ripe fruit and tannin on the palate. There is also a Reserve, more concentrated and intense, and two vineyard-designated wines, of which the Cold Creek, from the northern Columbia Valley, is held to be outstanding.

COLUMBIA CREST

Columbia River

> 1 Stimson Lane, Woodinville, WA 98072
>
> Production: 420,000 bottles
>
> Quality: 🍇🍇🍇   Price: ★★
>
> Best vintages: 1985, 1986, 1987

Columbia Crest, the second-biggest producer in Washington State, is owned by the Stimson Lane group, which also owns Château Ste Michelle, but is operated as a separate winery with its own facilities and wine-maker. The Cabernet Sauvignon, aged partially in American and partially in French oak, is a really refined and elegant wine with a complex, subtle bouquet – impressive in any company. There is also a most attractive plummy Merlot. It would be interesting to see how the two varieties blended.

COLUMBIA WINERY

Columbia River

> PO Box 1248, Issaquah, WA 98027
>
> Production: Cabernet Sauvignon, 60,000 bottles; Otis Vineyard, 8,000 bottles
>
> CABERNET SAUVIGNON
>
> Quality: ♥♥♥   Price: ★★★
>
> OTIS VINEYARD
>
> Quality: ♥♥♥♥   Price: ★★★
>
> Best vintages: 1985, 1986

Columbia, not to be confused with Columbia Crest, claims to be the oldest premium winery in Washington State, having been founded in 1962. An equally significant date in the winery's history is 1979, the year David Lake, MW, was employed as wine-maker. The Columbia Cabernet Sauvignon comes from six hillside vineyards in the Columbia River appellation; aged for eighteen months in *barriques*, it is relatively light, and strikingly Médocain in style, with tones of tobacco and spice. Very much more concentrated and impressive is the Otis Vineyard, produced in tiny quantities from the oldest Cabernet vineyard in Washington State, planted in 1957. Cedary, with a ripe, complex, red-berry nose, this is a firmly structured, beautifully balanced wine with the potential to age fifteen years.

GLOSSARY

AOC *Appellation d'Origine Contrôlée.* French system of vineyard areas defined according to grape varieties, yields, methods of viticulture and alcoholic strength.

AVA Approved Viticultural Area. American version of the French AOC system, but much less stringent. A guarantee of geographical origin only.

BARRIQUE Traditional Bordeaux barrel with a capacity of 225 litres.

BAUMÉ French system for measuring must weight (the sugar content of unfermented grape juice) as the determinant of the wine's potential alcoholic strength.

CÉPAGE Grape variety; hence *encépagement*, the composition of a wine in terms of grape variety.

CHAI Ground-level wine-cellar.

CHARTREUSE Single-storey style of architecture popular among wealthy eighteenth-century Bordelais for their country houses.

COULURE The failure of grape berries to develop after flowering.

CRU	Literally, 'growth'. Used of vineyards of particular quality.
CUVAGE/ CUVAISON	The period that red wine spends in the fermentation vat, in contact with the grapes' skins and pips.
CUVE	Vat; hence *cuvier*, a battery of vats, or fermentation cellar.
DO	*Denominaciónes de Origen*. The Spanish equivalent of AOC.
DOC(G)	*Denominazione di Origine Controllata (Garantita)*. DOC is the Italian equivalent of AOC. To qualify for DOCG, wines have to be passed by a tasting panel.
EN PRIMEUR	The term for selling wine before it is bottled, usually in the spring or summer following the vintage.
FINING	The clarification of wine after fermentation. Clarifying agents include beaten whites of egg, dried blood, gelatin and isinglass. The traditional method is to allow beaten whites of egg to fall through the wine collecting particles.
FOUDRE	Large wooden vat in which wine is aged. Usually oak but sometimes chestnut, with a capacity of upwards of 500 litres.
INAO	*Institut Nationale des Appellations d'Origine*. Responsible for setting up and overseeing the laws of AOC.

MACÉRATION
CARBONIQUE

Method of fermentation, designed to produce fresh and fruity red wines, low in tannins.

MALOLACTIC
FERMENTATION

The conversion of malic acid into lactic acid which occurs naturally in red wines, making the taste softer and smoother.

PHYLLOXERA

The aphid that destroys vines by eating their roots. Devastated European vineyards from the 1870s. There are worrying signs that it may be making a comeback in the USA and Australia.

RACKING

The process of running off wine from one barrel to another, leaving the lees behind.

RÉGISSEUR

Manager of a Bordeaux Château.

TERROIR

The French term for a particular piece of land and its microclimate; hence *goût de terroir*, the earthy taste or texture to be found in certain Cabernet Sauvignon wines.

VIGNERON

Wine-grower

VIGNOBLE

Vineyard

INDEX